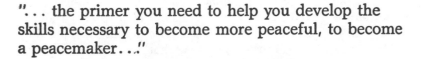

D0836844

".. . the primer you need to help you develop the skills necessary to become more peaceful, to become a peacemaker. . .."

"Our enemies today are not individuals or even nations of people, but the nameless and faceless threats posed by nuclear weapons and pollution and poverty and greed. As we confront these enemies all too often we feel powerless. *The Great Turning* is all about empowerment. It is an affirmation of our power as individual human beings to reach across borders and boundaries to humanize our conflicts, to ease our suffering, and to turn back these enemies. In that power is our hope and our future."

U.S. Senator Mark Hatfield (R/Oregon)

"When we look back from the year 2025, we will surely see *The Great Turning* as a classic of how we managed to create a more mature humanity, a more spiritual society, and a safer world. Craig Schindler and Gary Lapid, both longtime warriors in the best sense of the word, give us clear visions of how to proceed and courage for the journey."

Chellis Glendinning, Ph.D.
author, *Waking Up in the Nuclear Age* and *When Technology Wounds*

"Our future literally depends upon people reading this book. It is that critical. This is not just an important book — it is absolutely *vital* that people around the world understand its message. Our future depends upon the quality of decisions that we make in the next decade. Likewise, these decisions depend on our knowledge of what is shared so powerfully in these pages.

"As a Christian, . . . I would urge all people of faith to read this most significant book — and then give a copy to a friend. *The Great Turning* is timely and profound. It provides not only the necessary vision, but also the skills and tools to make that vision a reality."

Tim Hansel
founder and president, Summit Expedition
author, *When I Relax, I Feel Guilty* and *You Gotta Keep Dancin'*

"*The Great Turning* is an inspiring book. Craig Schindler and Gary Lapid have produced what could be called a do-it-yourself manual for global survival. They make it clear that world peace and an end to violence will not be achieved by leaving it to the experts. Rather it is a game that all of us must play, one in which our every move becomes important."

Raymond F. Dasmann
author, *Environmental Conservation*
professor of ecology, environmental studies,
University of California, Santa Cruz

"We can recognize *The Great Turning* as simple statement of fact, based not on wishful thinking but on recognition that the Gate of History is swinging. It requires no magic, no esoteric beliefs, but recognition of the common interests of the US and USSR that we not be blown up, and that we not see nuclear weapons scattered around the world. On these common interests we can build nuclear safety."

Admiral Noel A.M. Gayler
former commander of the U.S. Pacific Forces

"That we need to change our ways of thinking in order to survive is a given. This book, jargon free, and filled with practical suggestions, points us towards that path."

Dr. Anne H. Cahn
consultant on national security affairs

Drs. Schindler and Lapid discuss a visionary but not unreasonable technique, tested by extensive experience, for negotiation which is as powerful as it is novel.... [This] technique should be useful not only in arms control negotiations, but also in the resolution of other international issues ... and even family disagreements.... I recommend this book to the intelligent non-expert, which includes just about everyone."

Louis Rosen
senior fellow, Los Alamos National Laboratory

"Here is *the* primer you need to help you develop the skills necessary to become more peaceful, to become a peacemaker — at home and beyond."

Sam Keen
author, *Faces of the Enemy*

"*The Great Turning* is a courageous book that integrates spiritual, social, and ecological wisdom into a compassionate vision of a sustainable future, and then provides the practical tools of interpersonal communication to realize that future."

Duane Elgin
author, *Voluntary Simplicity*
executive director, Choosing Our Future

"A very encouraging book, going beyond the world's problems, and pointing us toward the solutions. *The Great Turning* is a great, inspirational book.... It's exciting to see that we *can* make a difference in creating a safer, saner world. 'We' meaning ordinary individuals. This book fills me with hope and inspiration. Thank you for spurring me on!"

Vivienne Verdon-Roe
Academy Award winning documentary filmmaker
president, Eschaton Foundation: a national media resource center
for a safe and sustainable world

"*The Great Turning* is an excellent book for anyone who wants to make a difference in the world today. It is a book of wisdom filled with useful information and practical exercises to be applied on both a personal and social level. It is an outstanding contribution to global consciousness."

Frances Vaughan, Ph.D.
author, psychologist
former president, Association for Transpersonal Psychology

"*The Great Turning* states, 'Albert Einstein once reflected that it would take just two percent of the world's population to make the change necessary to create real peace and security between nations.' Drs. Schindler [and Lapid are] emphatically among that two percent, ... with [their] basic ideas for conflict resolution.... The book is brilliantly conceived to lead the reader to a full understanding of the methods for conflict resolution. I heartily recommend it for international readership."

Dr. Victor Westphall
director, DAV Vietnam Veterans National Memorial, Inc.

"*The Great Turning* offers in simple, clear, and readable language, a vision of hope for human kind and guidelines for helping each of us play our role in making that vision a reality. The sincerity of the authors, the power of their vision, and the urgency of our situation, all combine to make *The Great Turning* a valuable guide to human survival."

Roger Walsh, M.D., Ph.D.
professor of psychiatry and social sciences,
University of California at Irvine, California
author, *Staying Alive: The Psychology of Human Suvival*

"A persuasive affirmation that individuals do matter — and collectively can solve world problems. The insights into communications, motivation, and conflict resolution are valuable in all human endeavors from our personal lives to corporate management."

Robert C. Wilson
chairman, Wilson & Chambers
former CEO, Memorex Corporation

"The problem addressed by *The Great Turning* and by Project Victory, which it vividly describes, is epitomized by the Chinese proverb: 'He who rides a tiger finds it difficult to dismount.' This book engrossingly explores methods that can help us and the world get off the course that is leading us to ecological and thermonuclear destruction. It is essential reading for those concerned with peace, preservation of our planet, and with justice for all the world's people."

Victor W. Sidel, M.D.
distinguished university professor of social medicine,
Montefiore Medical Center, Bronx, New York
former president, Physicians for Social Responsibility

". . . academically credible while exceedingly readable; comprehensive yet crisp; and accurately descriptive while being profoundly prescriptive as well. *The Great Turning* is the great calling to proven models of dialogue away from political duelogues and frightful duelings which plague the search for peace."

William F. Lincoln
president, National Center Associates, Inc.,
dispute-resolution training and services
former federal commissioner, U.S. Peace Academy Commission

"Here is a strong challenge to keep the 'inner' and 'outer' dimensions of our lives from becoming separated, along with many specific proposals and suggestions for creating a scenario of hope for the future. People in the midst of many different personal journeys will find a meeting-ground in these pages."

Robert McAfee Brown
professor emeritus of theology and ethics,
Pacific School of Religion, Berkeley, California

"A well reasoned and contemporary exposition of how and why each one of us is needed to save life on earth."

Richard Rathbun
president, Beyond War Foundation

"This book is a powerful manifesto that creates awareness of the necessity for humanity to turn now if we are to be saved from nuclear destruction or from the deadly effects of environmental decay. . . . One of its strengths is that it does not unrealistically project a general utopian vision and recognizes that sinful and finite humanity will continue to have conflicts, but now on some central issues it gives great hope that the converging of recognized necessities with the growth of conscience will bring about 'the great turning.' "

John D. Bennett
former president, Union Theological Seminary

"This book reminds us that we are, indeed, in the midst of a great turning in the planetary journey of our species. It helps us wake up to the countless choices presented to each of us, each day, for living in ways that can heal our world."

Joanna Macy, Ph.D.
author, *Despair and Personal Power in the Nuclear Age*
adjunct professor, California Institute of Integral Studies

The Great Turning

*Not for ourselves alone, but for all
humanity. . . . Let us hasten to find the path that leads
to liberty, safety, and peace for everyone.*
— Thomas Jefferson —

The Great Turning

personal peace • *global victory*

Craig Schindler, J.D., Ph. D.
& Gary Lapid, M.D.

BEAR & COMPANY
PUBLISHING
SANTA FE, NEW MEXICO

DEDICATION

For our children, Zeya Schindler (age 7), Zack Lapid (age 9), and Maya Lapid (age 7); and for all the children who will soon inherit the 21st century.

LIBRARY OF CONGRESS
CATALOGING-IN-PUBLICATION DATA

Schindler, Craig F., 1946-
  The great turning: personal peace, global victory / Craig F. Schindler and Gary G. Lapid.
    p.   cm.
    ISBN 0-939680-51-3: $9.95
    1. Interpersonal relations. 2. International relations. 3. Interpersonal communication. 4. Conflict management. 5. Peace. I. Lapid. Gary G. II. Title
HM 132.S3518 1989
302.3'4 — dc19   88-31583
                                                         CIP

Copyright © 1989 by Craig F. Schindler and Gary G. Lapid

All rights reserved. No part of this book may be reproduced by any means and in any form whatsoever without written permission from the publisher, except for brief quotations embodied in literary articles or reviews.

Bear & Company
Santa Fe, New Mexico 87504-2860

Cover, interior design and illustrations: Kathleen Katz
Cover illustration: Jim Finnell
Typography: Buffalo Publications
Printed in the United States of America by R.R. Donnelley

9 8 7 6 5 4 3 2 1

Contents

About The Cover Design

Shortly before his death, Joseph Campbell commented in his interviews with Bill Moyers that the primary symbols of the next century would be about the entire Earth: "When you see the Earth from the Moon, you don't see any divisions there of nations or states . . . And the only myth that is going to be worth thinking about in the immediate future is one that is talking about the planet . . . and everybody on it."

The ancient Zia sign represented the radiating power of the Sun to sustain life. It also symbolized the four cardinal directions and the great wheel of life, turning from season to season. In our cover design, we have put the Earth at the center of the Zia to represent the evolutionary shift of mind necessary to sustain and enhance life on Earth. It is a shift from an ego-centric view to an eco-centric view which recognizes the reality of our global interdependence. The Earth at the center of the Zia reminds us of the importance of taking conscious responsibility for our future and of the necessity of seeking understanding from all directions and points of view at this critical turning point in human history.

Our thanks to Kathleen Katz for her fine art work in designing the cover.

Acknowledgments

Why did we write this book? One of the primary reasons is that we both have young children. Like so many people in the 1980s, we came to an abrupt awakening that our world and our children's future were terribly threatened. As parents, we could not imagine caring for their welfare each day without also trying to do something to make their future more secure. In short, we wrote this book because we want a victory for our world, so that all of our children will live in a twenty-first century that is safer and more compassionate.

This book is based upon work we have done with thousands of people in mediated dialogues, communication workshops, policy conferences, and leadership training seminars around the United States. We want to thank and acknowledge all of the individuals who have participated and contributed their ideas and insight.

Whereas this book was a co-creative effort, most of the actual writing of the manuscript was done by Craig Schindler. Over the past four years, we have collaborated together to develop and systematize the concepts and methods in this book with our colleagues at Project Victory, particularly Theo Brown. Gary Lapid drafted language and supplied guidance throughout, especially on the methods for dialogue and conflict management. Most of the insights and examples about communication and dialogue are derived from the working experience of one or both authors. We refined the text together with the help of many people mentioned below.

There are three individuals who deserve special acknowledgement at the outset for their immense contributions:

Theo Brown — As the executive director of Project Victory, Theo has helped to inspire and sustain the creative process of writing the book, draft after draft, providing his analysis and wisdom based upon years of experience as a national organizer. Theo was pivotal in helping to develop the methods and tools described herein. He drafted language for several sections of the book and gave numerous editing suggestions essential to the text. More than any other person, it was his conceptual strength and unwavering commitment to the project which enabled us to succeed.

Bess Greenfield — Bess played a critically important part in helping to edit and refine the text. As an editor and computer master, she worked for hundreds of hours to input and revise the manuscript. She helped to design much of the format and layout. Her careful skill and immense work through late nights and weekends contributed tremendously to bring it all together.

Toby Herzlich — During the early stages of the writing. Toby helped to formulate many of the basic concepts and principles. She helped to draft the original version of the opening vision as well as several other pieces. Her vivid images and thoughtful examples contributed much. With her excellent writing abilities, she helped to improve and enliven many passages. Toby played an essential role in helping to conceptualize and launch the book

Our sincere thanks and deep appreciation to Gerry and Barbara Clow, our publishers at Bear and Company, who made this book possible. To Barbara Clow, our thanks for believing in, and sustaining the vision of *The Great Turning* long before it was on paper. To Gerry Clow, our thanks for his wise counsel and firm hand throughout the long process of seemingly endless revisions. We could not have asked for a more encouraging and mutually collaborative process with our publisher.

We are grateful to the people who read and commented upon drafts of the manuscript. No writer can really convey how much the constructive criticism of those who take the time to comment is appreciated. We were fortunate to have a diverse and excellent group of readers: Tom Johnson, Josh

Karter, Heidi Hamrick, Laura Paull, Bob Barrett, Carol Beaumont, Jim Baer, Phil Kline, Sylvia Rogers, Nancy Goodman, Chip August, Linda Povey, Hathaway Barry, Larry Ford, and Teddy McDonald.

Tom Johnson, and Josh Karter, in particular, provided in-depth analysis and conceptual breakthroughs which helped to reframe important parts of the text. They both deserve great acknowledgment for their significant contributions to the ideas and analysis expressed here.

Heidi Hamrick gave creative insights and excellent feedback through draft after draft. Laura Paull used her journalist's skill to clarity the language and sharpen the conceptual analysis. Chip August encouraged and contributed to the book in many ways, from editorial revisions to creative design. Barbara Lapid was very supportive of the process of creating Project Victory, the workshops, and the dialogues.

Chellis Glendinning and Duane Elgin, both working on parallel projects, provided essential mirroring and wisdom in the final stages. Chellis contributed data and insight from the research in her forthcoming book, and Duane gave us valuable feedback on the particulars of the vision for the year 2025. He also gave insightful comments on developing the overall tone of the practice.

A number of people provided valuable insights to the development of the methods and tools for dialogue and conflict management: Charlotte Lowry, Phil Kline, Lynn Gorodsky, Bob Barrett, Bruce Berlin, Mark Bennett, Meryl Lefkoff, Mark Rovner, Mary Helen Snyder, John Marks, John Parkini, Jim Laue, and Bill Lincoln.

Charlotte Lowry deserves special acknowledgment for her role in helping to pioneer some of the dialogue techniques. It was Charlotte who took the initiative to begin the first ongoing dialogue group with both military officers and peace activists in Albuquerque, New Mexico. With Theo Brown, she was largely responsible for organizing the first statewide dialogue in New Mexico.

Carol Beaumont provided many ideas and practical suggestions from her years as a teacher; she also helped greatly to lighten the load through her ongoing volunteer support in our office in Palo Alto. John Burkhardt contributed important ideas and conceptual analysis throughout the writing. Lynn Gorodsky helped to formulate some of the exercises in designing the Project Victory teacher training, "Beyond Ordinary Education." Liz Bond and Linda Goffen gave excellent suggestions for refining key language. Kimberly Carter was very helpful with editorial suggestions in the early stages. Phil Kline, Cathy McCowan, and Bobbie Collins contributed important research to the writing process. Kia Wood provided excellent computer assistance in the first rounds of revision.

We want to acknowledge and thank those who have offered personal and material resources to make the writing of this book possible. We could not have continued through the four years without their belief in and support for the project. Our thanks and great appreciation to Ed Goodstein, Hathaway Barry, Uli and Joan Spannagel, Jim Baer, Ann Marks, James Compton, Bob and Linda Barrett, Annie and David Wellborn, Hardy Sanders, Arnold and Nancy Greenfield, Val Kilmer, Foster and Dania Gamble, Miriam Lapid, Katherine McEntyre, Teddy McDonald, Austin Marx, Greg Heer, William and Katherine Slick, John Kielly, Pam Otis, and many others.

We are especially grateful to Patti Cavaletto, Michael Broome, and Leslie Jones for providing access to a wonderful place of retreat and renewal which was essential to the writing. Their kindness and wisdom created the supportive context in which much of the book could be written. Our thanks to John Wallace who believed in the vision of the book when it was still only a glimmer. We deeply appreciate his unwavering encouragement and help in many ways. And the great beauty of the western United States helped to inspire the book. Much of the manuscript was thought out while walking the high mesas of New Mexico and the coastal mountains of California.

John Burkhardt, Linda Arnold, Dan Lowrey, and Phil Kline provided inspiration with their original music and songs about a Great Turning. Steve Zeifman of On Tape Productions in San Francisco donated many hours of video studio time to help with the development of the dialogue methods. Mert and Tonya Carpenter of Los Gatos, California, generously provided their photographic expertise. Our thanks to Kathleen Katz and Debora Bluestone of Bear & Company for their work to design and promote the book.

We want to express our appreciation to other friends and colleagues who have contributed to the intellectual and spiritual development of the book: John and Diane McEntyre, Diedre Rye, Eve Eden, Tim Hansel, Bill Milliken, Jim and Cathy Corby, Ken Norris, Jim Baer, Hathaway Barry, Uli Spannagel, Caryl Turner, Roberta Bristol, Sara Wood, Linda Povey, April and Stuart Welsh, Katherine Harrold, Ann Niehaus, Glenn Barlow, Sandy Herrick, Frederick Van Rheenan, Judith Murphy, David Shulman, Ian Thierman, Daniel and Catherine Mountjoy, John Goldenring, Katherine Mann, John Walker, Werner and Christina Krutein, Nancy Goodman, Susan Junta, Mark Rovner, Sylvia Rogers, Roger Walsh, Sharon Simon, Anna Swartley, Kate Hamrick, Debbie Glovin, Jane Yett, Elisa Pederson, Alan Marks, Anne Rein, Carol Forest, Ann Harmon, Andy Carman, Helen Mehr, Ken Burrows, Joel Frankel, Hank and Pat Adams, Wendy Martyna, and Bill Leland.

We particularly want to thank and acknowledge our parents who have given us more than we can begin to express: C. Franklin Schindler and Nancy Schindler, and Gilbert and Miriam Lapid. They are the original source for the values and vision which we sought to express in this volume. More than anyone else, they have inspired a sense of commitment in us to want to contribute to the world. We hope this book can be a small testimony to our deep appreciation for their many years of encouragement and support.

Finally, we want to express our thanks and appreciation to our immediate families. Their loving encouragement throughout the long and sometimes arduous journey of doing the book and Project Victory enabled us to continue and to complete the process. To our partners, Heidi Hamrick and Barbara Lapid, we thank you for your wisdom, tolerance, and immense support. And to our children, Zeya Schindler, and Zack and Maya Lapid, we dedicate this book in appreciation for what you teach us and in the hope that you will inherit a beautiful world.

Projecting Victory

Project (v.)
to focus the mind; to throw an idea or image
forward in time, as in to project a vision for
building a more secure and peaceful future
for everyone.
Project (n.)
any organized effort; a disciplined activity or
cndeavor, as in the commitment to listen and
work together across different faiths, races,
and political points of view.
Victory (n.)
The old meaning: to win over, to defeat, to
conquer, as in war or battle; I win/you lose.
The new meaning: to defeat the threats to our
future; to win the peace for ourselves and our
children; to restore the environment; to take
charge of our lives and transform our relationship
to conflict; I win/you win.

A few years ago, we were working on the early stages
of this book in a mountain cabin. After working all day we
needed a change of atmosphere, and wandered down to the
little town. The only place open that late in the evening
was the Mountain Bar and Grill.

We were sitting at a table, absorbed again in the writing.
A guy at the next table leaned over with a smile and said:
"What are you guys writing?"

"It's a book."

"What kind of book?" came the surprised response. "What's it about?"

In the background, people were talking about the football game the next day and taking bets on which team was going to win.

"Well, it's a book about winning — about a victory we all can win. We're in the third quarter of the game to prevent disaster and build a better future. We're playing against ourselves and against time. We're going to win, because we have to."

The guy responded: "Nuclear weapons, man. Do you really think we've got a chance? And if the nukes don't get us, the pollution will. I figure the last fifteen years since I got back from Vietnam have been gravy. The human race is history. You know what I mean?"

He paused and then added, "Your book must be fiction."

"It is like science fiction now," we acknowledged, "but hopefully we all can make it happen."

He nodded, "Like Jules Verne writing about submarines 40 years before they were invented?"

"Right."

The Vietnam veteran wandered off. An hour or so later he came back, and said, "Maybe the world does have a chance but I wouldn't bet on it."

We shared with him that we thought the world would have an even better chance if we all put our money on it. The veteran, years of hard living creased in the lines of his face, smiled, "Yeah, I know what you mean."

That was a conversation neither of us has ever forgotten. Many people think it's too late. Many have given up on the future. Yet, maybe the world does have a chance. And maybe, each one of us has a chance to do something that really matters. So why not give it our best effort? For as Winston Churchill once observed, "Only when you play for more than you can afford to lose, do you really learn the game."

In 1985, along with Theo Brown, former executive director of Ground Zero, we founded Project Victory to help teach a new kind of winning. We began to work with thousands of Americans from across the political spectrum to develop effective methods for mediated dialogue and conflict management. We conducted communication workshops and "Dialogues on New Options for Peace and Security" in more than 40 cities across the United States, such as Medford, Oregon; New Orleans, Louisiana; Omaha, Nebraska; and Detroit, Michigan. In Washington, D.C., we developed working dialogue groups for the national staff members of conservative and liberal organizations. In New Mexico, we organized the first statewide dialogue which brought together community leaders from all points of view.

The methods, skills, and tools outlined in this book have been derived from the insights of thousands of Americans who have participated in our programs. We have facilitated dialogues involving members of Congress, nuclear weapons scientists, advisors to President Reagan, environmentalists, business executives, psychologists, military officers, religious leaders from the different faiths, and organizations which span the cultural and political spectrum, including: Young Republicans and Young Democrats, the Nuclear Freeze Campaign, the American Legion, Physicians for Social Responsibility, and The League of Women Voters.

In doing these dialogues, we have often been reminded of an ancient story called "The Eighteenth Camel." Once there was an old man who had three sons. In his will, he said: One-half of my camels go to my eldest son, one-third to my second son, and one-ninth to my third son. When he died, he had seventeen camels for the three sons to divide. The sons were dumbfounded. How could they divide up seventeen camels? After months of conflict with no success, they went to the village sage to ask for counsel.

The sage thought for a long time, then said, "I will give you one of my camels and now you have eighteen camels," whereupon they divided the eighteen camels: nine to the eldest, six to the second, and two to the third. This left one remaining camel which the sons gave back to the sage.

In the story of "The Eighteenth Camel," everybody wins. The three sons get their rightful share. The father's will is carried out. The sage gets his camel back and is recognized for his wisdom. There are no losers. Yet, all of this emerged out of a situation which previously looked impossible. The story teaches that through the discovery of new insight and new options, everyone can win.

Many of us have difficult conflicts in our personal lives which appear unsolvable. Similarly, the problems of international security and environmental degradation often seem to be without solution. Yet, when people in conflict come together with a shared intention to find new options, solutions can emerge where previously there were none. This is not to imply that it is always as easy as the wise man adding one extra camel. Sometimes, finding mutually acceptable solutions is difficult, but it is not impossible.

We experienced this when we were in Los Alamos, New Mexico in April, 1986. We were there to facilitate the first "New Security Dialogue" at Fuller Lodge, where Robert Oppenheimer had convened the scientists of the Manhattan Project more than forty years earlier. For the past four months, we had been organizing this first statewide dialogue. We went to leaders in the different communities throughout the state and asked them to participate. Many said they would come, but doubted that those who disagreed with them would be there.

Los Alamos sits on a high mesa in the Jemez Mountains looking out across the Rio Grande Valley toward the snow-capped peaks of the Sangre de Cristo Mountains. It is a magnificent spot with a view in all directions. It was here in this remote spot during World War II that the physicists of the Manhattan Project discovered how to harness the power that fuels the stars.

This first dialogue at Los Alamos was the kick-off for a nine-day educational campaign that involved 1000 community leaders in 24 dialogues in ten cities and towns all around New Mexico. There were representatives from the veterans, the military, the weapons laboratories, the disarmament community, the business community, the local colleges, the different religious faiths, and the diverse cultures of the Southwest.

Dr. Louis Rosen, who had come to Los Alamos as a young physicist to work on the Manhattan Project and stayed to build and direct one of the largest facilities, the Meson Laboratory, began his opening remarks by saying that communication was the key to our shared quest for peace.

"In the past," Dr. Rosen said, "wars could be fought without endangering all of human civilization. But a nuclear war threatens to do just that. Ten years from now I see equal horrors coming from biological weapons and chemical weapons. To solve these problems humanity must start communicating better than it has in the past, one with another."

The second person to speak up said, "I have been a nuclear weapons designer for 29 years. I have never been to a public meeting before. I read about this dialogue in the paper, and it sounded balanced, like I could really express my point of view. So I decided to come. My wife couldn't believe that I was actually coming." There was a pause, then his voice trembled: "What I want to say is that I am afraid. I fear that some war will erupt and in our madness we will use these terrible weapons on ourselves."

The sincerity of his comment broke the ice and made it easier for people of different points of view to share their thoughts and feelings. The next person said she had been a peace activist for the past decade, and this was the first time she had ever sat in a room, face to face, and talked to bomb builders. Soon the room was alive with discussion. The tone was not self-righteous or adversarial, but based on inquiry.

At the second dialogue at Los Alamos nine days later, our panel consisted of prominent figures from across the political spectrum — from the head of the Advanced Weapons Division at the Laboratory, to the former commander-in-chief of our naval forces in the Pacific, to one of the nation's leading advocates of arms control. The panel and the audience managed in a relatively short period to reach consensus on twelve proposals that our country could take "to reduce the risk of nuclear war, while maintaining our national security."

Two months later, as part of the Trinity Symposium, we had a third dialogue in Los Alamos. The panel consisted of esteemed scientists. Whether they were for or against the Strategic Defense Initiative, all of them agreed that ultimately technology could not get us out of the mess we are in. Only a change in human communication and thinking could do that. For the longer run, we need, as Dr. Louis Rosen put it that evening, "an evolution of thinking and feeling where people see that war is no longer an option and are compelled to find other ways to solve our problems."

Dr. Sheila Tobias and Dr. Richard Pipes participated in a dialogue on steps our country could take to reduce the risk of global war. Dr. Pipes is a Harvard professor of Soviet History and a former advisor to President Reagan on U.S.-Soviet relations. Dr. Tobias is a nationally known scholar and spokesperson for arms control from the University of Arizona. He is a forceful advocate of peace-through-strength. She is a forceful advocate of peace-through-disarmament.

After the dialogue, in which each listened and responded and sought to find common ground, they both commented on their experiences:

Dr. Richard Pipes: "I have never attended a conference quite like this one. It is a good thing. I think what it does is it narrows down some of the extreme points of view on either side and creates something more of a consensus. . . . I think you'll find it will have an effect on the public as well as the principals, the panelists. It will change their way of thinking."

Dr. Sheila Tobias: "I was skeptical to begin with that people who disagree fundamentally could look for commonalties, but I've been very impressed. I see what we have done here as a model for negotiation with the Soviet Union, because we are really looking not for where we disagree, but for where we agree."

At the outset of the new year in 1989, *Time* magazine

broke its tradition of naming an outstanding man or woman of the year. Instead, it named the "Endangered Earth" as the "Planet of the Year." "This year the Earth spoke, like God warning Noah of the deluge," said the editors of *Time*. "Its message was loud and clear, and suddenly people began to listen. . . . As man heads into the last decade of the 20th century, he finds himself at a crucial turning point: the actions of those now living will determine the future, and possibly the very survival of the species." *Time* concluded the article by calling for "a universal crusade to save the planet. Unless mankind embraces that cause totally, and without delay, it may have no alternative to the bang of nuclear holocaust or the whimper of slow extinction."

This book offers a description of the challenge that human beings now face and a vision of how we can emerge from this challenge with a personal and global victory. It offers skills to deepen our communication and handle conflicts more effectively. It is addressed to both our individual lives and our world situation. The book asserts that we are called to become the architects of a new era of human dignity, environmental restoration, and real peace.

It points out that our current adversarial politics are not effectively addressing the paramount issues of our survival. Factions and policies fluctuate back and forth leaving us with no clear sense of direction. In order to achieve longer-term comprehensive policies to address the threats to our future, we must change the way we formulate these policies. What is needed is both a personal transformation and a political transformation — a change in both the ways we communicate and resolve conflicts in our personal lives, and a change in the way we interact politically and make policies.

The book suggests that the journey to a future we all want begins with a positive vision: that humanity will not perish, and together we will build a more secure and peaceful twenty-first century. The next step is for each of us to step forward and say: "I will do my part." And then out of our common resolve we can reach across to people with whom we disagree, to learn from one another, to increase our understanding, and most important, to begin to work together.

Central to the book is Thomas Jefferson's invocation: "Not for ourselves alone, but for all humanity. . . . Let us hasten to find the path that leads to liberty, safety, and peace for everyone." The book is divided into four inter-related sections, each a different approach, or path, to the goal of a Great Turning. Part I is the path of vision and imagination. Part II is the path of analysis and commitment. Part III is the path of creative action. Part IV is the path of transformational strategy.

I: "With Hope for the Turn of the Century," begins in the year 2025 and tells the story, from the point of view of an old man, of the events that shaped the Great Turning, of how we rallied to address and overcome the human-caused threats to the future of life, especially the danger of global war and environmental catastrophe. It is a positive and shared story about our global future. Humankind needs to have a believable vision for the ending of war and the winning of peace in our time. The story told by the old man is one version, our effort to express what we hope can happen.

II: "Victory Over the Common Danger," is an analysis of the roots of our current predicament. Our common danger necessitates an evolutionary shift of mind: we are compelled to acknowledge our increasing, global interdependence and to take conscious responsibility for our future together. Interdependence requires a new meaning of victory — the ability to communicate effectively across our differences and the skills to resolve conflicts without violence toward mutual gain (I win/you win). The potential for species-wide destruction necessitates a species-wide ethic of respect for all persons and for the living Earth.

III: "Practice for Winning," is the how-to section of the book. It provides sixteen practical methods which can enable us to live the change we want for our world:

Four Principles for a New Kind of Victory
Four Steps for Shaping Our Future

Four Skills for the Art of Dialogue
Four Tools for Transforming Conflict

By using these methods, we can learn the art of dialogue and skillful communication. We can manage conflict in ways that are constructive and applicable to personal, national, and global concerns.

IV: "Getting to the Great Turning," outlines a broad strategy for the 1990s of how we can use these methods to create a politics of interdependence appropriate for the next century. It suggests a new model of mediated dialogue to arrive at the widest spectrum of agreement, methods to build a dialogue movement, ways to create more peace in one's life, to help restore the natural environment, and to create the beginning of a Great Turning by the turn of the century.

As we have travelled around this country listening to people from all walks of life, we have felt a remarkable depth of concern about our future. Facilitating a dialogue between the Young Republicans and the Young Democrats in Gainesville, Florida, we watched the stereotypes begin to break down and a deeper effort to discover workable alternatives emerge. Listening to six B-52 bomber pilots and six peace activists talk honestly with one another about their real fears of war and shared hopes for peace, we saw the power of human decency and common purpose cross ideological lines.

There are many hopeful signs that humanity is taking a turn toward life. The awareness and concern about the threat to our global environment has never been greater. There are increased possibilities for international environmental cooperation. The United States and the Soviet Union negotiated the I.N.F. treaty, agreeing to destroy an entire class of nuclear weapons through mutual verification and on-site inspection. A recent newspaper headline said: "Peace Breaking Out Throughout the World — Nations Seek End to Futile Wars." The article pointed to "the latest in a string of nations to opt for a peaceful solution to a bloody war that failed."

Our hope is increasing, based upon tangible breakthroughs. These breakthroughs reflect the beginning of a change in the way we are thinking and interacting with each other, and in our awareness of our relationship to the Earth. There is a growing recognition that if we humans are going to survive, we must acknowledge that we share a common goal — to preserve and enhance life on our planet. Again and again in dialogues, we have seen this shared commitment emerge between people who vehemently disagree — environmentalists versus developers, weapons manufacturers versus disarmament activists — and who then stretch to listen to one another and discover mutually workable options. In these "small turnings" of real dialogue across traditional battle lines, we have witnessed a new level of communication and problem-solving still in its infancy, yet growing more viable as an alternative to resolving conflicts through war. These small and important turnings are leading up to what we call the Great Turning.

Finally, this book is an invitation to everyone who is concerned about the future of our nation and our world to participate in a momentous period in human history. It is a call to help make the last decade of the twentieth century a time of profound transition to achieve a victory over the human-caused threats to our future. It is an invitation to help build the foundation for a more secure and peaceful twenty-first century.

With Hope
For The Turn Of
The Century

*If I were asked to name the most important date
in the history of the human race, I would answer
without hesitation, 6 August, 1945. From the dawn
of consciousness until 6 August, 1945, man had to
live with the prospect of his death, as an individual;
since the day when the first atomic bomb outshone
the sun over Hiroshima, he has had to live with the
prospect of his extinction as a species.*
— Arthur Koestler —

*In twelve years we will celebrate a day that comes
once in a thousand years: the beginning of a new
year, a new century, and a new millennium. For the
first time, on such an historic day, the choice before
mankind will be not just whether we make the future
better than the past, but whether we will enjoy the
future.*
— Richard M. Nixon —

*We still have it in our power to rise above the fears,
imagined and real, and to shoulder the great burdens
which destiny has placed upon us, not for our country
alone, but for the benefit of all the world.*
— Helen Keller —

*We do not have generations, we only have years, in
which to attempt to turn things around.*
— Lester Brown —

*It is individuals who change societies, give birth to
ideas; who, standing out against tides of opinion,
change them.*
— Doris Lessing —

*The day that hunger is eradicated from the earth,
there will be the greatest spiritual explosion the world
has ever known. Humanity cannot imagine the joy
that will burst into the world on the day of that
great revolution.*
— Federico Garcia Lorca —

*The future belongs to those who give the next generation
reasons to hope.*
— Teilhard de Chardin —

As we approach the end of the twentieth century, an
increasing number of people sense in a visceral way that a
time of great transition is at hand. We can no longer, as
in previous periods of human history, be certain that the
legacies of our time will be passed to future generations.
No longer is the survival of human civilization, and the
global environment which sustains us, assured. Our future
is at risk.

The twenty-first century, long viewed as a period of
science fiction, is now only a decade away. The high school
graduating class of the year 2000 entered first grade in the
fall of 1988. Most of us who have children, or know children
whom we love, can personalize the coming of the next century through the growth of our kids. The future is no longer
abstract. The future laughs and cries, runs and plays along-
side us in the present.

What will the world be like at the turn of the century?
Will it be staggering along the edge of crisis and terror? Or
will we have chosen a clear path toward greater security
and reduced hostility?

We face, at the same time, unprecedented threats and unprecedented opportunities. We fear the cataclysm of nuclear
war while simultaneously planning space flights to Mars. We
possess more wealth and technology than ever before, yet
hundreds of millions go to bed hungry at night. We double

the total accumulation of human knowledge every decade, yet much of the world remains illiterate.

The explosion of the first atom bomb at White Sands, New Mexico on July 16, 1945 marked the beginning of a new era in human history. For the first time, we are faced with the choice of becoming conscious agents of our destiny, or drifting unconsciously toward what Einstein called "unparalleled catastrophe." It is a critical moment, a crossroads in human evolution different in kind from any previous period.

There are two photographs of our time which most graphically depict this choice. The first is the mushroom-shaped cloud rising in purple and red hues off the desert floor. The second is the picture of the planet Earth, a blue sphere glowing with life in the dark recesses of black space. These two photographs represent a shift in the human capacity to perceive our identity. For the first time, we have a picture of our home, upon which we have evolved and are evolving. We can see more clearly than ever before that the unity of life on this planet is not only a theological tenet, but a profound ecological truth.

We humans not only possess the technology, but also the greed, ignorance, fear, and hatred necessary to destroy the world. We also have the insight, ingenuity, determination, and compassion to make this world a place of dignity and joy. We have the technology to end hunger. We have the scientific knowledge to stop the poisoning of nature and to restore our environment, while maintaining our economy. We have the ability to build a more secure and peaceful future for everyone on Earth.

The question of our evolution has come full circle. Have we traveled across the millennia only to end the journey? Or are we maturing to the stage where we will take responsibility to help shape our future with conscious dedication? The twentieth century has given us two archetypal images of our reckoning with destiny. We have an image of our interdependent life and an image of our collective death. We are standing in the moment of choice.

At the end of the 1990s, we will commemorate a day which comes only once in a thousand years. It is the turning from one century to another, the end of one millennium, and the beginning of the next — and if we choose, a turning away from the threat of destruction to a positive future. This "Great Turning" does not mean that we will have created some idealistic world. It does not mean that we will end greed, or eliminate all destructive conflicts. Rather it means that we humans will have ceased to be our own worst enemies. It means that we will have achieved a new level of problem-solving and ethical awareness appropriate to an interdependent world.

Our vision is that the 1990s will be a period of profound transition in which thousands, and then millions, of individuals take responsibility to address and overcome the threats to our future. This transition will start slowly, then build to a crescendo of shared commitment and celebration by the year 2000. The beginning of the twenty-first century will be remembered as a turning point in history, as individuals and nations begin to relate to each other with mutual respect and manage their conflicts so as to generate mutual gain. Out of the increased recognition of our interdependence, we humans will discover a new meaning of victory.

Our vision is that historians of the late twenty-first century — one hundred years from now — will look back on this period as the Great Turning. They will say that a movement for the survival and enhancement of life began in the last decade of the twentieth century. They will note that this movement had its roots in earlier movements for human rights and human dignity, and that this movement developed a process of communication whereby people of different points of view could treat each other with respect and discover common goals. As a result, the conditions which underlie the threat of global war were overcome, the ecology of the Earth was renewed, hunger was ended, and there were radical advancements in human health and technology.

And these historians will wonder about the literature of the late twentieth century which had predicted that we had reached the end of the frontier. They will say that we who lived at the turn of the century were actually poised on the edge of two frontiers — one to journey to the outer recesses of space, and the other to journey to the inner recesses of the human mind and spirit.

Vision precedes the creation of a new reality. "If we cannot envision the world we would like to live in, we cannot work towards its creation," writes psychologist Chellis Glendinning, author of *Waking Up in the Nuclear Age.* "If we cannot place ourselves in it, in our imagination, we will not believe it is possible."

A young man in a community dialogue we facilitated described his experience of learning how to hang-glide. In this sport, people jump off ocean cliffs and other high places on single-person kites, and if they are skillful, they glide down to safe landing spots below. The young man said that the first lesson his instructors taught was: "Never look where you don't want to land." If you focus on the rocks, he explained, you are likely to be drawn there. By looking where you want to land, the chances you'll get there are much greater.

Culturally, we have been doing a lot of looking where we don't want to land. For the past few decades, many books and movies have told and retold the stories of a coming apocalypse. These negative images of our future increase the sense of inevitability and helplessness. Fear-oriented versions of the future tend to function as self-fulfilling prophecies. Although fear can be useful to awaken us to the critical importance of the danger, it is not possible to build a positive future from foundations of fear and images of ruin. When we internalize such images, we feel powerless; as if history is being done to us, as if we are hypnotized by our own nightmares. Who, if not us, is telling the story about how our future will be?

What is needed is a vision which inspires us to come together across our different points of view and begin to relate to the coming of the next century as a time of great healing and social transformation. We can begin to change our national and global situation by transforming the way we think about its possibilities, remembering the first lesson of hang-gliding — to look where we want to land.

Through myth and story, Joseph Campbell said, we generate images which transcend the apparent limits of our past and give us glimpses of the next stage of our development. What follows is our vision of how this Great Turning can come to pass. It is intended to be a parable for how we can change the way we interact with each other, from the personal, to the national, to the global. Hopefully it will provoke you to envision your own version of such a future.

CHAPTER ONE

Looking Back From The Year 2025

We begin by looking back from the future. The time is August 6, 2025. The speaker is an old man who during the 1990s and the first decades of the twenty-first century was active in the movement which led to the Great Turning.

The sky is clearing, the air fresh from a desert rain. Lightning flashes in the distance. The storm has passed. The white sands of the New Mexico desert shimmer in the late afternoon sun. Looking out across this expanse, I am struck by its awesome beauty. It seems altogether fitting that this place should be the site for the first World Monument.

Standing at the base of the monument, I am moved by its grandeur and simplicity. Like the Jefferson and Lincoln memorials, the designers have captured some ineffable quality, a stirring tribute sculpted from the world's finest materials.

I remember being here five years ago today at the dedication ceremony, with 500,000 people from almost every country, gathered in celebration and prayer. The inscription carved into stone reads:

**World Monument
To commemorate a new era
of human dignity and world peace.
Together, we have achieved
a victory for the children
of all future generations.**

The inscription is signed by the leaders of nations worldwide and dated August 6, 2020.

Around the monument, there is a large reflecting pool laid out in a circle, with flags from the nations of the world. Beyond the flags are immense flower gardens. It is a shrine in the midst of the desert, an oasis of life. Thousands of people visit this spot each year. We come for many reasons: to remember, to relive the events with our children, to feel the joy of what we have achieved. And we come to recommit ourselves to the challenge of living with respect for all peoples and our Earth.

I am an old man now. I am in good health, but my time is short. I want to tell you a story. It is not my story, though I had a part to play. Rather it is the story of a generation which dedicated itself to achieving something very good and great. I am glad to have lived through this period which many historians now say is one of the most significant in human history.

For most of the twentieth century, the advancements of our technology far outstripped our wisdom. But we were compelled to mature. In the mirror of our nuclear/environmental predicament, we saw ourselves: our fears, our strengths, our obsolete ways of interacting, and our abilities to transcend our circumstances. Once we had committed ourselves to avoiding a self-inflicted global catastrophe, we were able to create the conditions for what we did want: a future built upon real peace and security.

Of course, we still have our problems. Greed has not disappeared, nor conflict, hatred, and strife. I would guess there are no fewer conflicts between nations now than there were in the twentieth century. What is different is how we deal with those conflicts. We have learned how to apply the principles of dialogue and conflict management in order to keep our differences from escalating into violence. War is not tolerated by the world community. It is viewed as a counterproductive tantrum which threatens everyone's survival. Conflict, however, is seen as largely a good thing. By breaking the connection between violence and conflict, we have been able to focus on the constructive uses of conflict. In this sense, we have taken an evolutionary step.

As I look out at the monument, I am reminded of the visionaries who across the centuries called for "peace and good will on Earth." What we have achieved is not some kind of ultimate peace. We humans seem to love our battles with one another, and I doubt we would ever want to give them up. But we have turned a great corner in terms of our ethical and spiritual development.

I was born in the aftermath of World War II and like most of my generation, I grew up wondering if there would be a future. We were raised on television and jet planes in a shrinking yet violent world. Below the surface there was always the question, "Will we live to be old and have grandchildren, or will our lives be ended by a World War III?" We grew up with this fear in the background, but most of us did not want to think about it, because it seemed like there was nothing we could do.

The nuclear era began here at Alamogordo, New Mexico in 1945: the Trinity site. At this place, just before dawn on July 16, several hundred scientists and military personnel watched the explosion of the first atom bomb. As one witness put it, "It was as if the Sun was rising in the wrong direction." Twenty-three days later, the first atom bomb was dropped on Hiroshima, Japan.

Alamogordo was Apache country. But the handful of cattle ranchers and homesteaders who lived here in 1945 called it by the Spanish name, Jornado del Muerto, "the Journey of Death." That was 80 years ago, the dawn of the nuclear age.

There were many times during the next few decades when it looked pretty grim. I remember in the early 1980s when my son was an infant, wondering if he would be killed in a nuclear war before he grew up, or if he would reach adulthood in a polluted and depleted world. We were closer to the edge than most of us were willing to admit.

Perhaps the hardest thing for us to grasp about these threats to our survival was that we could do anything to make a difference. At times, the world situation looked like "the Journey of Death." Many people were convinced that our self-destruction was inevitable. Like almost everyone, I lived in denial for many years, concerned primarily with my personal life and immediate goals. I suppose at some level I believed the world situation was hopeless, or at least beyond my capacity to affect the outcome.

We were on the edge. Little did we know that we were also on the edge of a breakthrough. Just like any major step, at the time it seemed so far out of reach. But now, looking back, historians of the twenty-first century refer to this period as "the Great Turning." It was a time like no other. What had appeared to be the Journey of Death became an impetus for us to wake up, to take charge of our destiny. Historians still debate how it all happened, although they generally agree there were several definite stages.

Individual Responsibility

The first years of the twentieth century's final decade were a time of transition for the United States and indeed for the whole world. Many people began to realize that an era was ending and a new one beginning. At the core of this change was a profound increase in our understanding of how interdependent the world had become. The daily realities of international trade, environmental problems which cut across national boundaries, and the threats of regional and global wars constantly reminded us that our fate was linked to that of all people. Breakthroughs in worldwide communication heightened our awareness. Interactive television where people in different countries talked with each other live via satellite became commonplace and symbolized our growing sense of a "global village."

In our country, this new attitude was clearly apparent in the messages used by advertisers and politicians. The image of Earth seen from space was everywhere we looked, in our magazines and on television. The more we recognized our interdependence, the more we began to acknowledge it was in our own best interests to find ways to communicate with one another and resolve our conflicts without resorting to violence. Millions of people now grasped that this was a pivotal time in history. With six billion people living on Earth and various technologies to destroy ourselves, we had to learn new ways.

Some argued that we needed a personal transformation — a change in the way we relate to one another as individuals and with the natural environment. Others argued that we needed a political transformation — a change in the way our politics addressed our problems. Both groups were right. And the movement which emerged addressed both together.

This ethical movement began with individuals taking responsibility for living the change we wanted in the world. The movement spread from person to person through circles of trust, neighborhoods, and professional associations. And what was the message? Hard to put into words. The way I understood it was: Each one of us matters. And the way we relate to everyone and everything in our lives has an impact on the world. The essence was for each of us to contribute our unique piece to the larger tapestry.

Thousands of us began to live with an ethic of respect for life and to deal more creatively with our conflicts. At the core of this practice was the principle of reciprocity — treating ourselves and others the way we wanted to be treated. Over the centuries, the wisest of humankind had pointed to this practice to heal the immense damage we had done to each other and to nature. What was different about living in the nuclear age was that the principle of reciprocity was no longer just a moral ideal, but a practical method for achieving our long-term security and happiness.

The preservation of nature demanded reciprocity also. Conservation became a way of life. We began to recycle everything from bottles and newspapers to all different kinds of solid-waste materials. Recycling and waste conversion became two of the major new business enterprises of the 1990s.

We began to create peace in our lives by resolving our conflicts more effectively with friends, family, co-workers, and strangers. Hundreds of neighborhood mediation centers were established in cities around the country. Corporations utilized principles of conflict management to promote the overall health and productivity of the organization. Thousands of schools developed educational programs to teach ecology and skills to resolve conflicts peaceably. In addition to resolving conflicts better, we became aware of the need to take care of our health and well-being. Methods to create peace of mind had been available for a long time. The real key was that we began to use them in our lives: reducing stress, taking time to renew ourselves and to experience the joy of being alive.

During the 1990s, this cultural change profoundly affected the way we did politics and made decisions regarding the paramount issues of our survival. Dialogue methods based upon reciprocity were developed and refined so that different factions could listen respectfully and work together to find new options. We began to listen to people with whom we disagreed, to look for common ground, and to help build the basis for a new kind of politics.

National Reconciliation

As the nation faced the beginning of another long and divisive presidential election, increasing numbers of us saw that the politics of narrow self-interest could not solve the complex and unparalleled threats to our future. At a time when we needed to be thinking farther ahead to address the real problems, our politics were too short-term and too narrow in scope. We began to see what some experts had been telling us for years — that without a national consensus our country could not steer a clear and steady course toward real security.

The challenge of complex problems — such as reducing the risk of global war while maintaining our national safety, or restoring the natural environment while strengthening our economy — required us to work together across our differences. Only through dialogue and consensual decision-making could we arrive at consistent and comprehensive policies.

By mid-decade the number of us who had made a personal commitment to improve our communication and conflict-resolution skills continued to grow steadily. One media observer estimated that more than half a million Americans were actively involved in regular conflict-resolution efforts. In addition, many times more than this number were exposed to educational programs on conflict management through schools, churches, and other organizations. There were clear indications that we were thinking very differently about how to deal with conflict and what it means to "win" in an interdependent world.

Some alarming studies on the environment helped to underscore our interdependence and re-define "winning" and "losing." Since the late 1980s scientists had been warning us about the depletion of the ozone layer that protects us from the Sun's ultraviolet rays. It took a shocking report, however, issued by the World Health Organization to finally get our full attention. This report concluded that a startling rise in cancer rates was directly attributable to the ozone depletion, and predicted catastrophic results unless worldwide cooperative efforts were made to halt this trend. Many of us were shocked and frightened and once again were compelled to grasp the reality that we are all inextricably linked together.

Soon people began to do something about their fears. Warily at first, people from opposing camps began to step across partisan boundaries to listen to each other and to understand each other's perspectives. There were discussion groups and national symposia all around the country bringing people with different points of view together in a common search for the way out of the predicaments we faced. It was quite remarkable when conservatives and liberals really listened to each others' concerns. Instead of making each other wrong, we learned to include other perspectives in our thinking and policy formation.

Previous interactions between these camps had been bitter and adversarial. Now, there was a growing recognition that the next step had to emerge from constructive dialogue. Corporate and environmental leaders participated in extended dialogues to formulate long-term strategies to reverse the greenhouse effect. Conservative and liberal groups joined in national dialogues to formulate new and inclusive strategies for peace and security.

All kinds of folks started to participate in the renewal of our democratic life. Business groups, civic organizations, and universities around the country sponsored public forums that included many points of view about the global threats we faced. Through dialogue we were able to break the stalemate and find workable solutions. The bitter divisions from the Vietnam era were increasingly healed, as more and more people from the "Baby Boom" generation became involved. Women, perhaps more than any other group, played a pivotal part in leading the Great Turning.

Christians, Jews, Buddhists, and people of all faiths renewed their commitment to the sanctity of life. By affirming our traditions of reconciliation, we were able to work together more effectively in the search for shared ethical principles upon which to base the policies of our nation. There was a quiet meeting of the ways, dedicated to preserving and enhancing life on Earth. I remember when we began to "pass the peace" from person to person, group to group, across denominations and creeds.

The dialogue process became so popular that it began to produce genuine national reconciliation. We began to bridge the differences that had divided us and acknowledge the need for an undivided national purpose to address the various threats to our life and liberty. A coalition of major organizations from across the political spectrum sponsored the first national dialogues between congressional and presidential candidates.

These mediated dialogues were quite different from adversarial debates. Basic principles of communications and conflict resolution which had become increasingly familiar to the culture were used to help candidates discuss how they agreed and disagreed on critical issues without the polarizing rhetoric. Skillful moderators facilitated at each event to make sure that this climate of mutual respect and open inquiry was maintained.

Television and media played a critical role in the dialogue movement, enabling us to conduct national "Electronic Town Meetings." Through interactive television we were able to discuss and give feedback to experts and national leaders. It also allowed us to have simultaneous dialogue between groups in Chicago, New York, San Francisco, New Orleans, or wherever.

The dialogue movement began to have a noticeable impact on the media itself. Reporters and television commentators began to report the discussion of critical issues in ways that were more informational and less adversarial. The role of the press in a twenty-first century democracy was much discussed and increasingly the networks began to devote more prime time to news coverage that was truly educational.

The media began to discover that a generation which wanted to bring about a Great Turning wanted to hear the full story. Indeed, the small steps and major breakthroughs in solving terrible human problems were what large segments of the population had been waiting to hear. I remember coming home from work in those days, and feeling glad to read the newspapers.

After twenty years of books and movies about the inevitable apocalypse, the stories changed. They became powerful tales of how the human race took charge to overcome the forces of death and destruction. A new generation of musicians gave us songs of hope. There were gatherings and celebrations. What I remember most is a profound sense of purpose. We felt connected to other people —

we were engaged in a common endeavor. The more involved we became, the more we felt the joy of knowing we were going to make it. In a sense, we began to celebrate the victory of our common humanity long before it was assured.

We began to appreciate and exercise the freedoms of our democracy directed toward choosing our future. This left millions of us hopeful that the final presidential campaign of the twentieth century might move beyond partisan rhetoric and actually arrive at new ways that Americans of diverse perspectives could work together. Fortunately, we were not disappointed. The tone and style of the campaign was the most respectful that I can remember. Candidates and their supporters really listened to each other. This allowed us to see areas of agreement and explore ways to bridge our differences. Candidates found that negative advertising just didn't work anymore, because it was no longer what we wanted from our politicians.

The candidates discussed the issues more carefully and substantively, particularly those relating to the threats to our survival. Through the use of mediated dialogue, they reached a level of clarity about their views that was unprecedented. Even more importantly, they identified broad areas of policy consensus. For the first time, a presidential campaign produced agreements about how opposing candidates and parties would cooperate together after the election was over. The results of this campaign created a renewed sense of hope for the vast majority of Americans. Although we realized that many international and domestic problems threatened our future, we believed, for the first time in years, that our country was now united enough to really do something about them.

New Directions

As a result of this period of national reconciliation, we were able to mobilize our energies and best talent to address the long-term problems that underlay the threats to our future. We were able to complete the transformation of our relationship with the Soviet Union, which had begun in the previous decade. Historians agree that the superpower summits between President Reagan and Secretary-General Gorbachev set the stage for a process that eventually ended the Cold War. During the early 1990s, reductions had been achieved in nuclear weapons systems and our two countries had increased economic and cultural contact. But we had not yet been able to achieve the kind of fundamental shift in the relationship that could free our resources to focus on other problems.

With broad, bipartisan support, our newly elected president undertook an initiative designed to create this breakthrough with the Soviet Union. His strategy was to seek an agreement that would result in drastic reductions in the conventional and nuclear forces that both sides maintained in Europe. Such an agreement had been talked about for years, but never achieved. Its success would signal a fundamentally new direction in East-West relations.

During the 1990s, the Soviet leadership struggled with the conflict between their need for internal reform and their ongoing desire to maintain strong control. The old guard in the Kremlin, forged under Stalin, had all passed away. The Soviet leadership was younger, less ideological, and more pragmatic. They were faced with pressures at home to strengthen the Soviet economy, as well as with increasing protests from independently-spirited satellite countries. As the decade progressed, those who supported restructuring gained more and more influence because it was clear that the Soviet Union could not compete internationally unless it became less rigid and more open.

The logic for a truly historic, mutual reduction in our nuclear and conventional forces was increasingly compelling. We needed to put more resources into regaining technological competitiveness in world markets; they needed to develop their resources and become a first-rate economy. We needed to maintain our standard of living; they needed to raise theirs.

In the past, the Soviets had often exploited the divisions in the United States, but now they saw it was no longer possible. After hard negotiation, the Soviets and Americans reached an agreement on an amended version of the president's proposal. It called for deep reductions immediately in all of the armed forces in Europe and, over a five-year period, led to a reduction and restructuring of remaining forces so that a successful attack by either side was virtually impossible. We were able to arrive at a new stage of arms management. The excitement that greeted the announcement of this historic treaty was heightened by the news that United States and Soviet representatives had also made progress on how to reduce superpower competition in regional "hot spots."

Again, these changes were in part catalyzed by changes in our personal lives. The number of people practicing conflict resolution and working to create peace in our lives continued to increase dramatically during this period, more than a million in the United States alone. This movement spread to other countries, and all over the world people were focusing on how to better communicate and problem-solve. Like millions of people, I came to see the direct connection between how I live my life, and what happens in the world.

I recall vividly how excited I felt as the momentum toward real peace began to accelerate. As we approached the turn of the century, world public opinion pressured the superpowers and all nations involved in regional conflicts to achieve breakthroughs before the new century began. The United States and the Soviet Union announced they had reached a set of agreements about their involvement in key regional conflicts. This agreement spelled out general "principles of restraint" that they would follow in trouble spots around the world.

At first, many of us were skeptical about whether or not the United States and the Soviet Union would comply with these "principles of restraint." However, our skepticism began to fade as both of the superpowers cancelled shipments of arms and began to curtail their involvement in escalating conflicts. When this happened, other nations started to believe that the United States and the Soviets were serious about a different kind of competition — and that it might be possible to create and sustain significant change in the world.

At the same time on the environmental front, the president called for a series of national dialogues. These dialogues held between environmental and corporate leaders produced a comprehensive strategy to help reverse the greenhouse effect. Legislation was passed to create incentives for conservation. Nationally, we reduced our fossil-fuel consumption greatly, while maintaining our standard of living. We began to seriously develop alternative, renewable energy sources. This increased public concern about the environment was reflected in American politics. The United States and other nations accelerated their efforts to prevent the destruction of tropical forests by buying the debt of Third World nations in exchange for their commitment to preserve the rain forests. Resources freed up from the de-escalation of international tensions were increasingly transferred to the challenge of restoring our natural environment.

World Convocation

The idea for a gathering of world leaders to make peace among nations was as old as human aspiration itself. Throughout the 1990s the seeds of this idea began to take root and grow, first within the religious communities, and then with the general public. The purpose of the World Convocation was to bring together representatives of all of the nations to use methods of dialogue and conflict resolution to find ways we could work together to achieve a more secure and humane twenty-first century.

Around the world there were dialogues and gatherings for national and cultural leaders to promote the concept. I think the Convocation caught hold because the war-weary people of the world seized upon the idea of the turning of the century and the dawn of a new millennium as a truly momentous time. Religious people everywhere across the creeds and traditions began to share the deeply felt aspiration that the turn of the century would mark the beginning of a different way in human relationships.

It was remarkable to hear leading cultural, scientific, and religious figures all speaking out for a World Convocation. There was a growing alliance of shared commitment across traditional divisions of ideology, faith, and culture. People of good will everywhere put out the call for the Convocation, and many nations, rich and poor, began to respond. After the success of their recent, unprecedented treaties, the leaders of the United States and the Soviet Union announced they would participate.

The World Convocation was different from any conference or gathering in the past. It was facilitated by the most skilled global experts in communication and conflict resolution. When a nation decided to participate in the Convocation, it committed itself to an irrevocable process of negotiation. Every nation which sent a representative committed itself to stay throughout the negotiations until just and durable agreements were reached. However long it took, the purpose was to identify actions that could assure human survival and dignity.

By December 31, 1999, many of the clearest thinkers and most respected citizens on Earth had gathered in Geneva, Switzerland. There were leading religious figures, men and women representing each of the different faiths, recipients of the Nobel Prize, world renowned environmentalists, and dozens of esteemed scientists. The world business community was represented by top executives from national and international corporations; the leadership of the labor unions were there. Doctors, lawyers, psychologists, educators, and other professionals from all over the world were present. There were the people who had achieved worldwide recognition for their excellence: musicians, performing artists, astronauts, Olympic champions, movie stars, writers, and statesmen.

Almost all of the nations on Earth had sent official representatives to Geneva. Religious leaders from the various traditions opened the Convocation:

> We come together on the eve of the first day of the twenty-first century from all nations, races, and religions, representing the communities of the world. For centuries, war has been the final arbiter in our conflicts. Now with the threat of mutual destruction, war is no longer an option.
>
> Given the magnitude of what is at risk, we are compelled to find ways to work together: to reduce the risk of global war, to restore the ecology of our Earth, to stop the abuse of human rights, and to end hunger on our planet.
>
> As we begin the new century and the new millennium, let us resolve that on this day, the nations and peoples of the Earth turned toward peaceful ways of resolving the conflicts that divide us.

The great hall erupted in a standing ovation which continued for a long while. At midnight the delegates participated in a candlelight ceremony for the turning of the century. Religious leaders called upon those present to join with millions around the world for five minutes of silent prayer or meditation in support of the work of the Convocation.

New Year's Eve 2000 was a time of great celebration. In houses all across our nation and the world, people lit candles to give thanks, and to welcome the third millennium with the flame of peace.

Mutually Assured Development

Within a year, the World Convocation had adopted a bold plan for action. If it was not obvious before, by the first years of the twenty-first century it was unmistakably clear that nations of the world could not continue massive military expenditures and at the same time undertake the challenge of the next stage of human advancement. We could not afford to restore the natural environment, reduce hunger and poverty, and explore our solar system if we continued to devote so much of our resources and expertise to arming our planet.

The United States, the Soviet Union, Japan, and most of the European countries announced the beginning of a massive economic development plan for the underdeveloped countries, which had been conceived by the World Convocation. The President of the United States challenged the Soviet Union to an all-out peaceful competition to eliminate hunger on Earth, to restore the quality of our global environment, and to explore the outer recesses of our solar system.

Soon the race was in full swing. Instead of trying to arm the world, we began to offer the tools of real development to the peoples of the less developed nations. Just as the Marshall Plan served to rebuild and stabilize Western Europe after World War II, so this massive effort served to advance the interests of the poor peoples of the world. We took the initiative to address and overcome the social, economic, and environmental conditions which underlie war and prevent lasting peace.

As the world's strongest democracy, the United States took responsibility to articulate a policy which came to be called "mutually assured development" — the establishment of economic and cultural relations between countries in order to achieve the largest mutual gain.

Now in 2025, our world is very different than it was in the late twentieth century. Those who had preached doom and gloom proved to be mistaken. Once again, those who said we had reached the end of the journey were limited by their own narrow view. Actually, we were on the edge of two journeys: one, the exploration of outer space, and the other the exploration of human compassion and global development.

To my mind, perhaps the most remarkable consequence of this

period has been the emergence of a deep appreciation for life and
the beauty of our own planet Earth. It is a great paradox that often
when we are about to lose something, we realize how precious it
is to us.

Through a concerted campaign to promote conservation, we
have managed to slow the greenhouse effect. Temperatures in many
parts of the world have risen one to two degrees, but this is far less
than the three to eight degrees predicted in the 1980s. By making
profound adjustments in our energy producing technologies toward
renewable sources, we have averted catastrophe. Breakthroughs in
space-based solar technology have enabled us to transfer much of
our energy production away from fossil fuels.

Unfortunately there was little we could do to reverse the damage
already done to the ozone layer, but through international agreements
we were able to ban the use of chlorofluorocarbons (CFCs) throughout
the world. The intelligent application of technology produced perfectly
suitable alternatives to products such as the styrofoam container
and the aerosol spray can. Our food now comes in biodegradable
packaging, without the need for any preservatives.

Superconductivity has allowed us to create energy-efficient mass
transit systems which decongested our metropolitan areas. The industrialized countries have provided incentives to the less industrialized
countries to develop in ways that are ecologically sound. The preservation of the remaining tropical forests, plus the rapid reforestation
of large areas of the Earth, is having a slow but steady effect on
stabilizing climate and absorbing carbon dioxide.

As part of our personal commitment, many thousands of us
planted trees, especially in areas that had been damaged environmen-
tally. We revitalized Arbor Day. Tens of thousands of school children
planted millions of trees. By the late 1990s, the custom of planting
trees as a way to affirm our shared commitment to the future gained
widespread popularity. It was both symbolic and practical, a small,
yet significant step toward restoring the ecology of the Earth. Within
a short time, planting trees to commemorate the Great Turning
spread to other countries around the world.

Now, twenty years later, I see the results wherever I travel. Areas
that were once denuded are green again. Groves of small trees
planted two decades ago are beginning to look like forests. Other

foliage and wildlife have returned. The reforestation of the Earth is well under way.

Relations between the superpowers improved steadily throughout the first two decades of the twenty-first century. While there are many ideological and economic conflicts between them, the United States and the Soviet Union have learned how to defend their basic interests without threatening the other's security. As a result they were able to restructure and substantially reduce their military forces. They also worked together to solve problems in South Africa, the Middle East, Central America, and other troubled areas of the world.

Monies freed from military spending have been directed toward better medical care and education for all citizens, and particularly toward the massive task of restoring the Earth's environment. The oceans which had reached a state of deadly pollution are now well along the way toward recovering their ecological balance. Through international cooperation, we have established a network of ecological reserves and a worldwide park system for the preservation of wildlife and plant species. Most urban complexes are now designed to include city gardens and "nature-reserves." And agriculture has shifted almost entirely from the use of chemical fertilizers to sustainable and ecologically based systems.

Historians are already referring to the first two decades of the twenty-first century as a renaissance. It is no doubt one of the most creative periods known, often compared to Greece in the golden age of Socrates or to the Italy of Leonardo da Vinci. Many commentators are beginning to draw comparisons between our period and the time of the American Revolution.

Now, 80 years after Hiroshima, the spirit of mutually assured development has generated an outpouring of creativity. The pace of medical breakthroughs is astounding. After an intense international effort, scientists found a cure for AIDS. Organ transplants and laser surgery are standard fare. Perhaps most heartening is the renewed sense of responsibility to provide good medical care to all our citizens.

The average life-expectancy is between 85 and 90 years. Many thousands of people live to be over 100. This, of course, while beneficial to the individual, has created new problems. Currently, there are elaborate plans for the colonization of the Moon and

Mars to relieve population pressures at home. Large space transports should make it possible by the end of the century.

Again, the ethical aspect has been significant. There has been a resurgence of respect for our elders and a much deeper sense of their value to the human community than was current in the late twentieth century. As I have grown older, I have noticed the difference. My peers and I tend to experience ourselves as being of greater worth, able to be productive longer, and sought after for our insight and experience. Racism continues to exist, but world public opinion gives it no legitimacy. Recently I heard the UNESCO statement that only a few pockets of hungry people remain worldwide and the end of hunger is foreseen as a reality.

Just ten years ago, the human race took another major step forward in its quest to reach other planets when the joint United States-Soviet manned mission reached Mars. After a 280-day journey, across 100 million miles, the international crew of eight touched down on the Red Planet. Their stay produced new information about the evolution of our solar system which scientists are just now beginning to understand.

The vista of our solar system and beyond is opening before us. Now, the first generation of children raised on video games, computers, and space movies is preparing their own children to travel to the stars. We, like our ancestors, are about to set sail for the New World. As always in the past, we face the unknown — the terrors, the hardships, and the triumphs — of our continued encounter with the mystery of the Universe.

Looking back as an old man, I am proud and grateful to have played my part in the Great Turning.

It is peaceful here at Alamogordo. The Sun is setting on the monument. Nature has healed the scars on the land. The flower gardens are radiant in the last light of the day. Two eagles circle overhead. The Journey of Death did not come to pass. It was a warning, a call for ending our old ways, ushering in what this monument calls "a new era of human dignity and world peace." It is an elegant turn of fate that this place, which unleashed the instrument of ultimate death, should become a symbol for the renewal of life.

Victory Over
The Common Danger

*When our days become dreary with low-hovering
clouds and our nights become darker than a thousand
midnights, we will know that we are living in the
creative turmoil of a genuine civilization struggling
to be born.*
    — Martin Luther King, Jr. —

*We can all cheat on morals . . . but today the morals
of respect and care and modesty come to us in a
form that we cannot evade. We cannot cheat on
DNA. We cannot get around photosynthesis. We
cannot say I am not going to give a damn about
phytoplankton. All these tiny mechanisms provide
the preconditions of our planetary life. To say we do
not care is to say in the most literal sense that "we
choose death."*
    — Barbara Ward —

You cannot shake hands with a clenched fist.
    — Indira Gandhi —

*We are here to make a choice between the quick
and the dead. . . . Behind the black portent of the
new atomic age lies a hope which, seized upon with
faith, can work out salvation. If we fail, then we
have damned every man to be the slave of fear. Let
us not deceive ourselves: we must elect world peace
or world destruction.*
    — Bernard Baruch —

*I believe that in our constant search for security we
can never gain any peace of mind until we secure our
own soul.*
    — Margaret Chase Smith —

*We seek victory — not over any nation or people˙—
but over ignorance, poverty, disease, and human
degradation wherever they may be found.*
— Dwight D. Eisenhower —

*Each of us must accept total responsibility for the
earth's survival. We are the curators of life on earth,
standing at the crossroads of time.*
— Helen Caldicott —

*Victory at all costs, victory in spite of all terror,
victory however long and hard the road may be; for
without victory there is no survival.*
— Winston Churchill —

As we confront the problems of the late twentieth century, the critical mind in all of us may have difficulty seeing how it is possible to implement such a vision anywhere in the foreseeable future. We are aware of the realities of international power politics, driven by greed, domination, and the need for continued military force. Human history indicates that those in power do not easily make changes which benefit interests broader than their own. Frederick Douglass, the former slave and great abolitionist leader, said it clearly, "Power concedes nothing without a demand, it never has and it never will."

During World War II, when Winston Churchill called for victory, it was over the tyrannical nationalist systems that sought to dominate the world. Now we are confronted with a different kind of tyranny: the victory necessary for our survival is against the complex problems which threaten our future. What is different now is that the universal dimensions of the threat we face compel those in power to recognize it is in their own best interests to make the necessary and profound changes. This will not be easy. To deal with these unprecedented problems requires a different level of thinking and interaction. We will not be able to build a more secure and peaceful future by continuing to "make war" on those with whom we disagree. As H. L. Mencken once reminded us, "For all the world's complex problems, there are simple solutions — and they are all wrong." Realistic solutions can only be discovered step by step by changing the process of the way we interact with one another, as individuals, groups, corporations, and nations.

We saw a vivid example of this change a couple of years ago as we helped to facilitate a weekend dialogue with six B-52 bomber pilots — Air Force colonels and majors — and six long-time peace activists. It rained for most of the weekend, so we were mainly confined to a large mountain lodge. Here were twelve people of extremely diverse perspectives and life experiences trying to listen to each other and find ways to work together toward a more secure world.

One late night session, between a lieutenant colonel who had been a prisoner of war in North Vietnam and a peace activist who was a former protestor of the Vietnam War, was particularly memorable. Everyone else had retired and we stayed up talking. Both the colonel and the peace activist were from the Midwest, both graduated from college at about the same time, and then their lives had taken profoundly different directions.

When the weekend began, neither could fathom the other's point of view. At 1:00 A.M. on the second night, they shared their two stories representing the bitter divisions of a generation. Each was utterly sincere, each related the depth of his own experience, and each was willing to listen with respect to the other. For both of us, this was a moment of real hope, that people of opposing views can come to understand one another and affirm the human bond which transcends mind set. It is this ability which will allow us to come together and work together to overcome the common danger.

CHAPTER TWO

Our Common Danger

All things are possible once enough human beings realize that the whole of the human future is at stake.
— Norman Cousins —

In our early experiments to develop methods of dialogue, we discovered how important it was to create a shared context before any real exchange of information could take place. We were, after all, inviting people to talk with each other in a new way. When participants were able to see that it was in each one's best interest to be in dialogue, that they each had a "stake" in finding a mutually beneficial outcome, their willingness to really listen to each other was greatly enhanced. This chapter is, in essence, the stakes-building foundation of the rest of the book. While some of the material covered may seem familiar, we hope it will be approached as a reflection on what is at stake, and an impetus to strengthen our resolve to take positive action.

Many of us have resistance to learning about the threats to our future. We fear that the more we know, the more bleak it will seem. Yet, if we are going to achieve a Great Turning, it is essential that we inform ourselves about the dangers we face. To live in denial or ignorance is a choice which may appear to be more pleasant in the short-term, but it renders us powerless to take effective action.

Imagine that you are driving along in your car and the engine begins to make loud, frightening sounds. In response, you turn up the radio, so you no longer hear the bothersome noise. Having dealt with the problem, you drive on, at least until your engine dies. With regard to the common danger, we have convinced ourselves that the problem is not getting fixed because it is too big, too overwhelming. But perhaps the problem is not getting fixed because we keep ourselves from fixing it.

Human-Caused Threats to Life

A thousand years ago, the civilized world faced the millennium with an almost frantic sense of foreboding. Religious leaders, having consulted Biblical prophecy, had predicted that the end of the world was imminent. In the year 1000, they feared God's power would destroy the world. In the year 2000, the danger is that man's power will destroy the world — unless we take decisive action to prevent it.

Richard M. Nixon

We are living in the shadow of tremendous problems which threaten our personal, national, and global future. Throughout history, humankind has had to contend with serious threats, but the nature of the current danger is unique — and much more ominous. What is different in kind is the scope of the threats. No previous generation has had to deal with dangers that were truly global in scope. Always before, human beings have known that even if the worst were to happen, life on Earth and the potential for human civilization would continue. This is no longer the case.

Now, we are in a situation where *all people face a common danger.* There is no geographic, economic, or cultural exception to that fact. At its core, the common danger can be defined as: the human-caused threats to the future of life. The danger we face is that human beings may precipitate some form of global catastrophe from which we cannot recover.

There are two main ways this common danger manifests itself in our world: the threat of *global modern warfare* and the threat of *environmental* catastrophe. Both of these are extensions of ancient problems that have plagued humankind for centuries. Yet, both have become many times more lethal because of our greatly increased ability to control the physical world.

Global Modern Warfare. After the 1962 Cuban missile crisis, President Kennedy reflected on how close the superpowers had come to war and what the results could have been in the nuclear age. "Everything the United States has built in three centuries could have been dissipated within 18 hours," he said. "Even the fruits of victory would have been ashes in our mouths." Since that time, the world's nuclear stockpiles have multiplied more than tenfold. In the early 1980s, President Ronald Reagan said:

> I can't believe that this world can go on through our generation and on down to succeeding generations with this kind of weapon (nuclear missiles) on both sides, poised at each other, without someday some fool or some maniac or some accident triggering the kind of war that is the end of the line for all of us.

Here are a few of the most compelling statistics on the threat of modern warfare:

• There are now more than 50,000 nuclear weapons on the planet, with a total firepower that is more than 6,000 times the firepower generated by all the combatants in World War II. The vast majority of these nuclear weapons are in the hands of the two superpowers and thousands of them are loaded on intercontinental missiles that can strike the other country in a matter of minutes.

• The explosion of even a small percentage of these nuclear weapons would create death and destruction on a scale never seen before in the world. One nuclear weapon could kill more Americans in two minutes than all of our 400,000 countrymen who died in World War II. If several dozen of them were exploded in major American cities, the United States would cease to exist as a functioning modern society. It is literally true that hundreds of millions of people could die in the first day of a major nuclear war.

• Nuclear weapons are qualitatively different not only because of the size of the blast, but because of the radioactive fallout which is, in effect, a kind of poison that can be breathed in, absorbed through the skin, or eaten. After a major nuclear war, radiation would contaminate vast portions of the world.

• In 1984, the National Academy of Sciences endorsed the "nuclear winter" theory. This theory concluded that the fires created by even a relatively limited nuclear war would burn for many weeks, lifting millions of tons of debris into the atmosphere. The skies would be blackened by the smoke from these fires and this would cause temperatures to drop by many degrees. The results would be extreme weather conditions that could threaten the ecological basis of life on Earth.

• Both superpowers possess enough chemical weapons to kill millions of people if they were ever to be used. The use of chemical weapons in the Iran-Iraq war during the 1980s was a somber testimony to the fact that these destructive technologies are increasingly available to other nations. According to the *Christian Science Monitor*, there are 22 nations that now have the ability to make chemical weapons.

• Currently, there are five nations who admit to possessing nuclear weapons: the United States, the Soviet Union, Great Britain, France, and China. Knowledgeable experts point to four other countries who almost certainly possess nuclear weapons but who do not admit it: India, Pakistan, Israel, and South Africa. In addition, nations known to be actively seeking to develop nuclear weapons include: Brazil, Argentina, Libya, Iraq, and Iran.

• George Gallup, Jr., in his extensive polling of experts about the future, recently found that the threat of a regional nuclear war and nuclear terrorism are among the most probable dangers we may face. Some experts estimate that by the end of the century more than twenty nations will have the capacity to make nuclear weapons. Despite the U.S.-Soviet agreement on banning intermediate nuclear forces, comments Senator John Glenn, "the danger of nuclear war is rising, not because of what the Soviets are doing, but because of what smaller or less industrialized nations are doing to develop ... nuclear weapons."

Environmental Catastrophe. If modern warfare is a form of potential "fast death," then the threat of an unparalleled and irreversible environmental disaster is a "slow death" which could be just as catastrophic. Although urban civilization has always had environmental problems, the situation we face today is unique. In the past, humans believed the Earth was large enough to absorb whatever abuse we dealt it. Increasingly, scientists are saying this is not the case, that we have arrived at a critical threshold in our relationship to the global environment. In its call for "a universal crusade to save the planet," *Time* (January 2, 1989) declared:

> Let there be no illusions. Taking effective action to halt the massive injury to the earth's environment will require a mobilization of political will, international cooperation and sacrifice unknown except in wartime. Yet humanity is in a war right now, and it is not too Draconian to call it a war for survival. It is a war in which all nations must be allies. Both the causes and effects of the problems that threaten the earth are global, and they must be attacked globally.

There are two global environmental threats which have recently received widespread attention: the depletion of the ozone layer and the "greenhouse effect." Scientists agree that both could cause irreparable damage to the delicate climate and atmosphere that make life on Earth possible.

Concerns about damage to the protective ozone layer first began to surface in the mid-1970s. Recently, a report by more than one hundred scientists working under the auspices of NASA, the World Meteorological Organization, and the U.N. Environment Program, concluded that the hole in the ozone layer above Antarctica is larger and widening more rapidly than expected. They unanimously agreed that it is the release of chlorofluorocarbons (CFCs) into the atmosphere which is causing the ozone depletion. The problem is clearly tied to human consumption and behavior since chlorofluorocarbons are used in our refrigerators, air conditioners, plastic foam, aerosol cans, and throwaway food containers.

The ozone layer plays a vital part in making life possible on Earth. The ozone envelops the planet and shields us from the Sun's ultraviolet rays. With a diminished ozone layer, more ultraviolet radiation will reach the Earth. Scientists tell us that this has already resulted in significant increases in the rates of skin cancer. Eventually there may be many other destructive results as well. Some scientists believe that increased ultraviolet radiation will induce mutations in the organisms that anchor the food chain of the world's oceans. It could damage the human immune system and leave us defenseless against infectious diseases. It could also threaten many of our crops and, in many ways, make it much more difficult for life to exist on Earth. As David Doniger of the Natural Resources Defense Council recently warned, "It is no exaggeration to say that the health and safety of millions of people and the world are at stake."

The warming trend which scientists have observed world-wide is another development which may have severe long-term consequences. Evidence is mounting that the climate is being forced out of equilibrium by a variety of gases, primarily carbon dioxide, produced by industrial emissions — and intensified by deforestation. These gases trap solar heat in the atmosphere. Some scientists believe that the world is already experiencing dramatic changes from this "greenhouse effect." As the World Resources Institute recently pointed out, the five warmest years in the 135 years that global average temperatures have been kept are 1980, 1981, 1983, 1987, and 1988. The United States and the Soviet Union account for 45 percent of the emissions of carbon dioxide causing the greenhouse effect — what *Newsweek* called "a different form of Mutually Assured Destruction."

Many scientists contend that unless current patterns of fossil-fuel consumption are dramatically reduced, temperatures around the world will increase by as much as three to eight degrees in the next fifty years. Such an increase would have catastrophic effects across the globe. Some areas would dry up and become uninhabitable; much of the polar ice caps would melt, and oceans would expand dramatically and cause massive flooding and erosion. It is hard to know all of the effects of such enormous climactic changes, but, as Senator Robert Stafford (R-Vermont) recently commented while reflecting on this problem, "If we fail to act, it will be a world hostile to humanity and the rest of life in dozens of ways; it will be a world which I would wish on neither my children nor grandchildren."

While these two global environmental problems are the most dramatic examples of threats that could lead to massive destruction, other types of environmental degradation may produce catastrophic results we currently cannot foresee. Here are a few examples:

• Our tropical forests, which contain 40 percent of all species on Earth, are being cut at the rate of two acres per second. Approximately 27.2 million acres of tropical forest are permanently lost each year. These forests convert carbon dioxide to oxygen and thereby replenish our atmosphere. By cutting our forests we accelerate the greenhouse effect.

• Another consequence of deforestation is the loss of habitat to countless animals and plants. The extinction of various species is now happening at a rate unequaled since the mass disappearance of the dinosaurs. Between 1600 and 1900, there were 75 known human-caused extinctions; by 1974, that rate had reached a loss of 100 species per year. Current estimates are that one-fifth of all the species on Earth may disappear during the next twenty years.

• Acid rain, a by-product of the combustion of fossil fuels, and other types of air pollution are killing lakes and pine forests in North America and Europe. In West Germany, at least one third of all forests have been affected. In Canada and the eastern United States, fish have been killed in thousands of lakes.

• U.S. industry alone generates 80 billion pounds of toxic waste per year. Estimates say that a large percentage of this is not disposed of safely, causing the contamination of our water and soil. We continue to produce and accumulate large quantities of nuclear waste with no consensus about a safe storage plan.

• The "garbage crisis," as it has been called, has reached staggering proportions as cities and states try to figure out what to do with the waste they have generated.

• The pollution of the oceans is now a serious worldwide problem. In the cover article, entitled "Our Filthy Seas," *Time* (August 1, 1988) wrote: "The blight is global, from the murky red tides that periodically affect Japan's Inland Sea to the untreated sewage that befouls the fabled Mediterranean. Pollution threatens the rich, teeming life of the ocean and renders the waters off once-famed beaches about as safe to bathe in as an unflushed toilet."

All of these global environmental dangers make it clear that we are approaching a day of reckoning — that we are on a collision course with our own future. In summarizing the environmental crisis, *Newsweek* used the headline: "Stretched to the Limit: Five Billion People Strain the Earth's Resources." As the director of the United Nations Environmental Program, M.K. Tolba, put it: "We face by the turn of the century an environmental catastrophe as complete, as irreversible, as any nuclear holocaust."

Clearly, these threats to life from modern warfare and environmental damage constitute something that is unprecedented in history. The danger we face is total in its scope. It is not limited in degree or isolated in location. It threatens all of us, and the destruction of life itself.

In addition to the two primary threats, there are a number of *destabilizing conditions*, which could, if we do not take decisive action, increase the likelihood of a global catastrophe. While these conditions do not in themselves threaten the future of life, they are part of a larger system of human imbalance which could precipitate a global catastrophe.

The first condition is the problem of the massive *population explosion*. In 1650, there were approximately 500 million people on our planet. By 1850, human population had doubled to one billion. Then, between 1850 and 1970, it quadrupled to four billion people. Since 1970, we have added another one billion to reach our current level of five billion. Estimates for the future are that this rapid growth will continue and that we will have more than six billion by the year 2000 and eight billion by 2025. The rapidly increasing global population will deplete already limited resources and intensify environmental problems worldwide.

Before 1960, basic biological systems stayed ahead of population demands. But since the population exceeded four billion in the 1970s, many ecologists believe that the renewal of life-supporting resources has continued to decline at the same time the demands of expanding populations are increasing. The result is a downward spiral: expanding populations use up the resource base, which lowers the standard of living, destabilizes the economy, and often leads to poverty, malnutrition, and social stress.

Second, the problems of *poverty and hunger* are a painful source of instability in many parts of the globe. According to Bread for the World, there are almost one billion people (out of a world population of five billion) who are classified as hungry, malnourished, or not having enough to eat. UNICEF cstimates that more than 35,000 children die each day from hunger-related causes.

Hundreds of millions of people are without adequate food and shelter across the world and tens of millions of them die each year from malnutrition. In the United States, the current estimate is that more than one million people are homeless during a year, 750,000 at one time, and more than 100,000 are children. The immense disparity between rich and poor creates frustration and anger, which are often at the core of tensions within a country or between nations. Until people everywhere have the basic necessities of life, it will be difficult, if not impossible, to create a truly secure and peaceful future.

Third, there is the threat of *economic instability*. Recently, many economists have warned that the massive debt of

Third World nations, coupled with the growing American debt and budget deficit, could set off a depression, or a recession, in the 1990s. Dr. Ravi Batra, in *The Great Depression of 1990*, argued:

> During the 1980s, wealth disparity has soared throughout our planet, generating a worldwide leap in stock prices, and a worldwide fragility in the banking system.. . . . The richest 5% of Americans have more income than the entire bottom 40%, and the richest 1% of Americans possess greater wealth than the bottom 90% . . . These are ominous figures, giving us advance warnings of things to come.

In 1986, the Federal Reserve Bank of New York reported that the total domestic debt was $8.2 trillion. By 1987, according to the *Economic Report of the President*, total domestic debt had reached $11.06 trillion. If we assume an average interest rate of ten percent, this means the interest paid by American consumers is about $1.1 trillion per year. Dr. John L. King, in *How to Profit from the Next Great Depression*, estimates that "out of every dollar we spent as consumers, about thirty cents went to pay interest on our collective debts." By 1987, the federal government's debt was $2.7 trillion. Many experts are increasingly concerned that economic instability due to debt and wealth disparity could set off a downward spiral that would be a serious threat to international peace and security.

Finally, there is the threat posed by *authoritarian governments*. During the twentieth century, authoritarian governments have taken the age-old tendency of state repression to new levels of terror. Nazi Germany, Stalinist Russia, the Khmer Rouge in Cambodia, Idi Amin's Uganda, and the brutal rule of the Nationalist Party in South Africa are just a few examples. Unfortunately, this list is painfully long. Both leftist and rightist dictatorships threaten the foundations of freedom around the world and make a fair resolution of genuine differences almost impossible. Authoritarian repression stifles the creative expression of the human spirit, prohibits dissent and creative thinking, and thereby inhibits the further advancement of what is best in human civilization.

It is this fear of the authoritarian state that is at the core of the danger that many Americans feel from the Soviet Union. The closed nature of the Soviet system and the examples of its repressive past — particularly the excesses of Stalinism — have put Americans on their guard. Many believe that any system which mistreats its own citizens cannot be trusted in international affairs. Indeed, they contend that such an authoritarian system which shows little concern about human life might be willing to risk a major world war in order to advance its communist philosophy. Of course, the Soviet Union is now showing signs of significant changes under President Gorbachev that move it away from rigid authoritarianism. His pledge before the United Nations in December 1988 to abide by "the primacy of universal human values" was an unprecedented statement from any Soviet leader. How far these changes will go and what will be their long-term result remains to be seen.

In this age of weapons of mass destruction, authoritarian governments are a greater threat than ever before. Any political system that is incapable of tolerating other points of view is more likely to find itself in conflict situations which could escalate out of control. Authoritarian governments are extremely dangerous in a world where one mistake could eventually threaten all life on Earth.

The Blind Men and the Elephant

We are all ignorant, just about different things.
Mark Twain

Our situation is reminiscent of the old fable of the blind men and the elephant. In trying to understand the nature of the huge beast they encountered, each blind man took hold of a different part. The one holding the trunk thought the animal was a snake. The one holding the leg thought it was a tree. The one holding its tail thought it was a rope. And the one touching its side was convinced that it was a wall. At first, the blind men argued about who was right. Each one assumed that his experience was the true representation of the animal, and could not understand why the other blind men were describing something which sounded very different. Only when they started to listen to each other did they come to understand the real nature and dimensions of the elephant.

Like the blind men and the elephant, different individuals and groups have focused on various aspects of our common danger. Each group tends to see its part as the most important, and like the blind men, we often do not grasp the enormity of the beast we are facing. For example, in the United States:

- Peace-through-strength groups focus on the threat of external aggression and terrorism, and the need for greater national and global security.
- Peace-through-disarmament groups focus on the threat of nuclear weapons and the need to end the arms race.
- Environmentalists focus on the threat of ecological disaster and the need to restore the natural environment.
- Human-rights advocates focus on the threat of authoritarian governments and the need to assure human freedom for everyone.
- Those concerned about the population explosion focus on the limits of global carrying capacity, and the need to achieve rough parity in our global birth and death rates.
- Advocates for the poor and the hungry focus on suffering due to hunger and desperate living conditions, and the need to provide enough food, adequate shelter, and basic medical care for everyone.
- Those concerned about the economy focus on the national debt, the vast, unmanageable debts in developing countries, and the need to create world economic stability.

Each of the above groups has its own primary description of the danger and an accompanying agenda for action. Like the blind men and the elephant story, each group is correct about its perspective. Yet, often we do not grasp that all of these threats are part of a larger web of imbalance. Just as the tail and the trunk are each part of the elephant, so each of these threats is part of an entire system of inter-related and human-caused dangers.

As we noted at the beginning of this section, these dangers that threaten life itself have one thing in common: they are all created or exacerbated by human beings. While it is deeply disturbing that the source of our common danger comes from within us, it is also encouraging. If we can come to understand why we act as we do, perhaps we can change our behavior and achieve a victory over the common danger. We live in an uncertain universe, where earthquakes can destroy whole cities, comets can go off course, and suns can explode. There is no way to guarantee or ultimately secure the future. But we must cease to be our own worst enemy. For this reason, it is important to look at some of the root causes of our predicament, both within the self and society.

Roots of Our Predicament

> *We have had our last chance. If we do not now devise*
> *some more equitable system, then Armageddon will be at*
> *our door. The problem is basically theological and involves*
> *a spiritual improvement of human character that will*
> *synchronize with our almost matchless advances in science*
> *... and all material developments in the past 2000 years.*
> *It must be of the spirit if we are to save the flesh.*
> General Douglas MacArthur

These are the words of General MacArthur on the battleship Missouri at the formal Japanese surrender ending World War II on August 11, 1945. At this key moment in history, Douglas MacArthur sought to reach future generations and alert us to the roots of our predicament, so that we might avert a more terrible horror than the world war just ending.

During the last four centuries with the revolutions of industry, science, and information, our growth in matters of external prowess has accelerated geometrically. We have conquered the physical frontiers of our planet — the great seas and the great mountains — and now outward to space. But our growth in matters of wisdom and ethics has not kept pace. "We have grasped the mystery of the atom and rejected the Sermon on the Mount," said General Omar Bradley. "Ours is a world of nuclear giants and ethical infants."

Our scientific and technological advancement has exceeded our moral and psychological development. General Douglas MacArthur sought to warn us that our long-term security is not so much a question of comparative military hardware as it is an evolutionary shift of mind. We can travel to the Moon and soon to Mars, but we have not yet learned to live in harmony with each other or with nature. We have not sufficiently developed our capacity for mutual respect and reverence for life.

Those who think that our technology is out of control often conclude that it is the technology which needs to be changed. Some argue that the solution to our current predicament will come from a breakthrough in our technology. Others believe that we must rid ourselves of nuclear weapons and other destructive technologies in order to be secure. Yet, technology is not the root problem or the fundamental solution. For example, history demonstrates any technological breakthrough in weapons systems by one country is often matched by its adversary. If we eliminated all such weapons from the Earth, still the knowledge of how to create them is widespread and will remain with us.

Technology itself is neutral. It is a tool. As Jacques Ellul has pointed out, technology generates its own imperatives and thereby helps to drive human culture, but still the underlying issue is one of human values and motivation. Technology in the service of greed, hatred, or injustice amplifies evil. Technology in the service of wisdom, compassion, or justice amplifies good. The terror of our destructive technologies is fundamentally a function of the fact that we cannot yet trust ourselves to act with respect for each other, or life itself.

Throughout our evolution as a species, there has been a reciprocal relationship between technology and consciousness. When early humans picked up a bone and used it as a hammer, they began to alter their thinking process. We created a series of tools which then altered our consciousness (our ways of thinking and perceiving) and our culture (our ways of relating to each other and the environment). This changed consciousness then facilitates the development of more advanced tools appropriate to the next stage of the human journey, which then require an advancement in our consciousness.

At the root of our predicament is our ignorance of interdependence. We have identified the interests of the self too narrowly. Our predominant world view is still based upon a nineteenth-century model, which asserts that humans are separate from nature, that nature itself is a machine, and that the "unlimited" resources of the Earth are ours to exploit as we wish. We act as though we were not part of nature and part of each other, and thereby threaten the finite Earth and foundations of our own human civilization.

We have emphasized the interests of the small self, while neglecting the reality of our larger self, our interdependent identity: the interests of the self as family, community, nation, and planet. It is of course true that we are separate and distinct individuals who need to protect and sustain ourselves. But it is also true that each of us is a part of the web of life, from which we have evolved and which sustains us, and that to survive and flourish we must protect the interests of the whole.

In our ignorance of interdependence we feel cut off and separate. This sense of isolation and separation engenders fear, especially the fear of loss. Out of this fear comes greed — the feeling that nothing is ever enough — an insatiable appetite for money, power, possessions, whatever looks like it may fill the emptiness we feel when we are cut off from a deep and abiding relationship to others and to our place in the universe. This greed facilitates and feeds the drive to dominate others.

The small self says, "I am at the center and others are here to serve my interests." Or it says, "We (our tribe or nation) are at the center and all other people and nature itself are here to serve our needs." The insight that each one of us is at the center is a profound truth. The distortion is that there is only one center. The lie is that "I am at the center, and you are not . . . . Our tribe or nation is the chosen one, and yours is not." This is the distortion of the absolutist mind.

The absolutist or true-believing mind says there is one and only one way. It asserts that one's group, race, religion, ideology, or point of view has the ultimate truth. The absolutist mind divides the world into "us" versus "them." It establishes a particular creed or belief system and then makes agreement with this point of view essential for participation in society. "Us" are those who see the world the way we do. "Them" is the enemy, the stranger or person who dares to disagree.

The absolutist mind cannot conceive of coexistence except on its own terms. For if I am ultimately right and you are ultimately wrong, then there is an unbridgeable gap between us. Unless you convert to "my" way, there can be no "our" way. For the absolutist mind, all interaction is reduced to an attempt to argue, convert, evangelize, convince or, in extreme situations, to persecute or eliminate the other. When the absolutist mind is collectivized, it becomes the authoritarian state, the rule of tyranny without equality and justice under law.

As we live out the end of the twentieth century, we live in the gap between our old values and beliefs, and the new values and wisdom needed to take responsibility for our advanced technologies. We live in a kind of "jet lag" between our old perceptions and the emerging realities of the next century. In his brilliant article, "It's Already Begun," futurist William Irwin Thompson writes:

We live in a culture that we do not see. We don't live in industrial civilization, we live in planetization. What we see is really the past; what we envision as the future is already the present.

We do not fully recognize what is emerging, because the vestiges of the industrial age, the institutions and beliefs, still form the basis of our perception. We are looking, as Marshall McLuhan once put it, through the rearview mirror at the past, at what has been. What will be is already unfolding as our present.

Just as the modern, industrial world view replaced the beliefs of the Middle Ages, so the belief structures of our current world view are being undermined. Science has discovered the interpenetrating ecology of all things and has thus replaced the view that nature is a machine and that humans are separate from nature. The belief in a world of objects separated by distance has been replaced by a world of almost total electronic linkage. Computers, television, and satellite "space bridges" now create the experience of simultaneous communication almost anywhere on Earth.

The fact that our modern culture has not yet adapted to these profound changes in world view is simply a function of jet lag. Seven hundred years ago, a feudal culture could not have conceived of nationalism. Two hundred years ago at the birth of our nation, the founding fathers could not have conceived of a world of modern nation-states with global technologies. And what now is unfolding that we are not yet able to consciously recognize?

Currently, we live in the gap between what we as a civilization are able to hold consciously about the reality of our destructive technologies and what we sense dimly. How can we comprehend that one nuclear bomb small enough to put in a suitcase can destroy New York City, Paris, or Leningrad? Or how can we fathom that the human use of chlorofluorocarbons in pressurized cans is damaging the ozone layer which has shielded life from ultraviolet rays for millennia?

From our old assumptions, we perceive a world of in-dustrialized nation-states separated by significant borders, which are often enforced by armed guards, fences, and inspection stations. Yet below this level of perception there is the invisible exchange of pollution which respects no national boundaries whatsoever. Acid rain needs no passport to kill fish and trees all across Europe, the Soviet Union, and North America.

Behavior which demonstrates the jet lag of our aware-ness is apparent in both capitalist and communist societies. United States officials have continued to operate out of the old assumptions that we need take no regard for the consequences of our acid rain — e.g. the industrial toxins which originate in the eastern United States and are killing the forests of Canada. Similarly, when Soviet officials first learned of the massive disaster at the Chernobyl nuclear power plant, they tried to suppress what was happening from the rest of the world. But it was no longer possible. The radioactive emissions from Chernobyl were being moni-tored by scientific tracking stations all over Europe. People in the West knew about the Chernobyl disaster long before the Soviet government told its own citizens.

Our old assumptions distort the way we perceive and interpret current realities. Much of our fear is a result of the fact that our level of awareness has not caught up to our technology. We are living in the transition between our old assumptions and the new understanding that we need to master our evolving technologies.

Divided Mind

We used to wonder where war lived ... and now we realize that we know where it lives, and it is inside ourselves.
                                                          Albert Camus

As we have worked with all kinds of people from na-tionally known experts to local community leaders, we have come to see that the divided mind is evident at all levels of interaction, from the personal to the global. This divided mind produces an adversarial model of human interaction: "It's me against you." Our goal has been to develop methods and tools to enable people to integrate the divided mind, to promote greater peace within themselves, and to increase their ability to make policies which include diverse perspectives. "The world hangs by a thin thread," wrote Carl Jung, "and that thread is the human psyche."

The UNESCO Constitution, written in 1945, states: "Since wars begin in the minds of men, it is in the minds of men that the defenses of peace must be constructed." At the root of our destructive conflicts is this divided or "warring mind." Many of us spend a great deal of time trapped in these conflicts: first within ourselves, then with those with whom we disagree — those of another creed, another color, another point of view. As nation-states, we are at war with each other, battling for power and resources. And finally, we are at war with nature — acting in ways that threaten the ecological fabric which sustains life on Earth. War in this sense might be defined as the inability to cooperate and coexist: "It's me against you." We are divided against ourselves. This divided mind is evident at four levels of destructive conflicts:

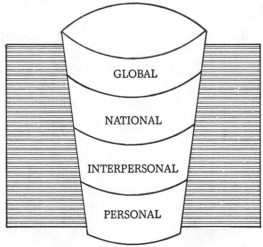

GLOBAL

NATIONAL

INTERPERSONAL

PERSONAL

Personal — War within the human mind. The roots of war begin in the human mind. Most of us have warring factions within our own minds. These factions are at times conscious and known, and at other times unconscious. Sometimes the conflict is between two or more competing needs, drives, or wishes. Sometimes the conflict is between parts of ourselves that we know and accept, versus parts we do not know or accept within ourselves. What we do not recognize or accept in ourselves, we tend to fear, judge, and reject in others. In part, war in the world grows from the seeds of self-denial, self-rejection, and self-hatred.

Thomas Merton, the Trappist monk and world-renowned teacher wrote:

> At the root of all war is fear: not so much the fear men have of one another as the fear they have of everything.
> ... It is not only our hatred of others that is dangerous but also and above all our hatred of ourselves; particularly that hatred of ourselves which is too deep and too powerful to be consciously faced. For it is this which makes us see our own evil in others and unable to see it in ourselves.

In the eyes of every small child, we see the clear flame of awareness, the one who is essentially alive and whole. Then the traumas of life leave many of us wounded and in battle with ourselves. The history of these distresses is recorded in our cellular memory, much like a computer program. When something reminds us of the original violation, we are reactivated. We carry the past with us like ghosts. Thus, we are often trapped in habitual beliefs and chronic patterns which prevent us from maintaining peace of mind.

When competing parts of our mind are in conflict, the result is anxiety. Anxiety can manifest as nervousness, agitation, decreased ability to concentrate, increased pulse rate, and insomnia; or it can be converted into an anxiety equivalent such as lethargy, guilt, depression, physical symptoms (nervous stomach, headaches, etc.). Anxiety can also be "acted out" against oneself or others. Some specific examples of intrapsychic conflict are: conflict between long-term and short-term needs or wishes, conflict between urges and defenses against one's urges, or conflicts about our desire to control versus our need to let go.

A recent news article in the *San Francisco Chronicle* reported that suicide has now become the third-leading cause of death for the 15-to-24-year-old age group. Accidents and murder are the first and second causes. As for the causes of suicide, the article said more children are victims of child abuse; more have only one parent; more have unwanted pregnancies; more are addicted to drugs and alcohol; more feel hopeless about the future; and more are depressed. These are all symptoms of destructive conflicts in the human psyche.

Interpersonal — War between individuals. Our parents and grandparents tell us of a time in America when, even during the Great Depression, you could leave your home unlocked without fear. No more. In many areas, our neighborhoods have become armed citadels of fear. The attempt to resolve conflicts through violence has become commonplace. We read about it every day in our newspapers. In Iowa, a 69-year-old man shot the mayor and two city council members because he was angry over a backed-up sewer. In Montana, a teenage boy killed his teacher because he was enraged over a failing grade. In Los Angeles during a recent summer, more than 30 freeway shootings occurred — motorists pulled guns and began firing at other cars.

This cycle of violation spreads like a contagion. Extensive research shows that children who are abused tend to pass on abusive behavior to their children. What was done to us across the generations, we tend to do to others. Hateful and oppressive actions tend to create hateful and oppressive responses. We can see this cycle of violation in many aspects of our society — the widespread use of drugs and alcohol, the high school drop-out rates, the celebration of violence on television and in the movies, the increase in crime and the overflowing prisons, the realities of continued racism. The chances of a woman in the United States being raped in her lifetime are currently one in six. In short, we are suffering from a deterioration in the conditions which promote our physical safety and the respect for the individual.

National — War between groups and factions. As Americans we face a common danger that threatens our lives, our liberty, and perhaps the future of civilization itself. Yet, we are factionalized. We are often driven and divided by our fears — the fear of economic collapse, the fear of external domination, the fear of nuclear war, the fear of environmental poisoning, the fear of terrorism, the fear of social and moral breakdown. At a dialogue involving liberal and conservative citizens from seventeen states, Dr. Sheila Tobias summarized the crux of the matter: "We are not so much divided by our dreams as we are by our nightmares." This division, as we will see in the next section, prevents us from taking bold and unified action as a nation to address the common danger.

Global — War between nations, and between humans and the environment. One estimate is that since World War II, there have been three hundred wars on Earth. There has been no single day free of war, and only a few areas of the world have stayed at peace. If we darkened all the countries on a map which have been involved in war since 1945, more than two thirds of the world would be in shadow. The major tenet of our world's current geopolitical reality is power. Armed camps compete to control and keep others from controlling the globe. Finally, humankind is at war with nature, treating our living Earth as though it were an object to be exploited, or an enemy to be vanquished.

The Politics of Gridlock

A house divided against itself cannot stand.
Abraham Lincoln

Given the reality of our common danger, one would

hope that our political process would be deeply engaged in effective problem-solving about how we can best overcome these threats to our future. But this is not the case. Our adversarial political process is currently not effective in finding solutions to the common danger.

Increasing numbers of people are aware of a crisis in our political process. The 1988 presidential campaign, with its negative tone and lack of substantive discussion, was an acute symptom of a deeper malaise in our democracy. George Will called the 1988 presidential election "a 10-month down-hill debacle. . . . With the presidential candidates setting the tone, the result has been trickle-down tawdriness . . ." According to a *Newsweek* poll, two-thirds of the public thought the election was dirtier than those in the past and three-quarters did not believe the candidates gave honest views on the issues.

For more than a year, candidates of both parties barnstormed the country and spent tens of millions of dollars on television commercials, yet rarely did they discuss the paramount issues of our survival and well-being for the 1990s. The tough questions were largely ignored like skeletons in the closet — how to reduce the trillion dollar debt, how to slow the greenhouse effect, how to stop the proliferation of chemical weapons, or how to build real security between nations. Both conservative and liberal commentators agreed the campaign left citizens uninformed and embittered. "Regardless of who wins or loses, the real tragedy for the nation is that Americans are learning nothing from the election," said Jonathan Kozol, author of *Illiterate America*.

A recent cover of *Time* featured endless automobiles bumper-to-bumper with the one word: GRIDLOCK. "Gridlock has gripped America," said the article, "threatening to transform its highways and freeways into snarled barriers to progress." It went on to describe "jam-packed freeways, bottlenecked bridges . . . overstuffed airports . . . grinding commutes: in many U.S. cities the rush hour has grown into a hellish crush that lasts virtually from sunup till sundown."

Gridlock is also an apt metaphor for our current political

process. Just as in a traffic situation, different groups are going in different directions in a headlong rush. Yet, we have little or no regard for the whole system. The politics of short-term interests, narrow greed, and divisive factionalism cannot get us to where we need to go. We are at an impasse; we are stalemated and ineffective in our efforts to find comprehensive solutions to the critical threats to our future. There are several reasons for this gridlock:

The political process is dominated by interest groups who work for their own narrow advantage. A country as diverse as the United States will inevitably have many groups that work to further their own self-interest. Unfortunately, many of those groups — whether their interest be economic, ethnic, religious, geographic, or single-issue oriented — lose sight of the needs of the overall political process. As they do so, they war against each other and make it extremely difficult to develop coherent, long-term policies that can serve the overall good. Allegiance to personal interests is natural, but in an interdependent world, problems cannot be solved without an accompanying sense of commitment to the good of the whole. Indeed, our modern world is now so interconnected that maximizing one's interests alone is often destructive to the very interests one wishes to protect.

The political discussion is too adversarial and divisive. The current way political campaigns and issue-debates are conducted exacerbates the divisions that exist in the country and makes it very difficult to unite for a common purpose. The 1988 presidential election is a recent, bitter example. Almost the entire focus is on winning short-term political victories and little attention is paid to the way that citizens of different views can work together for a common interest. Defeating the other side in a discussion about a problem, a vote in the Congress, or an election takes precedent over thoughtful consideration of what is really needed to deal with our common danger.

Our decision-making and our policies are too short-term in their focus. Our society is obsessed with immediate rewards, and this obsession seems to carry over to the way we approach political decisions. Both citizens and the politicians we elect seem generally unwilling or unable to examine the long-term implications of complex public-policy issues. As citizens we want results that benefit us as soon as possible; and politicians, who are focused primarily on winning their next election, gear their policies towards producing those short-term gains — even if it means that we all will pay a price in the future.

Few difficult problems in the modern world can be solved other than through a long-term commitment to implement a steady course. This is particularly true of the problems that constitute the common danger. For example, at a time when we are required to make thoughtful long-term decisions to reverse the greenhouse effect or to reduce our massive debts, our policies are too often based upon perspectives of a few months or a year. Solutions to such problems can only be achieved through policies implemented consistently for several decades.

The quantity and quality of citizen participation is not sufficient. The percentage of eligible Americans voting in national elections has been steadily declining since the 1960s. Because the number of people who vote is so low, Presidents Carter, Reagan, and Bush, were elected by less than 30% of all Americans of voting age. And the great majority of those who do vote never do anything else to help create effective national policies. Very few citizens have anything close to a working understanding of the complex problems that make up the common danger and are not informed enough to help formulate solutions for the problems they face. This need for citizen involvement and understanding is particularly essential to address the complex and paramount issues of the common danger.

Less than a week after the election, top analysts warned that there were growing fears worldwide that the Bush administration would not be able to cut the trade and budget deficits and could plunge the American economy into a devastating recession. So why was this discussion not central to the 1988 presidential campaign? Because both candidates concluded, probably correctly, that the American people did not want to hear that we are in debt up to our necks, and if we are not going to drown, we must make difficult choices. The *San Jose Mercury* said: "The stage may be set for four more years of gridlock between a stubborn president and Congress over budget deficits — a prospect analysts fear that foreign lenders may no longer tolerate."

Nowhere was the lack of real discussion more evident in the 1988 campaign than on those issues which directly relate to our common danger. While there was a great deal of rhetoric about environment, peace, and security, both candidates for president generally avoided in-depth discussion about what they would actually do to reduce the risk of war and restore the environment.

The politics of gridlock are dominated by short-term thinking and narrow-interest groups. Like hurried drivers on city streets, these groups are mostly concerned with getting to their own destination, not with helping the overall flow of traffic. Yet, once we are trapped in gridlock, then it becomes obvious that the system is not working.

So long as we are divided between factions at home, we will not be able to achieve consistent and comprehensive policies that will enable our nation to steer a steady course. Our policies will be partisan, contradictory, and short-sighted. They will vacillate back and forth depending upon which group is in the driver's seat. We will deflect, distract, and cancel each other out, thus weakening our efforts toward increased security and real peace. Our politics will remain gridlocked, and we will be unable to mobilize against the common danger.

CHAPTER THREE

An Evolutionary
Shift Of Mind

*Through the release of atomic energy, our generation
has brought into the world the most revolutionary
force since prehistoric man's discovery of fire. . . .
We shall require a substantially new manner of
thinking if mankind is to survive.*
— Albert Einstein —

For hundreds of thousands of years, our ancestors huddled
together in caves at night to protect themselves against the
cold. They gnawed at the raw flesh of their prey. They were
humbled by the darkness.

Then, after millennia of watching lightning strike and
forest fires burn, we humans took the flame as our own.
We learned to carry a torch from campsite to campsite,
and how to spark a fire ourselves. We had taken on godly
powers — the capacity to generate warmth, cook food, and
illuminate the darkness. Now, during the long winter months,
we could sit by the fire and tell our stories. We could paint
pictures of the hunt and the festivals on the walls of the
cave by firelight.

Ancient myths and stories from around the world express
the recognition that we had acquired the use of one of the
central powers of the universe. It opened a new dimension
of human existence. So, too, came the power to destroy, to
burn down forests, to burn each other, and the world we
knew. The mastery of fire changed our ways. It was an
evolutionary leap.

Our journey across time has been marked by a series

of leaps forward: the development of agriculture; the emergence of early codes of law and justice; the invention of the printing press; the Industrial Revolution; the abolition of slavery; the rise of the women's movement; and the placement of the first human on the Moon. Such advances have been provoked both by changes in our environment — where old ways were no longer suitable — and by changes in our capacity to comprehend and direct our fate.

At the dawn of the nuclear age, Albert Einstein recognized that the power unleashed at White Sands, New Mexico now required human beings to move forward to the next step of their evolution. Just as the cave dwellers had to learn to be responsible for the destructiveness of fire, so we who live at the threshold of the twenty-first century are compelled to take responsibility for an even greater power — the fire that fuels the stars.

Upon seeing the first mushroom cloud, J. Robert Oppenheimer, the father of the bomb, remembered a line from the Hindu scriptures: "I have become death — destroyer of the world." Later, when asked to comment, Einstein said, "Now all men have become brothers." Both insights are true: With the power to destroy ourselves comes the necessity to grow in wisdom and respect for each other and our living Earth.

The End of Adolescence

> *The world we have made as a result of the thinking we have done so far creates problems that cannot be solved at the same level at which we created them.*
>
> Albert Einstein

People who speak about a coming Armageddon have grasped a certain insight about the depth of the transition in which we live. In a sense, they are right that we have reached the closing of a world. Our adolescence as a species is ending: the challenge of our survival requires us to reach a more conscious stage of human development. In our adolescence, we have been mostly unaware of our capacity to shape our destiny. Now, as we mature into conscious adulthood, we are beginning to recognize that our destiny is, in part, a function of our own making.

The entire prehistory of human evolution, a period scientists now estimate at 3.5 million years, might be described as the childhood of our species. Early humans lived within the boundaries of nature and did not experience themselves as separate. They were not self-consciously aware of death. Nor did their primitive tools allow them to manipulate natural forces. Like all other animals, they lived in a primary dependency upon nature.

The childhood of our species ended with the emergence of agricultural civilization and the development of increasingly more powerful technologies to manipulate our environment. By this reckoning, the adolescent stage began approximately 5,000 to 10,000 years ago with the origins of recorded history. By inventing tools that enabled them to control the natural environment, our ancestors became more and more aware of their separateness from nature. Once they were able to objectify nature and recognize their own death, they were never quite at home again. They were no longer children who lived in the Garden at one with nature, nor were they adults who were able to be responsible caretakers of the Garden. They were adolescents.

Today, we are still in our adolescence. We have attempted to negate our dependency upon nature and to establish our technological autonomy. We have developed new technologies, yet use them with little maturity or discernment. As adolescents we have tested the limits of our power against nature, without thinking about the consequences of our actions. We have often acted with recklessness, with narrow, short-term judgment, and with the delusion of our own immunity.

As adolescents, we verge on the edge of losing control of our own technologies. Like the kid on the motorcycle who cannot resist racing through the next curve, we sense the danger, yet are drawn forward. We are tempted by our power.

Freeman Dyson, one of the physicists who developed the bomb, writes about the "technical arrogance that comes over people when they see what they can do with their minds."

> I have felt it myself. The glitter of nuclear weapons. It is irresistible if you come to them as a scientist. To feel it's there in your hands — to release this energy that fuels the stars. To let it do your bidding. To perform these miracles — to lift billions of tons of rock into the sky. It is something that gives people an illusion of unlimitable power and it is, in some ways, responsible for all our troubles.

The pain of our adolescence comes, in part, from sensing that we need to regain control of ourselves and our technology, but not yet knowing how to do so. It is the pain of growth and metamorphosis.

Currently, we are an endangered species. Anthropologists speak of the process of "adaptive radiation," whereby organisms change to become more suited to their environment. New conditions exert a pressure on the organisms. When mutations or changed habits occur which make the organism more suited for the environment, it is better able to flourish and produce offspring.

For example, in England before the Industrial Revolution collectors of the peppered moth, *Biston betularia*, found that almost all the moths were light-colored, although occasionally a dark-colored moth was captured. Yet, within a few decades after the Industrial Revolution, black moths made up to 90 percent of the moth population in air-polluted areas. The moths rested on tree trunks during the day. So long as the trees were light in color prior to industrial pollution, the light-colored moths were not visible to predatory birds and thus were not eaten. But once the trees turned black from pollution, the dark moths survived and reproduced to greater extent than the light-colored moths. After London took drastic steps to reduce air pollution following the catastrophic smogs of the 1950s, the peppered moth was observed to shift back towards a lighter color.

The human species has created the current stress of our common danger, which is creating pressure for us to adapt. If we do not learn to think, communicate, and solve problems at a different level, we are likely to perish. The development of weapons of mass destruction requires us to change our practices regarding conflict. Likewise, the hole in the ozone, acid rain, loss of top soil, pollution of our waterways, and the growing waste/garbage dilemma compel us to change our practices in the way we treat the Earth.

Our common danger necessitates an evolutionary shift of mind. As a species, we must become adults. We must mature toward a more inclusive awareness. What is required is a change in our basic relationship to our self, to each other, to the nation, and to our planet. We are compelled to acknowledge our global interdependence and to take conscious responsibility for our future together. This shift in consciousness must begin with the individual, because the center of conscience or consciousness dwells in the individual, not the nation-state or other institutions. We are experiencing an evolutionary pressure which calls for a shift from egocentrism to ecocentrism.

If we are going to master the fire that fuels the stars, we must master the human mind which invented these ingenious and destructive technologies. Since human ingenuity and determination created them, there is the potential for human ingenuity and determination to meet their challenge. The point is not to attempt an impossible retreat to the relative safety of the nineteenth century, nor to continue the dangerous imbalance of the twentieth century. Just as with fire, these technologies are an impetus for us to advance — to take on a new magnitude of awareness and responsibility. We are asked to be conscious agents of our evolution, to make certain that we don't "burn the tribe."

Coming of Age

Man's problem in the last analysis is not the atom bomb

> *or technology or the war-mad leaders and the false prophets,*
> *but is man himself. If he is to emerge a victor instead of*
> *a slave, he must explore his mind and his spirit so as to*
> *know himself.*
>
> Admiral Richard Byrd

In 1950, Admiral Richard Byrd, one of the great explorers of this century, described what he called the most important of all his journeys "exploration into the realms of thought and the human spirit." On one of his many expeditions, he spent an entire winter alone at a meteorological station during the long polar night in the shadow of the South Pole. His tiny shack was buried under snow on top of 800 feet of ice. He was cut off by the continual darkness, the cold, and the ice from any physical contact with the outside world.

In the middle of the polar night, Admiral Byrd discovered that he was being poisoned by carbon monoxide from the faulty burner of his oil stove. To eliminate the carbon monoxide, he had to keep the stove off for 12 hours of the 24. Most of the time, he was forced to lay in his sleeping bag in the dark, unable to read, with nothing to do but think. Here is how he describes his experience and the insights he reached:

> My thoughts, naturally enough, were on the gloomy side and they soon began to take charge of me. . . . And thus I began to explore my mind to see what I could find there in the realm of imagination and thought that might help me.
>
> Gradually I was able to control my thoughts more and more. I found that I could throw my thoughts backward or forward in the stream of time to any place I chose. It was as if my mind were a motion picture screen and I could run on it whatever picture I selected from an unlimited list. You may be sure that most of my scenarios took me to places as different as possible from my very gloomy surroundings, such as warm sunny lands.
>
> So I explored as best I could into the uncharted and unknown areas of the mind; and slowly, as the days passed, I came on to some things. I discovered how

much a man's world can be a world of the mind. And that a man himself determines or makes his world, which thus, to a degree, is the reflection of his own inner self wherein dwells the universal spirit of good.

A man beset by evil within and from without can mobilize his spiritual self to conquer that evil. Just so can the human race mobilize its moral and spiritual power to defeat the material power of evil that threatens it.

Admiral Byrd's insight offers a key to the necessary evolutionary shift of mind. Given the constant interplay of actions-changing-consciousness and consciousness-changing-actions, we can start by becoming more aware of our own mind. While none of us is likely to experience this kind of extreme isolation and freedom from distraction, each one of us can learn in our ordinary lives to observe our mind and to know ourselves at our depth.

In his isolation, compelled to begin to watch his own mental process, Admiral Byrd came to know that he was not the flux of images and thoughts in his mind. Rather he was the one who could observe and even learn to direct his own mental process. This achievement, he recognized, is a critically important step in the process of individuals and nations learning to direct their thinking toward greater peace and security on Earth.

Whenever we are solely identified with the content of our position or point of view, we have forgotten the depth of who we are. We might draw a comparison to the use of computers. Imagine becoming so identified with a particular program in your computer that you forget you are the user who can change the program at any time. This is analogous to the adolescent mind, which often sees itself as powerless to make any difference before the forces of history.

A few years ago, Dean Burke of the Harvard Graduate School of Arts and Sciences described a course he taught at Harvard on Nazi Germany. His class was designed to teach students about the situation in Germany in the 1930s. The lectures, readings, and movies sought to give the students an in-depth perspective of the conditions which led to the rise of the Nazis. He asked the students to write a paper in response to the question: If you had been alive in Germany in the 1930s, what could you and others have done to prevent the rise of Nazism?

The vast majority of students wrote papers saying they thought there was nothing they could do. It was inevitable. The little person does not matter in the broad sweep of history. Dean Burke was distressed by the papers. He called this "No-Fault History" — no one is responsible, we are all victims.

In our adolescence as a species, we have viewed ourselves as bystanders or pawns, with little or no capacity to determine the future. This belief in our powerlessness functions as a self-fulfilling prophecy. So long as we perceive ourselves as victims — whether for reasons of psychology, biology, economics, history, or spiritual ignorance — we are helpless and the situation is hopeless.

Transcending the victim mind is a critically important step of our maturation. Admiral Byrd was tempted during his struggle to succumb to the belief that it was hopeless and to allow the bleakness of his circumstances to prevail. What he discovered was that he could choose. Similarly, as long as we believe it is not possible to overcome our common danger, we will not succeed. But if we choose to discover a way out of our predicament, we will rapidly mature to be big enough for the challenge.

Being an "adult" implies taking responsibility, being more conscious, having more understanding and perspective. An adult, like any good parent, recognizes that he or she is in charge. Thus to move beyond our individual and collective adolescence, let us begin with the acknowledgment that we are the adults. No one else is going to do it — no Mom or Dad or great leader or government program or magical power.

We call this next stage of our maturation, "the Intentional and Observing Self:" *intentional* because we are able to take responsibility and direct the process of our lives more consciously; *observing* because we are able to see our humanity and the world more inclusively than we did as adolescents.

The Intentional Self

Those who believe they can do something, and those who believe they can't, are both right.

Henry Ford

The headline in the *Albuquerque Journal* (July 24, 1987) said: "U.S. Climber, 91, Becomes Oldest Woman to Scale Fuji." Hulda Crooks, a 91-year-old mountaineer from Loma Linda, California, reached the top of Japan's tallest peak at dawn after a difficult three-day climb. As she scaled the windswept, barren Fuji, Crooks said she hoped her adventure would encourage people to reject limitations society sometimes places on the old and the young. "Even when people say old age starts at 65, you don't have to settle for that," she explained.

Hulda Crooks began climbing mountains in her 40s after having pneumonia. Nicknamed "Grandma Whitney" for her 22 ascents of the 14,495-foot Mount Whitney, she has climbed 97 peaks since she was 66 years old. As a pink sun rose over the horizon, Crooks stepped through a special gate marking the top of the sacred 12,385-foot dormant volcano and waved an American flag tied to her walking stick. "It's wonderful," she said, bundled in a down jacket in near-freezing weather. "You always feel good when you make a goal."

The word, *intention*, comes from the Latin root, *intendere*, meaning to direct the mind toward something, to direct one's course. Intentional thinking is the shift from viewing ourselves as the pawns or bystanders of history to seeing ourselves as conscious agents who can help shape the future.

The future is not some fixed reality toward which we are going, but something we create by choices in the present. Certainly, we humans are not God and it would be arrogant for us to think that we are totally in charge of the Earth or our future. We are only one part of the whole. Yet, we can co-create the future out of the thoughts, aspirations, and actions which we generate in the present. This is the power of intention.

Our intention is our direction. It is both our goal (or underlying motive) and our determination to undertake the process necessary to achieve our goal. Thus, intention = goal + determination. For example, imagine yourself being in New York City and having the intention to go to Los Angeles. On the way, your car breaks down in Omaha. If you are not determined to reach your destination, you may just turn around and take an airplane back to New York. But if you have a clear and undivided intention, then getting your car repaired in Omaha is just another necessary step on your way to California.

Most of us have had experiences where we were drifting along in our lives without a clear sense of direction. Then we set a goal and became intentional. At the root of all human communication and interaction is our intention. Picture a pyramid representing three distinct, yet interrelated, aspects of human communication:

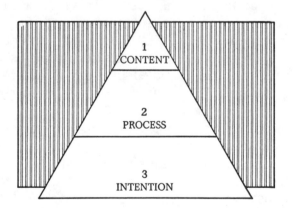

The *content* is <u>what</u> we say or do. It is the literal message of our words or actions. The *process* is <u>how</u> we say it or do it. It is the dynamic or the means of the interaction. The *intention* is <u>why</u> we do it, the goal we have in saying it or doing it. It is the spirit behind the words or actions, the underlying motive, or direction.

If someone accidently hits one of us with an elbow in a crowd, after the first moment of defensive reaction, most of us quickly recognize that it is not a threat. But if someone hits us on purpose, we perceive it as an entirely different event. It is the same act, but the intention alters the meaning of the action. Now we perceive it as an attack or threat to our person. Criminal law, for example, distinguishes between three different crimes: manslaughter, second-degree murder, and first-degree murder, all on the basis of the difference in underlying intent.

In human interactions, we often focus only on the upper section of the pyramid. We listen to the *content* of the interaction, but rarely do we pay attention to the *process* or to the underlying *intention*. Just like the tip of the iceberg is the only part that is visible above water, so the rest of the pyramid tends to be below the surface of our awareness. We hear the words that the other person is saying, but we do not monitor the dynamic of what is happening or the spirit of the communication behind the words. By not being mindful of the distinction between the three levels, we often debilitate our capacity to communicate and act consciously.

Another way to conceptualize the relationship between the three levels of communication is as three interlocking gears. The first gear is the *intent* which drives the *process* gear, which then drives the gear of *content*.

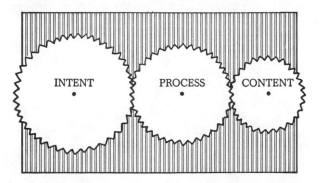

A few years ago, we both attended a conference which featured two prominent doctors representing opposite ends of the political spectrum on the question of how to prevent a nuclear war. One was a spokesperson for a conservative peace-through-strength organization, and the other a spokesperson for a liberal peace-through-disarmament group.

From the beginning, the two doctors took out their verbal scalpels and began to fight with each other. Neither was willing to listen to the other or to acknowledge there might be some insight in the other's point of view. Each escalated his rhetoric in response to the other. The two doctors, both sworn to protect life and both sincere in their points of view, ended up calling each other immoral and unethical. From the perspective of the audience, little was learned and no progress was made in addressing one of the most important questions of our time.

While the stated purpose of the conference was to discuss ways to reduce hostility and increase security, the *process* of the two doctors' interaction was a tension-increasing spiral, which generated more hostility, and facilitated little or no communication. The underlying intention of both physicians (judging from their actions) was to convert the other to his point of view, to defeat, to belittle. Since their *intent* was to fight it out, this generated a *process* that was bitter and divisive, which then produced a *content* discussion that was narrowly defensive and not productive of new ideas.

Imagine if the two doctors' intent had been to communicate constructively, to listen and learn from each other, and to discover common ground. By changing their *intention* from one of trying to convert or defeat the other to one of trying to listen and gain greater understanding, they would have generated a different *process*, and out of this process would come new insights, data, and options.

The Observing Self

The One you are looking for is the One who is looking.
Francis of Assisi

Recently, a close friend shared this experience of sitting with a dying friend on the day before she went into a coma:

I was holding her hand, sitting in her room, and in the hall, our young children were skirmishing. My friend appeared unaffected by the commotion. As I observed her serenity, I realized how often I let myself become affected by small irritations and minor disturbances. It occurred to me that those of us who believe we have substantial time left here on Earth go in and out of our "big selves" and our "little selves."

My friend, on the edge of death, was experiencing only the "big self." This self sees the big picture, it has no fear of loss — it is detached, and doesn't define itself by anything on the outside. This Observing Self is able to transcend time and circumstances. Though we often forget, it is the portal to the spiritual realm. The little self is entangled in our life's current drama. It is attached to worldly concerns and defines itself by its attachments. This outer self is often motivated by fear, and thinks in narrow terms of preventing loss.

There is a fundamental difference between our identity and those things with which we have become identified. We are not our cars, our houses, our jobs, our roles, or even our beliefs. Each one of us is an essential person, a unique individual who observes and transcends all. The one we are looking for is the one who is looking out from behind our eyes.

The error we often make is that we confuse the flux of images and thoughts in our own mind with our Observing Self. We forget who we are at the center and become identified with the ever-changing periphery of our lives. This forgetting of our essential identity might be compared to the experience of watching a movie. Often, we become so involved with the characters on the screen that we forget we are the person sitting in the chair. In other words, we become so identified with the content of the movie that we are not longer aware of the process of our Observing Self.

Recall the diagram of the pyramid and the three levels of human interaction. Now picture a circle around the pyramid, representing the Observing Self, the one who includes and transcends all three levels of interaction.

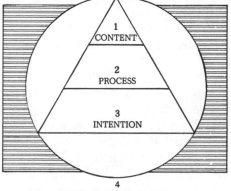

THE OBSERVING SELF

1. THE CONTENT — what we say or do.
2. THE PROCESS — the way we say or do.
3. THE INTENTION — the goal we have in saying or doing.
4. THE OBSERVING SELF — the essential person who observes and transcends all three levels.

Have you observed that you are not only the content of your words, actions, or thoughts? Each one of us is more than our physical forms, more than our clothes, status, ideas, feelings, or beliefs. All of these are items on a list called the contents of our lives. But we are not objects. Each one of us is an indivisible person, a whole who is greater than the sum of all the parts.

Similarly, you are not only the process of your life. You are the Observing Self who watches the entire journey from birth to death. Can you remember looking out from your eyes when you were a small child running and playing?

When you went to high school or college? When you had a child? Or when your parents died and you began to grow older yourself? Each one of us is there looking from the inside out, throughout the entire cycle of our life process.

Finally, you are not only your intention. Rather, you are the source of this intention, whether consciously or unconsciously. The more you are centered in the Observing Self, the more you are able to choose your underlying intent. It is a conscious choice. Intention generates the process which then influences the content; the more we are centered in our essential person, the more we can use the power of intention to determine our future with conscious care and dedication.

Just as the human eye cannot see itself, so the Observing Self cannot see itself as an object. For the Observing Self is a subject alone, which can be experienced and known by another subject, what Martin Buber called an "I and thou relationship." Looking out from within this observing subject, we can see the positions of the mind, and often we mistakenly identify the mind as the self.

To use another metaphor, the human mind turns like a wheel, rotating from position to position, mood to mood. Watch your mind during a normal day. In the morning when you first awake, perhaps the dreams of the night are still with you and affect your mood. Then, at work your experience of the day takes on an entirely different tone. Perhaps, you get into an argument and become very adamant about a particular point of view. Later in the day, as you reflect upon the argument, you realize that actually there are many other ways to see it. You are no longer as attached or identified with your position as you were earlier in the day. On and on it goes — the rotating wheel of our mental process.

But who are you? Who is the one that observes all those feelings and positions throughout the day? At the center of the rotating mind is the Observing Self, the whole person, the soul — whatsoever we choose to name our most essential presence.

From the center watching the periphery of our mental

positioning, we can observe: "I am not my anger. I am not my beliefs. I am not the various masks that I wear. I am not the various roles that I play. I am not my pleasure. I am not my pain. I am not all the ideas and things with which my mind becomes identified."

The holy place within each of us, to which Francis of Assisi refers, is the place that sees the whole. This place of awareness which sees the whole, is itself indivisible. Thus the more we are centered in the Observing Self, the more we are able to see how two apparently conflicting ideas or points of view are part of a larger, more inclusive whole.

In our adolescence, the human mind has been primarily reductionist, dissecting the whole into its component parts, whether it be parts of a person, nation, or planet. In the world of black-and-white thinking, the adolescent mind sees no underlying unity: either you are good or bad, friend or foe. There is no common ground, no middle path, no inter-connection. But beyond black-and-white thinking, the two are one. What looks divided is also connected at another level. When we can allow sets of paired opposites to coexist in our thinking, they provide access to greater wisdom. If we cannot allow competing ideas to coexist in our minds, how can we gain the increased understanding of listening to other people with widely divergent points of view?

The more we are centered in the Observing Self, the more we are able to be detached enough from the content of our own opinion to listen to other opinions, and together to look for clearer insights and more cogent solutions. From the Observing Self, we are more conscious of our underlying intention and hence able to direct the focus of our mind more effectively. Once we are clear that our shared intention is to build a more secure and peaceful future for everyone, we need not be so identified with the content of our current point of view about "how to do it." Quite the contrary, we will want to explore as many perspectives as possible in order to find the most workable and comprehensive strategies to achieve our goal.

CHAPTER FOUR

A New Meaning Of Victory

This is my battle hymn;
It's for a battle we're all in.
And while the battlefield's without and within,
It's a battle where everyone can win.

I've seen the clear bright rivers run;
I've seen the dark turn to the Sun.
And as I awake to a new coming dawn,
I see the world and I are one.

Within us without us, my friends,
There is a place where we all win ...

There is a great chain that must not live in vain,
It's led us to life, and life must not end.
Now do you — do you see this place?
Where everyone can win.
                    — John Burkhardt —
                    "A New Battle Hymn"

The word *victory* comes from the Latin root, *vincere,* meaning to conquer. When Julius Caesar and the Roman Legions took Gaul, he is reputed to have said, *"Veni, vidi, vici* ... I came, I saw, I conquered." The dictionary defines victory as:

1. the advantage or superiority gained in defeating the enemy or an opponent in battle; triumph gained by force of arms. 2. the defeat of an enemy in combat, battle, or

war. 3. success in any context, struggle, or enterprise; supremacy, superiority, or triumph in any effort.

Throughout most of recorded history, a victory has necessitated a vanquished party. To win the great war, there must be a loser. To conquer, there must be those whom you have conquered. The war model of resolving conflicts says, "My victory is your defeat." There is no other alternative. The only ruling principle is that the winner takes all.

Today, this model is fundamentally at question. As we saw in the chapter above, "Our Common Danger," the threat of modern war and environmental catastrophe have created an imperative to survive which is global in scope.

The 1958 movie, *The Defiant Ones*, is an apt and powerful metaphor for our global situation at the closing of the twentieth century. Two prisoners, one black (Sidney Poitier) and the other white (Tony Curtis), have escaped from a prison in the South and are chained together. Each hates the other, yet they are forced to flee for their lives together, chased by hounds and a posse. Often they come to blows with their one free hand. The folly, of course, is that if either were to seriously harm the other, it would mean almost certain capture or death for the other.

Chained together, they are compelled to cross a swift and dangerous river. At one point, the lead person loses his footing and both are swept away into the rapids. Finally, Tony Curtis manages to grab a branch and pull them toward shore. Lying exhausted on the beach, Sidney Poitier gasps, "Thanks for pulling me out."

Tony Curtis barks back, "Man, I didn't pull you out; I kept you from pulling me in."

Whether we recognize it or not, we are chained together crossing a perilous river, in a period of time when a combination of events could sweep the nations of the world into a global war or ecological catastrophe. As a result, we live in the transition between two different models of winning.

We all want to win in our lives. We want to be successful and respected. We want to have family and friends who love us. We want our children to grow up strong and healthy. We want our nation and our world to survive and thrive. We want our lives to be the best they can be.

In short, we all share the same desire to be happy and to fulfill our potential. And most of us want to make a contribution to help make the world a better place. Yet, the fact is that we cannot truly win, if our world is losing. If we are poisoning our air, water, and soil; depleting the ozone; watching the increase of drugs and violence; or fearing the momentum toward a regional or global war — there is no foundation upon which to make our lives a victory.

This chapter outlines certain prerequisites for redefining victory — for creating a world in which everyone can win:

Respect for All Life: We see that all life sustains us and hence we act from respect.

The Means Are the Ends: We recognize that the means are inseparable from the ends, and hence we use methods which are in accord with our goals.

A Spirit of Open Inquiry: We observe that greater understanding comes from exploring many points of view, and hence we operate from a spirit of open inquiry.

Real Dialogue: We cultivate empathy and engage in real dialogue with others across our many differences.

I Win/You Win: We recognize that in an interdependent world, it is in our own best interests to turn our conflicts into mutual gain.

Respect for All Life

> *Fundamental to all ethics is reverence for life: to protect and encourage life is good; to destroy and demean life is bad.*
>
> Albert Schweitzer

Only a few fortunate men and women have had the opportunity to see the Earth from space with their own eyes. Yet, the photographs and the awareness that these astronauts have brought back to us haved helped to create an expanded sense of human identity. We have begun to see the Earth in her magnificent totality.

> The Earth reminded us of a Christmas tree ornament hanging in the blackness of space. As we got farther and farther away it diminished in size. Finally it shrank to the size of a marble, the most beautiful marble you can imagine. That beautiful, warm, living object looked so fragile, so delicate, that if you touched it with a finger it would crumble and fall apart. Seeing this has to change a man, has to make a man appreciate the creation of God and the love of God.   James Irwin, astronaut, U.S.A.

> Before I flew I was already aware of how small and vulnerable our planet is; but only when I saw it from space, in all its ineffable beauty and fragility, did I realize that humankind's most urgent task is to cherish and preserve it for future generations.   Sigmund Jahn, astronaut, German Democratic Republic

> During a space flight, the psyche of each astronaut is reshaped. Having seen the sun, the stars, and our planet, you become more full of life, softer. You begin to look at all living things with greater trepidation and you begin to be more kind and patient with the people around you. At any rate that is what happened to me.   Boris Volynov, astronaut, U.S.S.R.

> The first day or so we all pointed to our countries. The third or fourth day we were pointing to our continents. By the fifth day we were aware of only one Earth.   Sultan Bin Salman al-Saud, astronaut, The Kingdom of Saudi Arabia

Imagine being in a space shuttle and traveling straight up toward the stars. Immediately after the launch, you see views of your home city; then these rapidly expand to include the entire country, which then becomes an aerial outline of the whole continent. From 200 miles up, all you can see is the vivid blueness of the oceans, the swirl of white clouds, and the rugged terrain below. All human-made boundaries have passed away.

As you orbit the blue planet, you watch the sixteen daily sunrises and sunsets. Astronaut Joseph Allen remembers, "You see clouds towering up. You see their shadows on the sunlit plains. It's like a stereoscopic view of nature."

Looking back at Mother Earth, you see her awesome mystery and her vulnerability — the limited boundaries of life against the black depths of lifeless space. As you pull further away, the blue Earth becomes a small sphere in the distance. There is no wind in space, no smells or sounds. It is silent. The only noise comes from your spacecraft and from yourself. You are alone with your thoughts in the infinite night sky of the Universe.

For some astronauts, space travel has been a spiritual experience. Recalling his experience of being on the Moon looking back at the Earth, astronaut James Irwin says, "The total power of God became abundantly clear to me. The lifelessness of the Moon versus the place where life abounds, the Earth, makes you think deeply about life in general." Similarly, traveling back from the Moon toward Earth, astronaut Edgar Mitchell had "an explosion of awareness, a peak experience."

It is this explosion of awareness — the recognition that life itself is sacred and that the Earth is a sacred totality — which will provide the ethical foundation for the next century and beyond.

As biologist Lewis Thomas eloquently put it:

> Viewed from the distance of the Moon, the astonishing thing about the Earth, catching the breath, is that it is alive ... the only exuberant thing in this part of the cosmos. ... It has the organized, self-contained look of a live creature, full of information, marvelously skilled in handling the energy of the Sun.

This was not always the case. Hundreds of millions of years ago, our planet was lifeless, a molten mass of hot gases and volcanic activity, with no atmosphere to protect its surface from the Sun's radiation. Then, scientists say, after eons it began to rain and it rained for perhaps a million years, forming the vast oceans which now cover two-thirds of our planet. In these ancient seas, the conditions ripened for the mystery of life to appear. First came single-celled organisms which had the ability to convert the methane gases of early Earth to oxygen. Over millions of years these simple life forms created the atmosphere and the ozone layer which shields us from the Sun's radiation and allows a vast diversity of life to exist on Earth. Similarly, our thin layer of topsoil was created by the living and dying of countless generations of life forms, who over millennia left their organic matter behind to become the soil that nourishes us today. The lifeforce created the conditions for more life.

Today there are millions of species of animals and plants that live within what we call the "biosphere" — the thin layer of water, air, and soil that surrounds the planet Earth. This layer which supports all known life in our solar system is like the skin of an apple relative to the size of the Earth. All of these living organisms have evolved with us.

So long as we humans believe that other animals are mere objects with no awareness, we are likely to continue to treat them as mechanisms only to be exploited for our own purposes. The wolf, the eagle, the dolphin — each has its ways of seeing and knowing life. While we humans cannot know what it is like to see through their eyes, scientists are currently making great strides in cracking the code of inter-species communication. There may well come a day in the next century when, through the use of computers, we will be able to decipher the intricate songs of the whales and dolphins and respond in kind. We will then perceive fully the ultimate folly, the unspeakable loss, that every time we bring another species to extinction, we have eliminated an entirely different way of knowing life which has evolved for millions of years.

Through respect for all life, we can begin to restore our relationship to nature and free ourselves from our narrow prejudices, as Einstein said, "by widening our circle of compassion to embrace all living creatures and the whole of nature in its beauty." If we intend to survive and prosper together on Earth, we must protect and honor this lifeforce.

At the root of human morality in the nuclear age is choice. "What is the use of living," wrote Winston Churchill, "if it be not for making this world a better place for those who will live in it after we are gone." When we choose to live as though we are responsible for helping to preserve and strengthen life itself, we renew the depths of our existence.

The Means Are the Ends

The means are to the ends as the seed is to the tree.
                    Mahatma Gandhi

Central to Gandhi's teaching about ethics is that the means are the ends in the making. The importance of this statement cannot be overemphasized. By utilizing means which contradict our ends, we never get to where we want to go. If peace is our goal and we do not change the hostile way we interact with each other, then peace will remain an impossible goal. As Gandhi put it:

> They say "means are after all means." I would say "means are after all everything." As the means so the end. There is no wall of separation between means and ends. Indeed the Creator has given us control (and that too very limited) over means, none over the end. Realization of the goal is in exact proportion to that of the means. This is a proposition that admits of no exception.

One spring a couple of years ago, we were asked to do a communications workshop for a regional gathering of peace activists in Northern California. We were scheduled for the afternoon after a morning of other meetings and presentations. As we entered the room, a man was standing and speaking angrily: "The people at Lawrence Livermore Labs tell us that the Russians are our enemies; well, I want to say that the people at Lawrence Livermore Labs are our enemies." (This national laboratory which designs nuclear weapons and other military technologies is nearby.) A wave of anger rippled across the room and some people murmured in agreement.

This is something most of us do: We try to convert those with whom we disagree. When that doesn't work, we escalate, attacking their position and often their person. Rarely do we sincerely listen to other people who have a fundamentally different point of view than our own. If someone agrees with our perspective, we feel affinity, as if we are part of the same club. If someone disagrees with us, we experience them as "not-me," as enemy, and we close down.

At one of our community dialogues on peace and security, there was a young man at the back of the room. As soon as the dialogue began, the young man began to glare angrily, shuffle his papers, and furiously take notes as though he was preparing a rebuttal to whatever was being said.

After about half an hour, the young man leaped up, interrupted the meeting, and in a loud and tense voice said, "You people are the problem. You think you are for peace, but you don't understand that our country needs to be strong. You are naive and you weaken our country."

Immediately, a few people in the room began to react angrily, as though they were going to attack him back. Various others assured him that the room was widely mixed with people who represented the political spectrum, from peace-through-strength to peace-through-disarmament. He relaxed and later participated thoughtfully in the exchange of views.

The young man turned out to be a rifle instructor at Fort Ord, a large army base near Monterey, California. Toward the end, he stood up once again and told the room that he had come with the purpose of disrupting the meeting, because he thought it was "a bunch of peaceniks." He said he had been mistaken. Before he left, he gave us his card and said he would like to bring some of his friends in the military to our next dialogue.

Both the angry peace activist and the angry rifle instructor have a good deal in common. Both were acting out of fear, both had created enemies in their minds, both were at war with the process of peace-making. Both represent a part of our collective psyche with which we all can identify.

Whenever we argue self-righteously for "peace" — meaning our own version of peace — while showing no respect for other points of view, our message is contradictory. It is *peace content, but war mind*. While the subject we are talking about is peace, the process of what we are doing is divisive and warlike. Our manner and tone are often angry and judgmental. In the name of "peace," we have turned the other person into a perceived enemy. And what is our motivation or intent? Is it to seek greater understanding and options that work for all parties? Or is it to be right about our point of view — to talk peace but wage war with our words?

If the means are the ends, then the process of making peace requires a spirit of reconciliation, a genuine intention to search for common ground. A few years ago, a reporter for the *Washington Post* interviewed an old woman standing outside the peace talks in Central America. He asked her, "What do you think the chances for peace are?"

"I don't know." She paused, "Everybody says they are for peace but nobody seems to be for reconciliation."

The Spirit of Open Inquiry

Central to the advancement of human civilization is the spirit of open inquiry. We must not only learn to tolerate our differences. We must welcome them as the richness and diversity which can lead to true intelligence.

Albert Einstein

One of the primary tasks of the human mind is to insure the survival of the individual and thereby the species. The mind accomplishes this purpose by imprinting memory traces of threatening events as they happen and calling upon these memories as needed. For example, as small children we all learned by experience that fire hurts and this memory has imprinted, so that we could avoid being burned in the future. The mind associates *being right* with surviving. Just as we want to be absolutely right that no car is coming as we step out into the street, so we also want to be right that our idea or position is the true one that will increase our safety.

Our challenge, heightened by the nuclear age, is to learn to communicate effectively with people of different political, ethical, and religious points of view. This requires us to be open to the fact that we are not always right; quite the contrary, our way of seeing something is only one way of seeing it. "The first problem for all of us," wrote Gloria Steinem, "is not to learn, but to unlearn."

Basic to the spirit of open inquiry is the acknowledgment of relativity. It has been said there are always at least three truths: your truth, my truth, and the truth. Most scientists would agree that individual expressions of "the truth" can only be approximate. Every one of us has a particular perspective influenced by our personal history, values, and beliefs. Our view is in large part a consequence of where we are standing. "We see," as Walter Lippmann once put it, "through the stereotypes and the pictures in our minds."

You see it one way, and another person sees it very differently. And we construct our realities around the way we see it. For example, from the point of view of someone on Earth, Orion is a constellation that has been seen for as long as humans have studied the stars. But if we travel in a spaceship halfway from Earth to the constellation Orion, we will notice that the configuration we saw from Earth is no longer visible. We are closer and the stars of Orion are no longer close enough from our new perspective to be seen as connected. Orion has disappeared. What we call truth is relative to where we are standing.

Much of our world is currently locked into seeing things from only one point of view: "I am right. You are wrong." As a result, we narrow our vantage point and only take into account those who agree with us. We cheat ourselves out of the experience of interacting with diversity. We mistakenly associate listening to another point of view with agreement or surrender to the other person's way of seeing things. Yet, the willingness to listen is not about agreeing or disagreeing, but rather about receiving information from, and insights into, the other person.

Once during a community dialogue in Medford, Oregon,

a man raised his hand and said, "I don't like to listen to people with whom I disagree, because I'm afraid what they have to say might be contagious." The room laughed in agreement.

The belief that our way is the true way gives us a sense of security. We fear that if we are receptive to a perspective that does not reinforce our own, it will confuse or disorient us. Watch yourself and see what happens when someone vividly disagrees with something you are saying. Do you feel attacked? Does your pulse increase? Do you break out in a sweat?

The problem here is attachment. By confusing our essential identity with our current position, we restrict our ability to listen to new ideas and practice open inquiry. Real inquiry requires a willingness to not know the answer, to have a beginner's mind, to inform oneself from many different perspectives. Again, the more we are centered in the Observing Self, the more able we are to maintain our own perspective while fully listening to the other's point of view.

There is a cartoon in which a man is wearing a T-shirt which says: "I wear this, therefore I am." The more we wear our current position as if it were our only identity, the more defensive we will tend to be toward those who disagree with us. We often interpret disagreement as an attack upon, or rejection of, who we are. Those who agree with our position we see as friend, and those who disagree with our position we see as foe. This is very dangerous for our survival as a species, because the data and insight we need to overcome our common danger require us to be in communication with our apparent adversaries. Yet, the roots of our resistance to doing this go very deep.

A primitive single-celled organism can be observed to move toward that which nourishes it and away from noxious stimuli that threaten it. In a nourishing environment, the organism becomes more porous and the flow across its cellular membrane is enhanced. In toxic or less supportive environments, the organism reduces its porosity and the flow across the cell wall is diminished. The single-celled entity therefore spends a great deal of its life moving toward "friendly" environments and away from "unfriendly" ones. So it is with more complex organisms as well. When a wild animal hears a rustle in the bushes, it becomes alert and must quickly determine whether the noise was caused by something that threatens it.

These basic oscillations of toward/away continue to shape a significant portion of human interactions. Upon encountering others, we tend to immediately categorize into me/not me, friend/foe. These instantaneous perceptions determine the distance we establish, toward or away from, and the amount of flow, i.e., exchange of information, that we allow.

When we perceive differences, we tend to be more cautious and less receptive. We shift into a protective pattern; we shut down. This shutting down is quite literal, manifesting in physiological fluctuations which are mediated by hormonal and chemical means. The most obvious example is the "fight-or-flight" response, which is triggered by an internal chemical release whenever we perceive danger.

It is easy to see the role that fear plays in blocking open inquiry and preventing constructive communication. As fear increases, our ability to perceive clearly becomes blurred. Attention to nuances and subtleties is diminished, and our mental functioning becomes more dichotomous — black/white, us/them. We move into an alerting pattern, as when a loud siren blasts near us, and we lose our mental fluidity that allows creativity and useful problem-solving. In order to increase open inquiry between people of different political, cultural, and ethnic points of view, we need to reduce the level of fear in our interactions.

Real Dialogue

At the heart of the problems we face is an interesting dilemma: Only when threat is gone can you communicate, but obviously you're going to have to communicate to get rid of the threat.... The dialogue process attempts to cut

through that cycle and teach people to communicate even
where there is fundamental disagreement ...

Sheila Tobias

In June 1987, one hundred citizens from seventeen states gathered in New Mexico for the Trinity Symposium Policy Dialogue, co-sponsored by Project Victory and the Trinity Forum. It was a four-day event: two days were spent training the community leaders on skills for dialogue and conflict resolution, and two days involved mediated dialogues featuring two U.S. senators and twelve national security experts of varying political views. There were representatives from conservative groups, such as the Hoover Institute and Americans for High Frontier, and from liberal groups, such as the Rocky Mountain Disarmament Project and the Institute for Policy Studies.

A weapons designer from Sandia National Laboratory said: "This kind of dialogue is critically important because often we are so divided. Conservatives and liberals are in the front seat of the same car driving along a steep mountain road. Each group has one hand on the steering wheel, but most of the time we are trying to pull the wheel in different directions."

The word *debate* is derived from *battre* (French), meaning to beat; and *battere* (Latin), meaning to beat or knock. In short, a debate is a "civilized" verbal battle, an adversarial model of communication and problem-solving. This adversarial model is the very cornerstone of our legal system and other institutions reflecting our culture. Generally, when two people have a difference in attitude, perspective, opinion, belief, or point of view, each will attempt to convert or dominate the other. Each seeks to find the hole in the logic, reasoning, or facts of the other and uses the "knife tongue" to inflict maximum damage. This scenario is particularly evident when playing to an audience.

It is as though we have all been trained in the "Perry Mason School of Interpersonal Relationships." The adversarial process is often passionate, interesting, and even amusing.

It does not, however, facilitate communication, if we define communication as a genuine exchange of information. The adversarial process does not beget understanding, tolerance of differences, or empathy — all qualities that are increasingly appropriate and necessary as we move into the twenty-first century. To the contrary, the purpose of an adversarial interaction is to win and not to lose; to make your opponent wrong while self-justifying and extolling the rightness of your own perspective.

Our current public discussion on issues pertaining to world peace and national security has been plagued with this adversarial mode of communication. Conservatives and liberals rarely have a true exchange of information. They debate; they posture; they battle. They talk *at* each other, not *with* each other. Each side tries to convert the other to its vantage point. "My idea can beat up your idea" prevails as the process. Fear diminishes receptivity and turns potential dialogue into a win/lose competition in which the participants tend to become more convinced of the rightness of their particular position.

The spiral of escalating rhetoric which often erupts between factions in this country is a mirror reflection of the tension-increasing spiral that currently engulfs many of the nations of the world. We will remain deadlocked in this "dialogue of the deaf" unless we advance our means of communication, so as to respect the fears and needs of different points of view. With the fears rendered not only visible but validated, the rhetoric of escalation can give way to creative problem-solving.

If we are going to create a de-escalatory spiral at the level of our global conflicts, it must begin by de-escalating the process of our personal and national interactions. An evolutionary shift of mind requires us to develop models of communication which facilitate peaceful interaction among differing points of view. In a world where the difference of interests and beliefs will continue to be a source of tension between nations, we must create real dialogue across different points of view.

Martin Buber, the great twentieth-century philosopher, distinguishes between two kinds of interactions: an "I-It" relationship and an "I-Thou" relationship. At any moment, we have a choice. We can relate to the other as an object to be manipulated, a thing to be used, an exterior to be judged. Or, we can relate to the other person as having an inner self behind the costumes, masks, and mind set, just as we do. Dialogue is the communication from depth to depth, from "what is essentially human in me" to "what is essentially human in you."

Too often we focus only on the external appearance. Our minds make judgments based upon how someone looks or fits into our categories. If we approve of a person's costume or point of view, we include that person as part of our world. But if we dislike that person's exterior or point of view, we exclude that person from our world. Similarly, the more we objectify and neglect our own inner person, the more we will tend to treat others as though they were objects as well.

Empathy is the practice of extending our awareness to include the experience of others. Empathy has nothing to do with co-dependency or merging with the other. To the contrary, the more centered we are in the Observing Self, the more we can extend our awareness to a wide diversity of people. Empathy is the antidote for the absolutist mind, for the place in each of us that thinks, "I am totally right and you are totally wrong; my way is the only way." By putting ourselves in the shoes of another person — feeling his or her needs, fears, and hopes — we come to know that the other is not an object, but a breathing/thinking/feeling subject like ourselves.

It is very difficult for many of us to listen to another person without judging and rejecting because we disagree with his or her beliefs. Yet as the world-renowned photographer, Margaret Bourke-White emphasized: "To understand another human being you must gain some insight into the conditions which made him what he is . . ."

It takes discipline to listen fully; our minds react and we are reminded of many things we want to say or comment upon. The urge to interrupt, give advice, or try to convert gets in the way of genuine listening. But if you want to help launch the next century into safety and peace, start by taking the initiative to listen with empathy. Seek to create a climate of mutual respect in which the people in your life feel empowered to express themselves fully.

Every time one of us listens to the other — not because we agree or disagree with the content of his or her position, but because we value the essential person — we achieve a small victory for the advancement of human dignity. The commitment to honor and respect what is essentially human in oneself and the other is at the heart of real dialogue.

With regard to conflicts within ourselves, the use of inner dialogue can also facilitate integration and peace of mind. Whenever we are divided between two or more competing voices inside, we can initiate an inner dialogue to listen to each of our conflicting points of view. Theo Brown, one of the founders of Project Victory, calls this "the town meeting of the mind." By listening to the different factions and caucuses within ourselves, we see from a larger and more integrated perspective. Rather than suppressing or denying competing parts of our psyche, we can extend our awareness to include them. The more we treat our own inner process with empathy, the more able we are to engender real dialogue with others: peace within, peace without.

Whether the goal is personal peace or global victory over the common danger, dialogue is critically important to help heal the divisions that threaten our future:

Personal — Dialogue within the mind can help to heal the inner divisions and provide access to the whole person.

Community — Dialogue between individuals and groups can help to heal the outer divisions and provide access to increased understanding and workable solutions.

National — Dialogue between factions within the nation can generate a different level of policy-making and help to formulate comprehensive policies which will enable us to steer a steady course toward real security and peace.

Global — Dialogue between nations can help us to arrive at global strategies of mutually assured development and thereby facilitate a way out of our world-threatening situation.

I Win/You Win

If we win here we will win everywhere. The world is a fine place and worth fighting for ...

Ernest Hemingway

During most of human history, the option of all-out combat has followed the breakdown of diplomacy. This war model of resolving conflicts assumes that the conflicting sets of interests cannot be mediated or reconciled in a way that serves all parties. When it comes to disputes of territory, resources, or status, we must fight it out to determine who is superior. Yet, with the advent in recent times of weapons of mass destruction, the boundary between homicide and suicide has become blurred. This creates a global imperative to curb our violence and find new means — other than "might makes right" — to solve conflicts.

It is as if the nations of the world are sitting in a house which is filled with canisters of gasoline. The two super-powers have the most matches. Other countries are competing to get more matches, and many countries have enough matches to set off small explosions which might create a chain reaction. Most of these countries are playing a game of power, but nobody knows for sure by what rules. The central purpose in all the different variations seems to be to get as much power as you can in order to be dominant and secure. Yet, there is little or no security.

Whether recognized or not, all of the nations are caught up in one paramount game of survival, because they all live in the same house. Implicit in this ultimate game is the power of any one of the players — should they get too far behind or too crazy — to light a match and throw it into the canisters of gasoline. If they cannot win at the game of getting power, desperate and fanatical players may decide to ruin the game for the others.

If we want the house to survive, we need to start by acknowledging that the rules are different now, that if we burn the house down, everyone loses. Everyone must "win" the paramount game, or no one will. Here the meaning of winning has changed profoundly. The old model of "winner takes all" is not viable in this new context. For if one country "wins" to the point where another country has nothing left to lose, and the second country has the means to destroy the first (and perhaps human civilization), then everyone is threatened. World leaders and citizens are increasingly recognizing that real stability must be based upon a shared commitment to our common security.

The increasing interdependence of our global economy and ecology compels us to find "I win/you win" solutions to our conflicts. The obsolescence of the old win/lose model is vividly illustrated by a quote from the Federal Emergency Management Office in the early 1980s: "Victory in a nuclear war will belong to the country which recovers first." If we want to WIN — in terms of our survival and long-term prosperity — we must redefine the meaning of victory.

Yet, this "new" model of winning is not really new. What is new is that we are compelled to implement it, on a much broader scale. The model of "I win/you win" is in fact deeply rooted in the human experience. Every time a group of people, a tribe or nation, has banded together to overcome a common threat — like hurricanes, floods, earthquakes — there has been the experience of a shared victory. Every time a team has mastered a common challenge — climbing a peak, diving to the depths of the sea, or designing a new computer — there is this experience of *winning together*. It is a remarkable experience: We not only obtain the thrill of victory, we share it with those who made it happen with us.

The key to the constructive use of conflict is our underlying intention. If the intention between two parties to a dispute is to find workable solutions, those solutions are possible in most, but not all, circumstances. Workable solutions can be found to clashes based on a conflict of real interest — things both parties want or need; to clashes based on prejudice and historical animosity; and to clashes arising from psychological and inner-driven needs. Workable solutions cannot be found, however, for clashes based on greed and domination. In the short-run, this means we will have to rely at least in part on the deterrent power of military force. The long-term need is to create a personal and societal dis-incentive against greed and domination. Given a positive intention, here are a few ways in which we can constructively use conflict:

We can change the way we view conflict. Many of us have been taught that conflict by definition is bad, and we should avoid it at all costs. We have also learned from our movies and television that the appropriate way to deal with conflict is to be violent — pack a gun and, if necessary, blow our adversary away. (If not physically, then at least psychologically.) Neither of these two positions offers much hope for dealing effectively with conflict.

We need to begin by recognizing that conflict is an inevitable and important part of our lives. Eliminating conflict is not possible, nor would it be desirable. Conflict dealt with constructively promotes growth. If there were no tension or conflict in our lives, we would become stagnant. For example, conflict is at the core of the western dramatic tradition. We experience the movement of the plot through the setting up, and then the resolution of conflict.

To be able to distinguish between the creative and the destructive use of conflict is extremely important. The creative use of conflict contributes to our growth and development, and serves to enhance the dignity and well-being of oneself and the other. The destructive use of conflict violates the integrity and diminishes the well-being of oneself or others, whether it be another person, a nation, or nature.

We can change the way we hold opposites. At the source

of much conflict is the fact that we see things from very different points of view.

By learning how to hold two conflicting ideas or points of view at the same time, we can move beyond black-and-white thinking. This is a profound step. Every time we expand our frame of reference to include the insights of two or more divergent perspectives, we become larger than the perceived conflict.

There is a drawing of two women, one old and one young. Their faces are interwoven so that initially it is difficult to see both at the same time. If you focus first on seeing the young one, you cannot see the old woman and vice versa. The mind jumps back and forth, seeing one and then the other. The breakthrough comes when you can hold both viewpoints simultaneously.

We can change the way we resolve conflicts from win/lose to win/win. The process of finding win/win outcomes to a dispute is equally relevant to our personal lives, to policy discussion between factions within the United States, and to interactions between nation-states worldwide. If each party can discover what the other party really wants and what the other party really fears, many times a solution can be formulated which meets the goals and protects the concerns of both parties.

We can promote reciprocal tension-reduction. War is the ultimate escalation of destructive conflict. In the nuclear age, there is an unacceptable risk that regional conflicts will flare into a global war. An ever-increasing number of people must make it their goal to implement a process of reciprocal tension-reduction at all levels of destructive conflict. The key word here is *reciprocal.* For example, in a hostile situation, the attempt to unilaterally disarm, whether personally or nationally, can be destabilizing. But where there is a mutually verifiable process, tensions can be reduced, step by step.

History shows that it is possible to reduce tensions and generate a climate of mutual restraint, even in extreme circumstances. Robert Axelrod in *The Evolution of Cooperation* described an example from World War I, where Allied and German soldiers faced each other in trenches along the Western front. This close combat was among the most gruesome in the history of warfare. Yet, over a period of time, German and French troops developed systems of interaction in which each side implicitly agreed not to slaughter the other, based on the same treatment in return.

Long periods would elapse in which the only shots fired were well above the enemy's heads, or directed in some way to demonstrate each side's willingness not to kill the other. Yet, both sides made it clear that violation of this unspoken agreement would be reciprocated at least as strongly. For example, a French soldier noted that if his side launched a grenade into the German trenches, they could expect three grenades to be shot back. Frequently, both sides would demonstrate the precision and prowess of their weapons by blasting areas immediately adjacent to the trenches, communicating that their restraint was not due to weakness, but to an acknowledgment of mutually perceived advantage.

It was not that the two sides liked each other, nor were they primarily concerned about each other's survival. They were at war, but they knew that establishing a system of reciprocal tension-reduction was better in the long run for each of them. Such a relationship evolves when one side takes the initiative to de-escalate the tension. Through the process of testing and retesting the opponent's intent, a spiral of tension-reduction begins to evolve.

Currently the United States and the Soviet Union are engaged, at least partially, in a process aimed at reducing tensions and cultivating a climate of mutual restraint. The trench warfare example is analogous to our global situation in a number of ways. In the World War I situation, the same battalions of enemy soldiers were stationed across from each other for long periods. Hence, they could begin to send consistent signals to each other. Both sides knew they had the weaponry to decimate their adversary and both also knew that if they did, they would almost certainly be destroyed themselves. The only way for either side to survive was to establish a relationship based on reciprocity.

CHAPTER FIVE

Riding
The Tiger

He who rides a tiger finds it difficult to dismount.
— Chinese proverb —

The reality that everything is at risk will be with us for the foreseeable future. We cannot put the genie of these destructive technologies back in the bottle; we cannot go back to a time before they were invented. Most people would agree that the need to maintain some kind of deterrent against the use of force is essential. The Adolph Hitlers and the Idi Amins cannot be stopped through conciliation. Not to recognize that greed and the lust for power will continue to influence human events is to be deluded by a kind of utopian naivete.

The ancient image of "riding the tiger" is a profound metaphor for the challenge we face — not only in our time, but for generations to come. If our common danger is a tiger, then we must learn to ride the tiger without falling off and being devoured. The ride is exhilarating, but it also can be deadly if we are not vigilant.

At present, the common danger is the ultimate enemy. Riding the tiger requires us to focus the energies of war and aggression toward the battle to overcome the common danger. This battle is no less threatening than those in previous epochs. To the contrary, if we do not win this battle, it could be our last.

In 400 B.C., the Greek statesman Pericles wrote: "Dead men know no victory." Yet history since then is strewn with millions of dead from our countless wars. Since the wisdom

103

of the need to move beyond domination and to redefine victory is not new, why have we not done it? What is in our way? What are the obstacles to creating, as Robert Fuller put it, "a better game than war?" What after all is our resistance to peace?

At War With Peace

My argument is that war makes rattling good history, but peace is poor reading.

                                                      Thomas Hardy

Everyone says they want peace. Protestors march for peace. The military defends us to maintain peace. Our political leaders speak out for peace, our religious leaders pray for peace. So why don't we have peace? "Peace" is one of those words, like "love" and "God" that has become a convenient screen for everyone's unrealized yearnings. We can all be for it, without having it interfere very much with our daily lives, whether as individuals or nation-states.

In recent years, there has been increasing discussion about the obsolescence of war and the compelling need to "move beyond war." But we do not as yet have a positive and shared image of what it is that we want when we call for peace. Quite the contrary. Our actions tell us that we are ambivalent about peace. Our vision of what peace can be has been distorted by at least two false images in our collective human psyche.

First, "peace" has often been defined only as the cessation of war. "Peace" is the interim period between wars, i.e., the peace between World War I and World War II lasted from 1918 to approximately 1938, a fleeting twenty years. Peace, in this sense, is viewed as the absence of armed conflict. War is the rule, peace is the exception. War is the constant, peace is the pause. Peace has no independent meaning; we have difficulty in creating a vision of the world at peace. If peace is the lull between wars, war seems to be where the excitement is, where the action is. Peace is like the pit stop, the time-out in a very exciting and dangerous road race.

In December 1983, the *Los Angeles Times* reported that sales for children's war toys (miniature soldiers, tanks, guns, khaki uniforms) had risen dramatically during the year. The article speculated that the successful American invasion of Grenada had apparently served as an inspiration. How many times did you play the game "Peace" as a child? What would you do? Sit around quietly and hold each other's hands? Nobody plays peace as a kid. Our images of peace are so empty that we have no such children's games.

How about the game "War"? Didn't you, at least the boys and perhaps the girls, play some version of war? The cast of characters changes over time, but the underlying drama of the war game remains essentially the same: the struggle of the good guys versus the bad guys. Which version did you play: cowboys and Indians, cops and robbers, Americans and Nazis, Luke Skywalker and Darth Vader, Rambo and the Reds? War, not peace, is the game of the backyards and the sandlots.

The second image of peace we have imprinted in our collective psyche is a kind of ultimate resolution of the drama. Peace is the coming salvation, the end of history: hosts of angels singing hosannas on high; the ultimate triumph of the forces of good over evil; Gregorian chants forever; Peace Everlasting.

The universe, as perceived through most human eyes, appears to be a dance of opposites: sunrise and sunset, male and female, life and death, light and dark, good and evil, creation and destruction. It is a dynamic dance, intensely and pervasively in motion. The two halves of the whole are as necessary to the dynamism as two banks of a river, or two players in a chess game. It takes two to tango, two to tangle, two to have a game. Otherwise, there would be no movement, no drama, no dance.

Any image of peace which promises to resolve or "flatten" this dynamic movement is not going to capture our full commitment. If we think of peace as the final goal, we will be partially resisting. We say we are for it (who after all can be publicly opposed to peace?) but we don't create it, because we don't want the game to end. If peace is viewed as the opposite of conflict or as the end to all conflict, who wants peace? Imagine being married to someone with whom you never disagree, never have a fight, never experience any conflict. It would be a flatland of repression and denial, the peace of the walking dead.

The legacy of these two images has left us with a rather twisted relationship to peace. Either peace is the absence of war or it is the ultimate resolution of the drama, as in "rest in peace." In either case, we, the human species, have demonstrated a profound ambivalence towards what we call "peace."

George Lucas did not make a trilogy of movies called "Star Peace," and if he had, most of us would probably not have gone to see them. "Star Peace" sounds boring. When we say we are only for peace, we are fooling ourselves. We are not telling the whole truth. Peace is only a part of the whole, only half the story. At the end of the *Star Wars* trilogy there is a kind of heavenly resolve: Obi-wan Kenobi, Master of the Jedi Knights, and the former Darth Vader, servant of evil, appear together in a transfigured state. But mind you, it is only at the end, after many chapters of the conflict. Such is the projection of the human psyche: we want both the struggle and the transfigured resolution to the next round.

War represents the adversarial struggle, the battle to live and win against death. War represents catharsis, uncivilized freedom, an opportunity for us to release our collective madness. During World War II, there was a significant drop in the suicide and homicide rates worldwide. All the tension, guilt, and aggression that had built up could be released like a pressure cooker blowing its lid. War provides a sense of common purpose and a shared passion to unify against the enemy.

Alfred Kazin wrote that war is the enduring condition of the twentieth century. War has also been the enduring condition for all recorded history. The cycles of war and non-war date back for millennia. "As for wars," said historian Will Durant, "well, there's only been 268 years of the last 3421 in which there was no war."

Why do we go to war? There are many reasons, many justifications, but they do not seem to go to the heart of the matter. Three million French, British, and Russian soldiers died in muddy trenches in World War I because a student shot an archduke. "The truth," wrote William Broyles, Jr., in an eloquent article, "Why Men Love War," "is the reasons don't matter. There is a reason for every war and a war for every reason."

What is perhaps most difficult to admit is that we go to war in part because we want to. When we are honest with ourselves, we can admit that we both hate and love war. Immediately after a war, when the killing and horror is fresh in the public mind, the opposition grows. Then, after a decade or two, some primal urging takes hold of the next generation like a fire in the mind, as though nothing of the terror of the past has been learned.

William Broyles, Jr. wrestled with the taboo of talking about why men, decades after the end of the war, still remember these experiences as some of the most vivid of their lives. Reflecting upon his memories as a combat veteran in Vietnam, Broyles wrote: "War is ugly, horrible, evil, and it is reasonable for men to hate all that. But I believe that most men who have been to war would admit, if they are honest, that somewhere inside themselves they loved it too, loved it as much as anything that has happened to them before or since."

Broyles deserves our acknowledgment for his candor. Who wants to admit that war is so intimate to the human experience? "Civilized society" says that all war is bad, but the same society spends billions of its dollars preparing for war. If we are not honest about why we are drawn to war, we are more likely to continue our repetitive behavior.

Broyles suggested that we love war because in battle we are compelled to be totally alive. We are brought to the terror and the beauty of the present moment. Our awareness is heightened by the "now" of surviving and experiencing whatever joy or sorrow is possible. "War stops time," wrote Broyles, "and intensifies experience to the point of a terrible ecstasy." We love war because it offers a mighty purpose, something greater than ourselves.

In the past, we have rarely been able to mobilize ourselves to such human unity except by facing a shared enemy or confronting a shared danger — storms, fires, hurricanes, earthquakes. Exceptional human beings, our poets and prophets, have made the solitary journey to the mountain top, but our culture has often used the myth of battle against the great enemy to create historically transcendent experiences. For example, Exodus is the story of a battle: Moses and the Israelites against the Pharaoh and the Egyptians. In Revelations, Armageddon is the final battle between the forces of good and evil in order to create Heaven on Earth.

We project "battle" as the way to peace, because within the human psyche, we are in battle. Today we stand in a central paradox of the human condition, especially heightened by the weaponry of the late twentieth century; we want the battle to continue because we want to keep winning the great victory, to be in mythic time.

The reality of the human experience is that we want both conflict and the resolution of conflict taken to the next level of integration. We want to struggle, to pass through conflict, and to advance to higher stages of development. This growth happens through the interaction with, and the integration of, perceived opposites. It is paradoxical. The two are separate, and also two parts of a greater one. Male and female, war and peace, life and death are interdependent elements of a larger whole. Luke Skywalker needs Darth Vader in order to become the real Luke Skywalker. In fact, Darth Vader turns out to be Luke Skywalker's father. The good guy is the son of the archvillain — a terrific metaphor for the interdependence of all existence. Likewise, Lucifer was God's favorite angel before his decision to captain the underworld.

Our language is rarely able to express meanings which point beyond dualistic perception. For example, life and death perceived from a dualistic level are opposites. Yet, in terms of an ecological or systems perspective, life and death are two halves of one cycle. When the fir tree falls to the ground, it becomes the home for termites, worms, and countless other life forms. As the old tree rots back into the ground, it renews the soil and makes it possible for the new seedling to become another fir tree. Unfortunately, we do not yet have a word in English which expresses the interdependent relationship of life and death (life/death).

Similarly, we do not have a word which expresses the creative unity of war and peace, conflict and the resolution of conflict. We do not yet have a vision of what this "larger peace" will look like in our lives and world. The image we are seeking is not "peace forever," but a dynamic and passionate process which inspires our total involvement, the energies of the warrior dedicated to the victory of a Great Turning.

Winning-Peace

To map out a course of action and follow it to an end,
requires some of the same courage which a soldier needs.
Peace has its victories, but it takes brave men to win them.
                                        Ralph Waldo Emerson

What, after all, is peace? We asked participants in two workshops, one for senior citizens and one for high school students, to respond to the question: What is peace for you? Here are a few of their answers:

"Peace is being able to live in a world where there is constant conflict, coexisting with one another."

"Peace is my hope for the future: Every country getting along, not wanting to blow each other up; people in America being more peaceful — no murder, kidnapping, crimes."

"Peace is a lack of fear and anxiety."

"Peace is . . . when people live their lives without fear;
with the rights to the necessities of life: food, shelter,
clothing, the opportunity for education, the means of
creativity, and a system of justice."

"Peace, to me, is being safe at home and not having to
worry about bad things happening to friends or family;
having clear air, fresh water, and enough resources to live."

"Peace is global equality, where every person is a winner,
and 'war' does not have meaning."

"Peace is a state (of consciousness) where people have
open minds — the ability to be flexible, so that people
with conflicting ideas can be open to try to understand
each other better . . ."

Perhaps the most compelling insight from all of these
definitions is that *peace is not an end,* it is a process of managing conflicts constructively. The challenge is to re-orient our
thinking to a concept of peace that is not an end point.
Most of us have a strong desire to find total solutions to
our life-threatening dilemmas. We want to fix the problem,
once and for all. It is very difficult for us to live with an
on-going and unresolved tension. Yet this is the reality of
our situation for the foreseeable future.

For too long, our concepts of peace have been confined
to half-truths and unappealing images. We need a new word
to describe the process of peace as a dynamic balance of
tension. George Lucas created a new word: "light-saber,"
by putting together two contrasting ideas. Just so, let us
invent the word: "winning-peace," to represent the concept
of a dynamic and passionate process of sustainable balance.

Winning-peace combines the discipline, courage, and
totality of the warrior with the patience, compassion, and
wisdom of the peacemaker. Winning-peace certainly sounds
more fun, more alive. Winning-peace is triumphant, not in
some ultimate way, but in the sense that we have succeeded,
for our time, in overcoming the threats to our future. We
win against the common danger and the result is that the
human journey continues.

The world-shaking fact is that now we are all in this together: The danger we confront is common to all nationalities, races, and creeds. The consequences of global war or environmental catastrophe affect everyone. It is therefore in the self-interest of every individual and nation to work together. Once enough of us comprehend this fact, the stirrings of a movement to preserve and enhance life will become everywhere apparent.

Mastering the Ride

In 1999, we will remember the twentieth century as the bloodiest and the best in the history of man. One hundred twenty million people have been killed in 130 wars in this century — more than all those killed in war before 1900. But at the same time, more technological and material progress has been made over the last hundred years than ever before. The twentieth century will be remembered as a century of war and wonder. We must make the twenty-first a century of peace.

Richard M. Nixon

Riding the tiger is the on-going, dynamic process of working together to achieve and maintain the balance needed to prevail over the common danger. The conflict of interests between nations will continue. The challenge of our era is not to deny or eliminate conflict, but to learn to manage conflicts in our lives and our world, so as to minimize their destructive potential and maximize their creative outcome.

The tiger is not only our destructive technologies but also our aggressive energies: the hunter, warrior, and killer who has lived inside us for millennia to guard our survival. Riding the tiger requires us to develop the ability to negotiate effectively between our own aggressive and nurturing impulses. Riding the tiger involves integrating and transcending opposites. It is an apt metaphor for combining the best qualities of the warrior and the peacemaker. The opposites are never ultimately resolved, but as we mature, we learn to use the power of each appropriately.

In times past, much of our excitement and sense of purpose has been associated with war and the celebration of war. Now the warrior spirit is needed once more, but this time the real challenge is to manage our conflicts without resort to violence and domination. This is not something which will happen overnight. It may take most of the next century, or however long. The point is, there is no alternative.

In 1950, Admiral Richard Byrd suggested that the human race could mobilize its "moral and spiritual power to unite the world behind our common global purpose." He described this purpose and the method to achieve it as follows:

> All decent men and women the world over, of whatever creed or race or color, desire for themselves and their loved ones *a chance for the pursuit of happiness, and liberty and freedom of worship.* This is our common global purpose.
>
> And to achieve this purpose there is a workable method — the Golden Rule, which men and women of all religions can understand. . . . It is the realization that the well-being of one man depends upon the well-being of his neighbor, the well-being of one group depends upon the well-being of its neighbor group, and the well-being of a nation depends upon the well-being of its neighbor nation. And all nations are now neighbors.
>
> But we must not make the mistake of considering what the Great Teacher told us 2000 years ago as a teaching based on weakness. Above all things, it is important for man to base his fight for brotherhood and unity upon firmness, strength, and fortitude behind what is right and just.
>
> We know . . . that it will take time to mobilize the moral and spiritual force of man so as to unite the world behind our common, global purpose. And we also know that until the world is so united, the war-like leaders and false prophets must be held in leash by physical force.

At the outset of the twentieth century, the Wright brothers took their first flight, for a few seconds, at Kitty Hawk. Now, at the end of the century, the technology is emerging for us to plan colonies on the Moon and Mars. Yet, as we contemplate the journey outward to the stars, we are also confronted with the other great journey of human beings toward a more harmonious relationship with each other and the living Earth. How can we travel to space without resolving our self-made threats to the future of life? The challenge is to learn to live together and to live in balance with nature. Once we have mastered this challenge well enough to have turned the corner away from self-destruction, we will be ready to begin to explore the infinite reaches of the universe, to ride the tiger to the stars.

The Tiger —
A Parable For
The Twenty-First Century

Tyger, Tyger burning bright
In the forests of the night
What immortal hand or eye
Could frame thy fearful symmetry?
— William Blake —

Once upon a time in the childhood of our species, we lived in the Garden. We were at one with existence. There was enough for everyone. We walked in beauty and balance with all things. Then, in our adolescence, we ate of the fruit of the knowledge of good and evil. We began to think in opposites. We invented tools and machines. After a time, the power of our machines exceeded the bounds of the Garden, and we were cast out.

We found ourselves in a jungle, fighting to survive. We taught each other that there was not enough to go around, nor would there ever be. Soon, we encountered the Tiger loosed in the jungle. He was the most deadly Tiger ever known by the people of the villages. He killed men, women, and children. He destroyed entire villages in a few hours.

The fear of him, just the fear of him, caused the people to tremble in terror. He stalked the countryside. No one was safe. In their fear, people saw him everywhere. Generations of warriors went out to find and kill him, but always they were killed.

For centuries, the Tiger haunted the hearts and minds of

the people. Villages became towns. Towns became cities. Cities became nations. And the people noticed that as the nations became more powerful and fearsome, so also grew the fearsome power of the Tiger. Now, the Tiger could destroy entire countries in a matter of minutes. He was a scourge upon the entire Earth. There was nowhere to flee.

The people split into groups, arguing bitterly about what to do. Some said the only way to be safe was to kill the Tiger — to destroy the mountains and forests, all the places where the Tiger might be. Others said the way to be safe was to appease the Tiger, to offer up the young warriors of each generation to be devoured. Some said it was hopeless: There was nothing to do but wait until the Tiger destroyed everyone. And others gathered provisions and built underground caves where, they said, the Tiger could never enter. Some argued it was possible to contain the Tiger. Some wore claws and skins to be more fierce than the Tiger itself. And others said they were the chosen people whom God would lift up to the heavens before the Tiger came to devour the rest.

The more they argued, the more everyone was certain they were right. But the Tiger was oblivious. He stalked the land. He stalked the hopes and dreams of the young. He stalked the fears and nightmares of the old. He grew mightier and more terrifying. A dark age of fear descended upon the people's hearts. They neglected the hungry and polluted the land. They robbed and killed each other. They used "the Tiger is coming" to justify doing anything.

Then, a handful of people arose who began to question, "Where is this Tiger of whom we are so afraid?" And no one could answer, because no one had ever seen the Tiger face to face. They had seen the trail of the Tiger — the dying children, the ravaged countryside. "What is the Tiger?" they asked. Again, no one could answer, for they had believed only what they were told, generation upon generation.

The few who questioned grew to be many, and the word went out through all the lands, to all the peoples: "We must find the Tiger!" The call was carried far and wide, from person to person, nation to nation, to the furthest corners of the Earth. And all who knew what was at risk, be they women or men, old or young, answered the call.

They were called from all the nations to gather at the top of the sacred mountain. And so they climbed together. Sometimes the way was steep and difficult, and sometimes the way was beautiful and gracious. They faced all manner of challenges and dangers. And yet they continued. At the top of the mountain, they saw a vision of their journey stalked by the great Tiger. Again, they were afraid.

A voice spoke to them from out of the Wind, through the depths of their own hearts and minds, "Fear not. I am with you. You are able to do all that is asked of you."

Then they saw the Tiger, burning awesome and bright in the black night. Each person stepped forward and in the eyes of the Tiger saw a reflection of his or her own image. And the Tiger spoke:

> *In me, you see what you are. When you are cruel and murderous, I am your weakness. When you are loving and creative, I am your strength.*
>
> *Your hunger is the hunger of ignorance and fear. You thought I was separate from you and you made war against me. I am your wildness. I am your fire. Without me, you are nothing.*
>
> *When you were a child, you rode me without fear. But since then, there has been war between us, all these long years. Now, you have come of age: You are standing in the moment of choice.*
>
> *Continue to abuse me and I am the fire next time — I will burn the world. Ride me and you will feel the flame of life again. Ride me and you will see the Garden once more, even as you travel to the stars.*

Practice
For Winning

It is by forgiving that one is forgiven.
— Mother Teresa —

Whether humanity is to continue and comprehensively prosper on Spaceship Earth depends not on political and economic systems, but on the integrity of individuals.
— Buckminster Fuller —

While we exist as human beings, we are like tourists on holiday. If we play havoc and cause disturbance, our visit is meaningless. If during our short stay — 100 years at most — we live peacefully, help others and, at the very least, refrain from harming or upsetting them, our visit is worthwhile. What is important is to see how we can best lead a meaningful everyday life, how we can bring about peace and harmony in our minds, how we can help contribute to society.
— The Dalai Lama —

Words can destroy. What we call each other ultimately becomes what we think of each other, and it matters.
— Jeane J. Kirkpatrick —

I count him braver who overcomes his desires than him who conquers his enemies; for the hardest victory is the victory over self.
— Aristotle —

Without discipline, there's no life at all.
— Katharine Hepburn —

It isn't enough to talk about peace. One must believe in it. And it isn't enough to believe in it. One must work at it.
— Eleanor Roosevelt —

A human being is part of the whole, called by
us "Universe," a part limited in time and space.
He experiences himself, his thoughts and feelings as
something separated from the rest — a kind of optical
delusion of his consciousness. This delusion is a kind
of prison for us, restricting us to our personal desires
and to affection for a few persons nearest to us.
   Our task must be to free ourselves from this
prison by widening our circle of compassion to
embrace all living creatures and the whole of nature
in its beauty.
                                    — Albert Einstein —

Albert Einstein once reflected that it would take just two percent of the world's population to make the change necessary to create real peace and security between nations. What did Einstein mean — two percent? Einstein's call for a new level of thinking and problem-solving does not mean converting other people to one's own point of view. More likely Einstein meant that two percent of us can change history by changing the way we live, the way we communicate and resolve conflicts with each other across our differences. Two percent to be mediators, reconcilers, facilitators of a process between individuals and nations which decreases hostility and increases understanding.

Those who say that what is needed is a personal transformation, and those who say that what is needed is a political transformation, are both right. What is needed is a change in both the way we live our personal lives and the way we do politics.

Given the reality of our increasingly interdependent world, our nation is challenged to formulate policies which serve both our own national interests and the interests of global security. How, then, can we generate such national policies for an interdependent world? We must change the way we formulate policy so that our political process is consistent with the goals we are seeking to reach. And what does this political process reflect and depend upon? It is derived in part from our personal and cultural values.

By changing our personal values, we change the cultural foundation of our politics. Personal change does not always precede political change. Rather, the two are linked in a reciprocal process. When one changes, so does the other. As we make personal changes in our understanding of winning, we need to change the political decision-making process from a short-term, adversarial model — "I win/you lose" — to a long-term, cooperative model — "I win/you win."

What we are suggesting is a simultaneous, two-track approach: one, the development of a new cultural understanding of winning based upon the accumulative impact of the changed behavior of millions of individuals; and two, the creation of new models for political decision-making based upon, and supported by, this new cultural understanding of interdependence.

The idea of a personal practice of peace-making is certainly not new. Many of the great teachers and visionaries throughout history have called for such an ethical practice. What is compelling about our time is that the implementation of practical methods of dialogue and conflict management, both for individuals and for nations, is an imperative for our survival.

This practice for a new kind of victory is addressed to all of us who know that the future of our civilization, and perhaps life as we know it, is at risk. It is addressed to those of us who grasp that the potential consequences of not changing our lives, of not taking responsibility for our future, are so grave as to be almost unthinkable. "Practice for Winning" is addressed primarily to Einstein's two percent — to all of us who see that any Great Turning in the direction of nations will happen through the impact of thousands of "small turnings" in the lives of individuals.

CHAPTER SIX

Living The Change

We must be the change we wish to see in the world.
— Mahatma Gandhi —

Once a woman came to Gandhi with her son. "My boy eats too much sugar," she said, "and I am worried about his health. He respects you very much. Would you be willing to tell him about its harmful effects and suggest he stop eating it?"

Gandhi paused and thought a moment. Yes, he told her, he would do it, but she should bring her son back in two weeks, no sooner.

After two weeks passed, the woman returned with her son. Gandhi talked with him and suggested he stop eating sugar. The boy listened carefully and subsequently stopped.

As she was leaving, the woman thanked Gandhi profusely and then lingered for a moment. "What I don't understand," she said, "is why you asked us to wait two weeks when my son was with me the first time."

"Because," said Gandhi with a smile, "I needed the two weeks to stop eating sugar myself."

The point of telling this story is not that we should stop eating candy bars. It is rather that we cannot expect to have much impact by telling others to do things that we do not live. Instead of holding some distant goal, such as national security or world peace, and then living in a way which contradicts our ultimate goal, we can choose to create a unity between our ends and our means. We can live our goal as the path.

Practice, as the old saying goes, makes perfect. No one becomes a great violinist or basketball player or dancer without practice. If you aspire to be a great athlete or a great musician, it will require discipline. Great parents do not just magically appear; parenting requires patience, and renewed commitment in each moment.

Whatever we practice, we tend to become better at doing. To strengthen your body requires regular exercise and a good diet — a discipline you commit yourself to do, even when you don't necessarily feel like it. The practice toward your goal is the process of getting there. The paradox, of course, is that in order to get there, you have to also be able to visualize yourself being there. In order to sink the jumpshot from the backcourt, you have to be able to see it happening before you can put the ball through the hoop.

In this sense, the journey or practice cannot be separated from the achievement of the goal. The practice of projecting victory begins with the insight that the future unfolds out of the present. If you and I want to improve the quality of our lives and our world, we must live the desired change now.

For too long we have suffered under the mistaken belief that the future is beyond our control, that we were victims in the past and therefore we cannot affect the future. Stop and think about it. The future is a link in a long chain of cause and effect. What happened in the past helped to generate circumstances which created the present. Similarly, the conditions for the emergence of the future are in this moment.

If we want to make our life and our world a victory, we must begin in the present. Practicing the violin three hours a day does not guarantee that we will become Pinchas Zukerman, but it is clearly moving with gusto in the right direction. Practice is not everything, but it is an essential prerequisite to achieving our goals. "Practice for Winning" begins with the affirmation: "I see the goal is possible and I will do whatever is necessary, step by step."

If we want to be in dialogue with those with whom we disagree and learn to resolve conflicts at a different level, we must practice. One does not learn to be a great listener or problem-solver without continuously practicing the attitudes and skills necessary to achieve the best possible outcome. This practice is not something we master all at once, and then proceed to do automatically: It is a conscious endeavor.

By taking responsibility, and listening to each other, and working together across diverse points of view, we can create a new direction, a Great Turning, in the way we as individuals relate to one another, and how our country relates to other nations of the Earth.

Partners For the Turning

> *I am only one,*
> *But still I am one.*
> *I cannot do everything,*
> *But still I can do something.*
> *And because I cannot do everything,*
> *I will not refuse to do*
> *The something that I can do.*
>   Edward Everett Hale

Whether the circumstances of our lives are rich or poor, happy or sad, if we have no sense of purpose, most of us feel that something is missing. There is an emptiness, a lack of real satisfaction and joy. At the very least, we recognize that we are not acting in a way that develops and uses our full potential.

We humans are creatures who seek meaning. Yet, happiness and meaning do not come by trying to chase them. It's like running towards the horizon: the more we try to "capture meaning," the more it eludes us. It seems the experience of meaning often comes from dedicating oneself to a purpose larger than just our narrow concerns. And if we are dedicated to nothing which transcends ourselves, we become self-absorbed.

What do individuals like Thomas Jefferson, Harriet Tubman, Ralph Waldo Emerson, Henry David Thoreau, Sojourner

Truth, Frederick Douglass, Abraham Lincoln, Harriet Beecher Stowe, Clara Barton, John Muir, Susan B. Anthony, Teddy Roosevelt, Albert Schweitzer, Winston Churchill, Mahatma Gandhi, Eleanor Roosevelt, Douglas MacArthur, Helen Keller, Albert Einstein, Rachel Carson, and Martin Luther King, Jr. have in common?

They all dedicated themselves to some kind of service for others. They were all committed to a purpose larger than themselves. They all had a sense of the sanctity of the human person and all tried to live an ethic of respect for life. They all were fighters. They fought against all kinds of domination over the human mind and spirit. They all believed in a Creator or higher power which has endowed human beings with the spark of illumination.

They did not submit to the belief that it is impossible for the individual to make a significant contribution to the betterment of our world. Instead, they responded to the challenge of doing what one person can do to protect and improve the quality of life for future generations.

Most of the great ethical and religious traditions have the concept of an individual who takes responsibility not only for his or her own welfare, but also for the welfare of the whole community. Each tradition expresses it differently, but the basic idea is similar. Here are a few examples:

In Judaic tradition, such a person is often called a "tzaddik" or righteous one — an individual who seeks to live a just and merciful life in accord with the law. "What does the Lord require of you?" asked the prophet Micah (6:8). "Nothing but to do justice, to love mercy, and to walk humbly with thy God."

In Christian tradition, such a person is often called a "disciple" or a peacemaker. Francis of Assisi said: "Lord, make me an instrument of thy peace. Where there is hate, let me bring love. Where there is offense, let me bring pardon. Where there is discord, let me bring union."

In Buddhist tradition, such a person is called a "bodhisattva," one who seeks to live in truth and compassion, dedicated to the betterment of all beings. As the Dalai Lama, spiritual and secular head of Tibetan Buddhism, put it: "Compassion is the real essence of religion. Everything depends upon good motivation: compassion without dogmatism; just understanding that others are human brothers and sisters and respecting their rights and human dignity."

In Native American tradition, such a person is often called the pipe-carrier or peacemaker, one who seeks to walk in the way of beauty and honors all living creatures. Black Elk, the great Sioux elder, said:

> The first peace, which is most important, is that which comes within the souls of men when they realize their relationship, their oneness, with the universe and all its powers, and when they realize that at the center of the universe dwells the Great Mystery, and that this center is really everywhere, it is within each of us.
>
> This is the real peace, and the others are but reflections of this. The second peace is that which is made between two individuals, and the third is that which is made between two nations.

Mahatma Gandhi used the term "Satyagrahi," one who seeks to live nonviolence or "satyagraha," which means soul-force. "Some friends have told me that truth and non-violence have no place in politics and worldly affairs. I do not agree," wrote Gandhi. "Their introduction and application in everyday life has been my experiment all along."

Each of these different traditions, plus many more around the world, asks the individual to take responsibility, to seek reconciliation, to be a mediator in conflicts, to forgive oneself and others where there has been violation, and to live one's daily life with a sense of justice and compassion.

Also, in our modern secular traditions, we have a number of different ways of expressing the same kind of commitment. For example, in the environmental movement there is the concept of a conservationist or an "Earth steward," one who seeks to conserve and protect the natural environment and all living creatures. Rachel Carson helped to launch our modern environmental movement with her book, *The*

Silent Spring. "Wildlife, water, forest, and grasslands — all are part of man's essential environment," she wrote. "The conservation and effective use of one is impossible except as the others are also conserved."

The ideas, principles, and practices of dialogue and conflict resolution have been in part developed, and often lived out in the women's movement. At the beginning of the nuclear age, Eleanor Roosevelt articulated a call to women to exercise their leadership on behalf of world peace and human dignity:

> Women, whether subtly or vociferously, have always been a tremendous power in the destiny of the world, and with so many of them now holding important positions and receiving recognition and earning the respect of men as well as the members of their own sex, it seems more than ever in this crisis, "It's Up to the Women."

In the growing field of conflict management, there is the concept of a mediator or principled negotiator, one who seeks to resolve conflicts into mutual gain wherever possible. As Roger Fisher and William Ury, authors of *Getting to Yes*, put it: "Principled negotiation shows you how to obtain what you are entitled to and still be decent. It enables you to be fair while protecting you against those who would take advantage of your fairness."

For the field of humanistic psychology, there is the concept of the "global therapist," one who seeks to address and heal the divisions of the human psyche both within and between persons and nations. Roger Walsh, author of *Staying Alive: The Psychology of Human Survival*, wrote:

> There may be no more urgent or rewarding task facing each and every one of us than to acknowledge and fulfill our role in creating and applying a psychology of human survival: a psychology linking all those from all nations who wish to apply their skills to ... the most urgent issues of our time, unveiling the psychological forces that have brought us to this turning point in history, and working to transform them into forces for our collective survival, well-being, and evolution.

In the worldwide human-rights movement, individuals take responsibility to stop political torture and free prisoners of conscience around the world. Ginetta Sagan, imprisoned by the Nazis as a young woman during World War II, was primarily responsible for the rapid growth of Amnesty International in the United States. "As long as we know even one person is unjustly imprisoned and tortured anywhere in the world," she said, "we must take action to oppose that tyranny over the human mind and spirit."

For those who think in terms of our global future, the concept of a "planetary citizen" has begun to emerge — meaning one who takes responsibility for the betterment of life on Earth for all races, creeds, and nationalities. Dr. Martin Luther King, Jr., who lived this ethic, said: "If we are to have peace on Earth, our loyalties must be ecumenical, rather than sectional. Our loyalties must transcend our race, our tribe, our class, and our nation; and this means we must develop a world perspective."

No matter what our primary focus, if our commitment is to take personal responsibility for the survival and enhancement of life — be it our community, nation, or planet — then we are all partners in the Great Turning.

Experiments in Personal/Global Potential

Never judge the limits of what you can do until you know there's no going back.

Dag Hammarskjold

Gandhi called his autobiography, *The Story of My Experiments with Truth*. In explaining how he was able to do what he did, he said essentially: Look, I'm not fundamentally any different from you. I'm a human being, with clay feet. But there is one thing that has enabled me to direct my life more effectively. I inquired into what might help myself and others toward greater development. Whenever I came across some method or change I thought might be of assistance, I

would ask myself, "Is this true for me?" And I would try
it. If it contributed to my growth and to the betterment of
others, then I would pledge to continue to do it. Slowly,
over many years, I developed a set of personal disciplines
which helped me to take charge of myself. These were my
experiments in truth. If you will do your own experiments
in truth and discover what works for you, you will be able
to do things that equal and surpass anything I have done.

To break old patterns and to change our behavior requires
discipline and patience. It is like the process of building
new muscles. The first few times we jog or bicycle or ski,
it seems difficult. Our breath is short, our muscles weak.
But if we exercise gradually, day by day, the muscles grow
stronger until one day what seemed impossible is now the
foundation for new possibilities. So it is with the conscious
development of our personal and global potential.

Each one of us has the potential to help alter the course
of history. Yet, if we are pulled in many directions, divided
against ourselves, we will not be able to fulfill our own
lives or to live the change we want for the world. "Practice
for Winning" offers methods to assist us in becoming more
skillful in our personal lives and more effective in our dedication to help build a more secure and peaceful future.

This practice for a new level of winning is divided into
four parts, each one a different chapter, as follows:

- Principles for a New Kind of Victory
- Steps for Shaping Our Future
- Skills for the Art of Dialogue
- Tools for Transforming Conflict

We have developed these methods from our experiences
with thousands of people in community dialogues, national
security conferences, public policy symposia, and communication trainings. People from all geographical and political
persuasions have helped refine these techniques through
experimentation and feedback.

These methods are not a rigid set of teachings to be
done in some legalistic fashion. Rather, we invite you to use

them with an attitude of experimentation. See if it works for you. See if it can help you direct your life more powerfully, communicate more effectively, or manage conflicts more creatively. If it works, you can choose to incorporate the change into your behavior. It is always your experiment and your choice. Remember there is nothing fixed about these methods. By experimenting with these different methods, you can design new and more workable "practices" for yourself.

Making a commitment to practice is a step that can transform your life. The intention to take personal responsibility for shaping your future, sustaining dialogue with those with whom you disagree, and finding outcomes that will work for all parties to a conflict is profound. Sustaining your intention to do this over time, little by little, will help you to be more detached, more centered, and more powerful in your life-commitments.

"Practice for Winning" is designed to enable individuals, groups, and nations to take conscious responsibility for shaping their future and beginning a Great Turning by the end of the century.

Practice
For Winning

SKILLS FOR
THE ART OF DIALOGUE

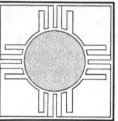

STEPS FOR
SHAPING OUR FUTURE

TOOLS FOR
TRANSFORMING CONFLICT

PRINCIPLES FOR
A NEW KIND OF VICTORY

CHAPTER SEVEN

Principles For
A New Kind Of Victory

*The possibility of species-wide destruction creates for
the first time the necessity of a species-wide ethic.*
— Erik Erikson —

The evolution of human ethics can be seen as the expansion of a sense of identification with an ever-widening circle: from the individual to the family, tribe, race, and nation. As our ethics mature, our concerns include the needs and interests of a larger group. We recognize that their survival and well-being is linked to our own.

We have arrived at the threshold of a more inclusive identity. With the capacity to destroy human civilization, and perhaps all life, comes the responsibility to make certain this does not happen. While the twentieth century has been a time of world wars and massive violence, it has also brought the acknowledgment of a more inclusive identity.

Now there are signs that we are evolving a global sense of self. The "We are the World" spirit is growing. More and more people are beginning to grasp that when someone starves to death in Ethiopia or is homeless in Los Angeles, all of us are diminished. In the words of Michael Jackson and Lionel Ritchie in their USA/Africa anthem: "We are the world, we are the children. . . . There's a choice we're making, we're saving our own lives."

The image of the Earth is more and more evident wherever we turn; from advertisements to logos to television documentaries, it is imprinted in our consciousness. And with it comes the dawning recognition that we humans are one species among many others, all living on a small, beautiful planet in endless space. Astronaut Russell Schweick-art describes his experience of orbiting the Earth: "When you go around the Earth in an hour and a half, you begin to see that your identity is with the whole. There are no frames. There are no boundaries." Both modern psychology and ecology teach that the individual and the world are linked. If "we are the world," then we will want the world to win. Here are four principles which provide a foundation for achieving this new kind of victory:

Principle One: Interdependence
Definition: *Everyone and everything is interconnected as part of the living Earth. We are bound together in a web of mutuality.*

We need each other to survive and flourish — humans and all of nature. Our fates are inextricably linked one to another. Ecologically, we are connected to the green plants that replenish our atmosphere, to the water we drink, to the sunlight and soil that grow our food, to the rocks, reptiles, fish, birds, and animals with whom we share the planet — and to our fellow human beings.

Many of us have been raised to think of ourselves as ruggedly independent, as though we could function utterly separated from the world. Yet, a human being living apart from the environment is an abstraction. In ecological reality, no such being exists. At any particular moment, the human body, like the body of any other animal, exists in a state of dynamic exchange — losing or gaining water, taking in or expelling gases, absorbing or giving off heat.

We are not alone. We are surrounded and sustained at all moments by the miracle of evolution and the great mystery of life. Every organism partakes from and contributes to the fundamental energy flow of life. Nothing exists separately from the conditions that are created by all other beings. Life is a single, organic tapestry with an infinite number of threads that tie together several billion years of evolution.

Life on Earth has been compared to a great pyramid. At

the base are the plants and the process of photosynthesis which provides the food for the more complex animals, all the way up to the mammals. Human beings exist near the top of this amazing pyramid, dependent upon millions of other organisms for our survival. Thus, the greater the diversity of species, the stronger the pyramid and its ability to survive given drastic changes in the environment. For example, if there is a great drought or the climate grows warmer, the probabilities that more species will survive increase in direct proportion to the diversity of species.

Every time we bring a species to extinction, destroy rain forests, eliminate wild habitats, or reduce the number of green plants, we diminish the capacity of our biosphere to sustain life. Acting in such an unconscious fashion, we weaken the ecological foundation upon which human civilization is dependent for its survival and prosperity. Thus, it is in our own self-interest to provide for the greatest possible diversity and richness of life on Earth.

We can also see this interdependence in our social and political systems. For example, the health of our children is related to the quality of our air and water; this quality is dependent upon the level of environmental pollution and the effectiveness of our waste disposal systems, which are dependent upon our political and economic policies. The quality of our personal lives is interwoven with our relationship to both natural and human systems.

Most of us live in a kind of perceptual box of our own making. While the size of our boxes may vary a great deal, each of us perceives that we can go to the outer limits of our box, but no further. And we define the box as "me." "Me" is what I know and identify with — my family, my job, my friends, my nation. "Not me" is what is foreign, alien, and potentially dangerous. As we approach the next century, it is appropriate and necessary for each of us to recognize that we can change the boundaries of our box. We are challenged to extend the horizons of our sense of self and thus to identify with an ever-widening part of the whole of life.

You can practice being more aware of this insight of interdependence by observing the way that seemingly separate things are related. One experiment you might try is as follows:

Whenever you perceive someone or something as "not me" or outside your definition of yourself, expand your identity to include whomever or whatever you see. Start by saying to yourself: "This is me, too." Then look for the place in you that can feel some sense of identification. In this way, we experience something alien or "not me" as part of the whole of who we are.

Everywhere you look, see a part of you there also. Extend your sense of self to include your family, community, nation, and world.

This recognition of interdependence does not mean that you must like, agree with, or even trust the other person. It simply means that you recognize that we are all part of a web of mutuality.

Principle Two: Consequences

Definition: *We reap the consequences of our actions. For every action, there is a reaction.*

All actions have consequences. Drop a stone in the lake and it ripples outward in waves; similarly, whatever we do generates reactions that affect the lives of those around us. Nothing is done in a vacuum. The world outside us acts as a kind of mirror or echo chamber in response to our actions. This is difficult to see at times, because the response may not be immediate or it may be quite subtle. There is a deep insight in the old saying, "What goes around, comes around."

The science of ecology teaches us that every action sets off a chain of repercussions. As Loren Eiseley, the great paleontologist, once put it: "You cannot pluck a flower in this universe, without troubling a star."

What we put out, tends to come back at us. We can observe this in the ecology of natural systems. For example, when we dump radioactive waste in the ocean, there are consequences. The radioactive material is absorbed by plankton, consumed by fish, and eaten by people who catch the fish. Soon, the strontium 90 begins to show up in our bones.

A recent *Time* article entitled, "Our Filthy Seas," cites the example of New York City dumping its garbage at a site 106 miles out to sea. Within two years of the start of this practice, local commercial fisherman noticed that increasing numbers of fish were deformed or diseased. "New Yorkers," said a Montauk dockmaster, "are going to get their garbage right back in the fish they are eating." Since the health of our bodies is directly connected to the health of our environment, we poison ourselves by poisoning the natural systems which sustain us. This is the ecological consequence of our interdependence.

Chief Seattle, the great leader of the Nez Perce tribe, wrote a letter to President Franklin Pierce in the 1850s in which he warned of the consequences of polluting the land: "Whatever befalls the Earth, befalls the sons and daughters of the Earth. Continue to contaminate the bed you sleep in and you will one day suffocate in it." The reverse is also true: generate positive conditions and they will have positive consequences. If we plant trees in an area which has been deforested, we create the conditions to prevent erosion. As the trees grow, the birds and animals return. Eventually, we have a forest filled with life again.

At a societal level, studies show that children who are abused and mistreated often grow up to be violent and abuse their own children. On the other hand, in societies where children are given lots of nurturance and affection, violence is minimal. We reap what we sow. So also the entire world reaps what each one of us sows.

At a personal level, we can see the direct and indirect consequences of our actions. Someone who consistently tells the truth is usually trusted and respected. Alternatively, most of us have had the experience of the lie that boomerangs and has negative results. Acting unconsciously without the recognition of our interdependence tends to generate destructive consequences to ourselves and others. Acting consciously with an awareness of interdependence generates mutual benefits.

A problem we face is our tendency to deny, or exclude from our awareness, the potential long-term consequences of our actions, while grasping for the apparent short-term results. We substitute what is best for our real development for immediate gratification. It may look in the short-term that being focused solely on one's narrow self-interest will yield the maximum gain. But this behavior generates repercussions which often can undermine the advantage we have achieved or even worsen the situation.

Examples of the principle of consequences can be seen all around us: Honest Freddy opens a used-car business in a medium-sized town. He cleans them up, makes them shiny, sells them quick and fast. He tells his customers many things about the condition of his cars that are not true. For awhile Honest Freddy makes a lot of money. Then, word gets around that his cars are wrecks and people stop buying from him. Honest Freddy loses his shirt and is indicted for fraud.

Our newspapers are often filled with stories of public figures who reap the consequences of their dishonest actions. According to the Committee on Developing American Capitalism, made up of top executives of national corporations, as reported by the *Las Vegas Daily Optic* (August 9, 1988), there is increasing evidence of declining ethics in business in the past twenty years. In their survey of Fortune 500 companies, they report that between 1975 and 1984, more than 300 of the Fortune 500 companies were involved in one or more illegal incidents; and that the top 100 companies were involved in 55 percent of all incidents. These violations included bribes, illegal political contributions, money laundering by bankers, check kiting on Wall Street, insider trading, fraud, payroll padding, and cheating on defense contracts. The prestigious group of American executives concluded that the consequences of this "uncontrolled human greed and lust for fame and power," were threatening our culture:

> This sows the seeds of distrust and hatred among neighbors, between employer and employees, between voters and their elected officials, and between business and

government. In the extreme, it opens the door of government to anarchy.

The consequences of actions between nations can be even more serious. In the 1950s and early 1960s, when the United States and the Soviet Union conducted hundreds of nuclear weapons tests above ground, it quickly became clear that the food chain was being poisoned by radioactive fallout. The most alarming example was strontium 90 found in cow's milk. This was a dramatic and deadly example of the consequences that would accrue from unrestricted nuclear testing. It led to the Limited Test Ban Treaty, signed by the two superpowers in 1963, which is still in effect. We had realized that the consequences of testing nuclear weapons in the atmosphere were too harmful to continue.

Today, the United States, the Soviet Union, France, and other industrialized nations sell large amounts of advanced weapons and technology to other countries around the world. This includes nuclear reactors which produce materials that can be converted into nuclear bombs. Such countries are eager to "catch up" with the industrialized world and pay well for energy and weapons technology. Viewed from the short term, this is good for business and for political influence. However, if more countries — especially those with regional hatreds — develop nuclear weapons, the short-term gain could become a tragedy of irrevocable proportions.

As we seek to apply the principle of consequences in our lives, it is important to think in cycles, to see the long-term effect. You might try this practice: Take a moment and ask yourself, "What are the likely repercussions of this action?" In many Native American tribes, there is a teaching about consequences that we in the industrialized world would do well to utilize: "Whenever you are going to take an action, ask yourself, 'Will this serve the needs of the next seven generations?' " Given the high velocity of change in modern society, it may be impossible to foresee the consequences for seven generations. However, it certainly makes sense to reflect on the repercussions of our actions on our own children and grandchildren.

Principle Three: Responsibility

Definition: *The individual is the primary architect of human advancement. We all have a unique part to play.*

Our lives matter. The future is forged out of our present actions, however small. If we want the twenty-first century to be a time of greater security and peace for everyone, then we must create the circumstances now for that to happen, beginning with our own thoughts and actions.

Perhaps the awareness that human civilization is threatened can serve to awaken us. The choice to live fully, dedicated to the betterment of all, begins with each of us. No one can choose to value your life for you. The experience of profound value begins in the heart and mind of every individual.

History shows us that major social, cultural, and scientific changes are often initiated by individuals. For example, prior to 1952, polio crippled and killed thousands of people every year, particularly children. Had Jonas Salk been limited by the logic of his circumstances, he would have concluded that polio was an incurable scourge which had ravaged human lives for centuries. But Dr. Salk persevered and developed a vaccination which has largely eliminated polio. As a result of his actions, the experience of humankind has been profoundly altered. Though most of us do not have the genius of a Jonas Salk, each one of us has the capacity to affect what is going on around us, in ways that enhance or diminish life.

One of the most misguided notions of modern culture is that what we do as individuals does not matter in the world. We live much of our lives saying things like, "Well, it doesn't matter if I throw this beer bottle on the beach. It doesn't matter if I dump this toxic waste in the river. It doesn't matter if I only seek my own gain and pay no attention to the needs of the world . . . because I am only one, and what I do doesn't make any difference." We prevent ourselves from taking small positive steps because we believe that anything we could do is insignificant.

Responsibility is not a burden. It is not to be confused with blame or guilt. Blame seeks to determine whose fault it is. Guilt has variously been defined as unexpressed resentment, or the feeling that you have done something which violates your own moral code or sense of rightness. Often, guilt is a psychological mechanism through which we punish ourselves for doing something while continuing to do it. The dictionary defines *responsibility* as "1. called to answer; 2. being the cause or explanation; 3. able to answer for one's conduct, as in trustworthy, accountable, reliable." Responsibility is forward-looking. It is literally the ability to respond, to take constructive steps to address whatever situation in which we find ourselves.

The expression of personal responsibility takes on different forms in different situations. On the day the Nazis marched across the border into Holland, a young ambulance driver living in Amsterdam began to telephone families with Jewish-sounding names. He picked them up in his ambulance, checked them into hospitals under aliases, and set up an underground network to get them out of the country. In all, he saved over 300 families.

After the war, a team of researchers went to Holland to interview this young man. They asked him, "Why did you risk yourself to save these families?"

At first he was startled and said that he did not understand the question. When they asked again, he said, "How could I have done otherwise? I saw that it had to be done."

Rosa Parks was a black woman living in Montgomery, Alabama in 1955. At that time, Montgomery buses, as well as most of its other public facilities, were segregated. Any person of color was forced to ride at the back of the bus. One day Rosa Parks got on the bus and sat down near the front. The bus driver ordered her to move to the back. She repeatedly refused, saying that she had worked hard all day and was too tired to move. Rosa Parks was taken to jail. By that night, thousands of flyers were distributed to the black community urging them not to ride the bus as a protest against segregation.

This Montgomery bus boycott was led by an unknown, 25-year-old black minister, Dr. Martin Luther King, Jr. It grew into a year-long protest and served to launch the civil rights movement. Thus, Rosa Parks' small act was the beginning of a national movement which eventually led to the elimination of legally sanctioned segregation in the United States.

In preparing for the 1984 Olympic Games in Los Angeles, there was much concern that severe summer smog could impair the performance of the world's finest athletes. This would not only injure the Olympics, but would bring a bad name to Los Angeles and the United States. Out of this concern came a campaign to clean up the air for the Olympics. People pulled together — car pooled, took public transportation, chose to drive off-hours. Corporations shifted their work hours to reduce traffic flow at peak times. Though it had seemed impossible a few days before, the skies were clear as the Olympic torch was lit. It was a remarkable example of individuals acting in small ways for their own welfare, the welfare of their community, their nation, and the peoples of the world. If we can take personal responsibility for clean air at the Olympics, why not take responsibility for the future of our nation and our world?

In Ray Bradbury's story, "A Sound of Thunder," a time machine makes it possible for people to travel back to the early days of Earth's history. One company runs expeditions to take hunters to the time of the dinosaurs. The hunters are instructed to walk on special platforms and not to shoot until told to do so. They are not permitted to "kill" the dinosaur until the exact moment the animal would have died. This insures that the human interaction with the past does nothing to change it.

On the way back to the time machine, one hunter forgets, steps off the platform, and accidently crushes a butterfly. Immediately the guides are panicked. They pack everyone into the time machine and rush back to the present. Much to their horror, they find many things to be different. The president of their country, their language, the feel of the air — all have been altered. A small act by one individual, magnified over millions of years, has changed the world they now live in.

We cannot know the ultimate outcomes of all our actions. It is, therefore, essential that we carefully consider the effect that our actions may have on the world, remembering that small actions can create large consequences.

The Great Turning begins with the individual; whenever any one of us steps forward and says: "I will do my part. This is our democracy and I will participate to make it more effective and humane. This is our world and our future. This is the legacy we will leave our children. I have the ability to respond and I will do so. I will look around me and see what needs to be done and find a way to do it."

Principle Four: Reciprocity

Definition: *Treat yourself and others the way you want to be treated. Give what you want to get.*

All of the great religious and philosophical traditions teach a central, ethical practice: "Do unto others as you would have others do unto you." The wisest of humankind — women and men — are united across the centuries in pointing toward this principle as the way out of the immense harm which human beings inflict upon ourselves and upon nature.

In the past we have given lip service to this "golden rule," but we have distorted its meaning by erring toward one extreme or the other. We have either tried to love our neighbor without loving ourselves, or we have tried to love ourselves without loving our neighbor. Each of these extremes misses the real point — that we are related one to another in a reciprocal process.

What is different about living in the nuclear age is that the principle of reciprocity can no longer be viewed as an abstract ideal, but as a pragmatic method for achieving our long-term survival and security. Given that we are interdependent, that we bear the consequences of our actions, and that the common danger threatens our entire world — we are compelled to practice reciprocity if we want to build the foundation for a safer world.

While Christianity, Buddhism, Islam, Judaism, Hinduism, and many of the native religions disagree at the level of the *content* of their beliefs, they share a fundamental agreement at the level of both *process* and *intention*. They all teach that by changing the way we live toward reconciliation and reciprocity, we can arrive at the greater purpose and meaning of life. At the root of this ethical practice is a common intention: a reverence for life and respect for all persons.

All of these great traditions affirm that life is sacred and that every individual is a unique microcosm of the whole, a representative of the Source itself. In traditional language, the soul or Observing Self is to God as the flame is to fire. In ecological terms, this relationship between the part and the whole is quite analogous. Each part makes its own unique contribution to the workings of the whole system, yet each part is also a microcosm of the whole. Biologist Lewis Thomas writes that one single cell is a microcosm of the Earth itself. "There is a flower in the universe," says poet William Blake, "and the universe in the flower."

The example of holographic photography is useful here. If you take a holographic picture and cut it into pieces, each piece will reflect an image of the whole. For example, if it is a holographic picture of a mountain, when you shine X-ray light through it, you will see the whole mountain. As the pieces get smaller, the holographic image gets dimmer, but it is still a total representation. To use this metaphor, the great religious and ethical traditions teach that the individual is a holographic representation of the whole of life; therefore, we are called to act with the same respect toward the part as we would toward the whole which sustains us.

Reciprocity is based upon the recognition of our mutuality. It is not about appeasement or self-sacrifice. It is not about neglecting one's own needs and interests. Rather, reciprocity acknowledges that in the nuclear age, the challenge of our mutual survival requires that "my" needs and interests must coexist along side of "yours."

The practice of reciprocity begins with oneself. To treat ourselves with the respect and kindness with which we want to be treated helps to heal the larger world. Similarly, treating others with the respect and kindness with which we want to be treated helps to heal ourselves. In this sense, our giving and our receiving are truly reciprocal.

What happens if we lead with cooperation and the other person tries to dominate or exploit us? If we continue to cooperate, we are likely to encourage the other party's aggression. How does the principle of reciprocity apply here? Sometimes compassion is tough. It is not about being nice. The person who is causing harm or seeking to dominate needs to receive a signal that such behavior will not be tolerated. Individuals or groups seeking to dominate may reevaluate their behavior if they realize that they cannot get away with it.

In an interdependent world, where we reap the consequences of our actions, the practice of reciprocity is enlightened self-interest. Just as parents extend their sense of concern to include the health and well-being of their small child, so we are acting in accord with our best interests when we extend our concern to the needs of our family, our community, our nation, and the Earth.

In thinking about how to apply reciprocity in many specific situations, you might experiment with picturing that everything you do will be done back to you in the near future. Then experiment with giving to others what you want to get back.

Similarly, consider how our country can better formulate policies based upon the principle of reciprocity. What would it look like for us to treat other nations in a manner that we, as a nation, want to be treated? In an interdependent world, nations that take the lead in applying this principle, in ways that do not threaten national security, will gain greater respect from other nations.

CHAPTER EIGHT

Steps For Shaping
Our Future

*If you don't know where you're going, you might
end up somewhere else.*
— Yogi Berra —

The assertion that we are at least partly in charge of our destiny has been long debated. From Socrates to Shakespeare and down to contemporary times, we have heard the two polarities of human experience. One extreme says that we are the ultimate captains of our ship; the other says that we are powerless before the storms of fate. There is, of course, a middle way which acknowledges that both have insight. We cannot control the future and yet what we do today influences tomorrow. We are co-creative; we each play our part in shaping the future in conjunction with the larger forces of history and of the universe itself.

Things evolve. We know they do by observing evolution in our own lives. The future does not descend upon us from nowhere; it unfolds out of what is happening in the present. In the seeds of the present moment, we can see the future growing. Today's seedlings are tomorrow's trees. If this is true, then how we live in the present, our choices now, are acutely important in affecting the future.

While we cannot control the future through the power of our intention, we can co-create the conditions for the future we want. The act of choosing our direction consciously is the first victory. Next, we can acknowledge our responsibility in the present for our actions in the past. For if we view ourselves as victimized by the past, then we will ex-

144

perience ourselves as powerless with regard to our future as well. Finally, by changing the circumstances of the present through the way we live our lives, we can, in part, consciously shape the unfolding of our future.

Our intention, as we have seen, is the foundation of human interaction. It is the basis upon which we can take conscious action to shape our future. For example, if millions of us have the shared intention to address and overcome our common danger, then we have a clear sense of purpose. If we know that we want a Great Turning for the advancement of our humanity, then we have a clear goal. We know where we want to go.

Often life confounds our picture of the way we think things should happen. The more attached we are to the specific details of our projection of the future, the more we set ourselves up to be disappointed or discouraged. But this misses the point. Projecting victory is not about trying to control the future — this is the perspective of the ego. Projecting victory begins with the intention to hold a vision of what can be, while acknowledging the reality of what is.

Elie Wiesel, the great novelist and winner of the Nobel Peace Prize, wrote in *Town Beyond the Wall*: "Everyone should have their own personal prayer. My prayer is 'God, please surprise me for I am not large enough to know what I need.' " Thus we can be centered in our underlying intention, while being detached about the details of how things unfold.

Here are four steps to help us shape our future. The value of each of these steps can be illustrated by the analogy of what it takes to climb a steep and rugged mountain. First, you must have a *clear sense of vision* that you are going to reach the summit. Second, you must have an *unshakeable resolve* — the integrity that no matter what happens along the way, whether you are walking through gracious meadows or struggling up steep granite, you are going to continue until you reach the top. Third, you need to *inquire* about all the possible routes up the mountain and discover the advantages and disadvantages in order to most intelligently choose your path. Fourth, you must *take action* by walking step by step along the path you have chosen. Of course, a good climber will remain flexible, able to adjust his or her expectations and route along the way, based upon new data and unforeseen circumstances.

Step One: Clear Vision

Definition: *Seeing where we want to go. The ability to acknowledge what is, while sustaining a vision of what can be.*

To go anywhere in life with a conscious direction, we need to know two things: where we are currently and where we want to go. For example, when you buy an airplane ticket, you need to know your destination and your place of departure. Just so, for us to overcome the major human-caused threats to life, we need to know where we are now and then visualize where it is that we are intending to go. While there is no guarantee that we will succeed, the likelihood of getting there is increased by focusing our attention on the desired destination.

First comes the vision. It is essential to be able to imagine a new possibility. The dictionary defines *vision* as "the ability to perceive something not actually visible, as through mental acuteness or keen foresight; the force or power of imagination." Imagination is the process of visualizing or otherwise creating an image of what is not yet, but could be. Again, the dictionary helps to clarify: "*Imagination*, an act or process of forming a conscious idea or mental image of something never before wholly perceived in reality by the imaginer."

Leonardo da Vinci sketched drawings of a flying machine four centuries before the Wright brothers' historic flight at Kitty Hawk. The novels of Jules Verne, written in the middle part of the nineteenth century, offer vivid descriptions of submarines, airplanes, rockets, and trips through interplanetary space. Was this mere coincidence? Did Jules Verne foresee developments which were inevitable? Or, did the power of his imagination, expressed in novels read by millions, help to inspire the direction of the developments?

With any vision there comes doubt — the voice that says it can't be done. All through history there have been the

cynics who knew all the reasons why some great idea was
not practical. The president of the Royal Society in 1895
said, "Heavier-than-air flying machines are impossible." Four
years later in 1899, the director of the U.S. Patent Office
said, "Everything that can be invented has been invented."

Until we have a vision of where we want to go, the
task before us appears to be difficult, if not hopeless. It
is like believing we are in a box surrounded by walls without a door. The box is our limited world view, or frame of
reference. There are no perceived alternatives. Until we can
visualize a door, we feel stuck.

"Human beings construct social reality in their minds,"
wrote Elise Boulding, Professor Emeritus at Dartmouth,
"prior to the sociophysical task of constructing the external
reality. They can do this casually, unconsciously, never fully
aware of what they are doing, or they can realize, take responsibility for, and fully participate in what takes shape in
their minds."

The practice of clear vision is equally relevant to the
personal, national, and global dimensions of our lives. For
example, in our individual lives we can hold a personal
vision of what we intend to have happen in the future,
while also recognizing our current point of departure. Similarly, the United States needs a clear vision for how to take
leadership in an interdependent world. And we need a global
vision of how to create the transition from mutually assured
destruction to mutually assured development.

The power of the human mind to project images onto
the screen of the future can be compared to what happens
in a movie theater. Our minds are like the projector, and
the way we interpret our present circumstances is largely
in terms of "our movie" about where we are and where
we are going. If we are projecting a tragic outcome or negative scenario, we are more likely to find or create one. What
we are looking for, we tend to be drawn toward. Hence,
the discipline is to begin to take charge of our projections

— consciously — to visualize clearly what we intend to have happen.

Often we cut ourselves off from our own dreams, plans, goals, and visions. We don't let ourselves even entertain the possibility that we could achieve what we really want, because we might fail. The fear of failure, or loss, keeps many of us locked up and unwilling to risk. The first step is to dream. Whatever you dream can come to pass. It may not happen, and yet because you have dreamt it, there is now the possibility. A seed in no way guarantees there will be a tree, yet without the seed, no tree will be possible.

Clear vision is a profound and often misunderstood ability of the human mind. It is not wishful thinking or undisciplined fantasy. Great leaders and teachers across history have known that being able to visualize a goal was essential to ever achieving it. For example, early in the nineteenth century the abolitionists had a clear vision of the end of slavery. They foresaw that abolition was an inevitable necessity of human advancement and that our nation could not long endure if we continued to hold our fellow human beings in bondage. Although it took many years and a civil war before the Emancipation Proclamation was signed, the end result was already seen as inevitable by the abolitionists.

Similarly, if we look up ahead into the twenty-first century, we can see that overcoming our common danger is an inevitable necessity of human survival and advancement. The natural environment must be restored, the threat of global war must be overcome, the right to life and liberty for all peoples must prevail over authoritarian governments, and hunger must be ended. To accomplish this vision, we will need to manage conflicts and make policies based upon the reality of interdependence. This is as clear and compelling a necessity for our time as the end of slavery was for the Civil War period.

As you strive to get clear about the particulars of your personal vision, the following process may help: Start by listening to yourself. Stop and reflect on what you want in life. What are your real goals and deepest aspirations?

State these goals as specifically as possible. It might help to write your vision and, if possible, express it to at least one other person.

Next, express all the reasons why you believe or perceive that your vision is impossible. Express the cynical or doubting voice which says: "This can't happen." Let the self-doubting part of you have its way. This is important because by suppressing our fears and doubts, we increase their unconscious power over us. By expressing and making conscious our thoughts and feelings about why our vision is impossible, we clear our minds of negative projections.

Finally, write a detailed scenario of how your vision can happen. Get a clear picture; the more specific you can be, the better. Generate several more scenarios, each of which is possible. Think in multiple versions. Avoid becoming attached to any one scenario. The details of your vision will keep changing, as your life changes, and you take action that changes your life. Sustaining a vision requires us to dance with reality and lets the unknown and the unpredictable interact with our hopes and our projections.

With regard to the challenge of creating a positive vision for America and the world in the next century, we need to undertake a similar process. First, our national dialogue must begin by listening to one another across the many different points of view. What are our shared goals and values? We need to formulate these goals as precisely as possible. Next, we need to express our fears about how our country may not be able to achieve these goals. Finally, having expressed our negative projections, we can work together to discover specific policy options which we can agree upon across the widest possible spectrum. Thus, without becoming attached to any particular position, we can renew our national sense of purpose and take steps as a more unified nation to shape our future with conscious direction.

Step Two: Personal Integrity
Definition: *Building the foundation for our vision. The sincere*

intent to match our words and our deeds, to be undivided in
the resolve to achieve our goal.

The word "integrity" comes from the Latin root, *integritas*
or *integer*, meaning whole and undivided. This same root has
given us the words integral, integer, integrate, integration.
Integrity is not a "thing," not something we win or do or
accomplish once and for all. Rather, integrity is a process of
living in relationship to what is true for us and for our world.

We cannot reach our goals if we do not live these goals
as our path. Our integrity begins with the decision to actually
do what it is we say we are going to do. To return to the
metaphor of climbing a mountain, it is not sufficient to hold
a press conference and make great declarations about one's
forthcoming climb. By walking up the mountain, through
good times and bad, we build our integrity.

Without integrity, we have no cohesion, no inner unity.
When we say one thing and do another, we are divided
against ourselves and are therefore ineffective. Without
integrity, we are set adrift in a maelstrom of conflicting
currents pulling us here and there. Without integrity, we
have no base of respect from which to achieve our personal,
national, or global goals.

Integrity accrues from choice, moment by moment.
Every time we choose to take the action that serves our
clear vision, we experience a small victory over the force of
self-negation. Every time we keep our word and do what we
say we are going to do, we reaffirm our conscious intention.

Many of us at one time or another have cheated ourselves
out of our dreams because we have given up too easily. We
have given in to our own fears and inner conflicts. Or we
have acted in ways that breached our own integrity and
hence the foundation for our vision.

Integrity is not a public-relations device, nor is it a check
list of do's and don'ts. Integrity is first and foremost an inner
experience: we recognize that we are aligned with our real
goals; we trust ourselves to do what we say we are going to
do; and if we don't, we forgive ourselves and start again.

When we are in conflict inside ourselves about our

direction, we broadcast mixed signals to the outside world. Mixed signals tend to generate mixed responses. Thus, many of us are not fully aware of what we are really intending to do. We are operating out of half-hidden belief systems, unconscious images, and deeply felt experiences left over from our past. In this way, our inner conflicts get reflected in our outer experiences.

When we say we are going to do something and then don't do it, we tend to strengthen our identification with these inner conflicts. On the one hand, there is the voice which promises, "I will do such and such." On the other hand, there is the judging voice which says, "Look, you can't be trusted." A house divided against itself cannot stand.

Therefore, it is very important for us to be aware of what we say we are going to do. Integrity is the discipline to stay with the pursuit of our goals until they are realized. The key is to start with do-able goals, to set ourselves up for success, not failure. By winning small victories, we increase our confidence and build the base of our self-esteem.

An example of the principle of integrity in international affairs can be seen in the problem the United States and the Soviet Union have had in stopping the proliferation of nuclear weapons. It has been difficult to convince other nations not to acquire nuclear weapons when the two super-powers have made themselves so dependent upon them. More than one nation must have doubted our integrity as we urged them not to do what we have done on a massive scale.

Integrity is the practice of keeping one's word, of seeking to match our words and our deeds. By keeping our word to ourselves and others, we experience an increased sense of integration. Through this process of integration, we are freed from our inner conflicts and enabled to achieve our goals. Integrity is the base of our future. Just as with an individual, so also a community or a nation must sustain its integrity if it is going to survive and prosper. Without integrity, it cannot take action that is consistent and in accord with its overall needs and interests. A nation will deteriorate just like an individual if it is torn by warring factions, indebted, and irresponsible to future generations.

By staying current, we maintain our integrity. A good place to begin with the practice of integrity is to finish unfinished business. Uncompleted actions and debts from the past keep us in conflict about what is unfinished. For example, if you have a backpack and your goal is to reach the summit, "incompletes" are like carrying rocks in the pack. The more unfinished business you have, the heavier the burden you are carrying. Each time you complete something, you lighten your load and the journey gets easier.

You might experiment with finishing your unfinished business. Take an inventory of your life. What debts or unfinished business do you have, whether economic, emotional, or spiritual? If you were told you had one year to live, what actions would be necessary in your life to obtain peace of mind? Make a list of everything that feels unfinished and then start completing your list. Scratch off the things that are no longer real and let go of them. Forgive yourself for the things that are not in your power to change. Seek to forgive those who have harmed you, and ask for the forgiveness from those you have harmed. Make amends. Pay your debts. Clean up all the unfinished business until one day you are caught up. You wake up refreshed, not burdened by the past, able to greet the new day with the awe and wonder of being fully alive.

The process of completing unfinished business is not something we do once and for all. It is a way of living — of staying current and maintaining our personal integrity. By completing things as they happen, we bring ourselves into a relationship with present time and thereby greatly enhance our ability to act consciously and to experience joy.

Step Three: Open Inquiry
Definition: *Exploring understanding from all directions. The willingness to keep an open mind, to seek truth without prejudice, to inform ourselves from many points of view.*

The purpose of open inquiry is always to increase our

understanding, to gain access to more data, to expand our perspective. The human mind is like a parachute; it works best when it is open. Old patterns and prejudices keep us from being empirical. They lock us into judgments that are not appropriate to the current situation. Inquiry requires us to have a fresh perspective, a beginner's mind.

Open inquiry acknowledges that our own personal perspective is relative. We all have a particular point of view which is a function of where we are looking from — our personal history, values, and beliefs. In a room of 100 people sitting in chairs looking at a speaker, every person is seeing something slightly different. We all have our own bias or angle of perception. What we perceive is, in large part, a consequence of where we are sitting.

Our attachment to a particular point of view keeps us locked into a very narrow perspective. We are like the blind men holding different parts of the elephant. The more someone disagrees with our point of view, the more defensive we tend to become. Action and reaction. We often interpret disagreement as an attack upon who we are.

The central problem here is confusing our identity with the content of that with which we have become identified. It is fundamentally important to distinguish between our underlying intention and all of the ideas, opinions, and positions to which our minds become attached. If you are on your way from New York to California, and your car breaks down in Omaha, your predetermined plan for the trip must be revised. You will want to practice open inquiry to find out the best options for how to get your car fixed and get back on the road. Your intention is clear: you are going to California. By gathering data, you will discover the most workable options to serve your intent.

Our attachment to the rightness of our position keeps us from being empirical: "This is my idea or my opinion and I will not see it any other way." Often, this attachment is not even to the particular content of our position; we are attached only to being right. Our attachment to being right prevents us from co-existing creatively with people with whom we fundamentally disagree.

The practice of open inquiry is an essential element of the evolutionary shift of mind that is required for human beings to survive and live together with mutual respect. By listening to points of view different from our own, we gain access to a larger truth. We literally see the issues from many perspectives. Out of this kind of inquiry, new and more comprehensive options emerge.

Open inquiry requires us to cultivate an open mind: to step back from our opinion and to look for increased understanding with no concern for whose idea it was originally. The more we can detach our ego from our current position, the more we can gather real insight from many points of view. This is not easy; to keep an open mind requires practice. As Helen Keller put it, "Toleration . . . is the greatest gift of the mind; it requires the same effort of the brain that it takes to balance oneself on a bicycle."

So often we want simple solutions to complex problems. We would rather argue about our preconceived belief than engage in the difficult search for what is true. We want answers rather than questions. Open inquiry takes candor and detachment. Without detachment toward our own belief or opinion, there is no open space in our minds in which to think. We need to remind ourselves again and again that what we believe about a particular issue is often nothing more than our limited current point of view.

Open inquiry is at the core of real education. Without a grasp of the facts and issues from many perspectives, we remain caught in our own prejudices. Too often when we educate ourselves about a particular issue, we look for those sources of information that fundamentally agree with our own opinion. We educate ourselves in order to be able to prove the view we already hold. We "arm ourselves with the facts." This is not real education. Education requires seeking data and insight from those with whom we think we disagree, as well as those who are part of our club of agreement.

You might try this experiment. Choose a national or

international issue relating to peace and security which is of concern to you. Pursue learning about it from various points of view. Look at background materials from several sources, read the arguments of those on different sides, create situations where you can listen to individuals who have diverse views, and engage friends and colleagues in helping you to think about what you are learning.

Step Four: Conscious Action

Definition: *Taking the next step toward our vision. The commitment to take small actions, to make adjustments, and then take another step, again and again.*

The best of our goals and dreams remain fantasies until we choose to act. If we just think about something, no matter how hard, it will not come to pass. We bring reality to our vision by taking action. If we have a vision of climbing a mountain and have done many things to prepare ourselves, but never actually start, we cannot know the real journey.

Conscious action requires us to choose an appropriate and immediate next step toward our goal, and then do it. By taking specific action in the direction of our vision, we often generate new possibilities that we could not have foreseen had we not acted.

In 1968, Dr. Victor Westphall's son David was killed in Vietnam. Shortly after learning of his death, Dr. Westphall had a vision of building a shrine to honor the veterans of the Vietnam War and renew the commitment to world peace. For more than two years, he tried to obtain the funding for the Vietnam Memorial, but at that time no one was interested. So Dr. Westphall just started. He designed the plans for a simple chapel on a mountain ridge. He purchased building materials, donated the land, invited his friends to help. One day he and his friends began to pour the concrete for the foundation of the chapel. Here is how he describes what happened:

> Once we actually started the Chapel, then all kinds of financial support and offers to help appeared. What I

learned is if you want to achieve something in life, just start doing it. More than anything else I would tell you, just take the first step and keep doing it and everything else will follow.

The chapel was dedicated at Angel Fire, New Mexico in 1975, long before the national Vietnam Memorial in Washington, D. C. Tens of thousands of veterans and their families have visited this inspiring shrine, and have begun the process of healing the wounds from the war and making peace with themselves.

Similarly, with regard to constructing the foundations for a victory of real peace and security: We must just begin. Each small action deepens our integrity and our experience of our larger purpose. We can shape our future, but only by putting one foot in front of the other.

We live in a kind of dialogue with the universe. We evolve by being in conscious relationship with feedback we get from our previous actions. We cannot force things to happen, nor can we make the conditions ripen. Timing is essential to choosing an appropriate and viable action. What was inappropriate once may become critically important and vice versa. Our actions produce consequences which give us a sense of how to adjust our course.

Once again, the practice of detachment is essential. If we are attached to a particular action producing a particular result and it does not happen, we are likely to overlook the next real option that has become available. Real alternatives are actual and now-possible, as distinguished from all the ideas that are theoretical, intangible, or not-yet-possible. Often what is most valuable as a next step is right in front of us, but we don't see it, because we are searching for a "grand plan" or we are worrying about something in the distant future.

The key is to choose what seems to be the most workable option from what exists now. Real alternatives are those which are currently available. The practice is to recognize that what is, simply is. By taking action, however small, we ground our dreams. Act deliberately (based upon your analysis and open inquiry), then observe the consequences of your action, make appropriate changes or adjustments, and act again deliberately.

CHAPTER NINE

Skills For The Art
Of Dialogue

The situation of the world is still like this. People
completely identify with one side, one ideology. . . .
Reconciliation is to understand both sides. . . . Doing
only that will be a great help for peace.
— Thich Nhat Hanh —

Dialogue is a concept of immense importance for our
survival and creativity. Dialogue can free the human mind
in ways that help to heal the divisions threatening our future.
Like toddlers learning to walk, human beings living today
must learn the art of dialogue. The term "dialogue" is derived
from the Greek words, *dia*, meaning through, and *logos*,
meaning the word, not just in the sense of the sound of a
word, but also its meaning. Dialogue is meaningful exchange,
a flow of information between people in communication.

Dialogue must be distinguished from our ordinary interactions, where we hold fixed positions and argue in favor
of our point of view. The intent to convert others has no
place in dialogue. This kind of adversarial communication
may produce clarification of the issues, but it is unlikely to
produce anything which is fundamentally new or creative.

Dialogue seeks to create a meeting of the minds. It is
predicated upon a willingness to listen and to learn from
each other. Participants in a dialogue need to be committed
to thinking creatively together and discovering what is true,
rather than to proving one's truth is the only way.

The participant in a dialogue may prefer a certain position at the outset, but he or she must be willing to listen to

other perspectives with sufficient interest and attention to grasp their meaning. At the root of dialogue is the intent to seek greater knowing, and to be willing to change one's current point of view if you discover convincing data. Each participant in a dialogue should be willing to suspend judgment about his or her point of view and those of others, in order to focus full attention on what the other person is saying. By listening for the meaning behind the words, each person comes to an increased understanding of the other person.

To summarize, the three levels of human interaction are essential to understanding dialogue. In all communication, the underlying intent generates the process which generates the content. In adversarial communication, the intent is to convert, to convince, to win as in a win/lose game, to prove the other wrong, or otherwise to dominate. The process which is generated out of this motivation is contentious and aggressive. There is usually very little listening or receptivity or creative thinking. The content which is discussed is limited by the unwillingness of the adversarial mind to even consider the data or the insight of anything but its own position.

In dialogue, the intent is to learn, to increase mutual understanding, to discover new insight, and to think creatively together. The process which is generated out of this motivation is cooperative and based upon a spirit of good will. The content which is discussed is not limited by old prejudices and habitual patterns. It is creative, emergent, and offers the potential for real breakthroughs.

Skill One: Establish Ground Rules.
Definition: *At the outset, express your commitment to listen and to learn with mutual respect. See if the other will agree to proceed using these guidelines.*

If you want to create a dialogue, it is essential to establish a shared commitment to certain guidelines based upon the spirit of open inquiry and mutual respect. Much of the time we humans are creatures of habit. Our old patterns of interaction are like the well-worn grooves of a phonograph record. Without conscious effort on our part, we will be pulled back into these all-too-familiar grooves. Therefore, one way to make the process of communication more conscious is to establish agreement between the parties at the beginning about their operating principles.

The parties in a dialogue may radically disagree about the content of their position or beliefs; however, if they can agree to observe certain simple ground rules, this will change the way they interact with each other. If there is a facilitator, as in the case of a public dialogue, the facilitator's role is, in part, to call the participants back to remembering the ground rules. If there is no facilitator, then it is incumbent upon all participants to remember their commitment to a different kind of process.

The purpose of establishing simple ground rules is to create a climate of genuine safety and honest exchange. At the root of these guidelines is the shared commitment to practice reciprocity — to treat the other person with the respect with which you want to be treated. These ground rules are the fulcrum upon which we can leverage the process from being adversarial to being mutually creative.

Here are four suggested ground rules for a dialogue:

- Be open to learning from each other's point of view.
- Be willing to listen and share the allotted time.
- Attempt to use precise language and avoid exaggeration.
- Don't dominate and don't let yourself be dominated.

It is important not to become legalistic about these rules or guidelines. If you don't like this particular set of wordings, make up your own. Nor should they be used in a heavy-handed or holier-than-thou fashion; this will prove counter-productive to the real intent of being in dialogue with someone. Simply use the guidelines to create a climate of good will and real listening.

The way you establish agreement to certain guidelines will vary greatly from situation to situation. The key is to be appropriate to the circumstance. For example, in a public dialogue the facilitator should state the ground rules at the beginning and ask all participants to agree. Then later, if participants fall back into adversarial modes and interrupt or demean others, the facilitator can remind them of their prior commitment to the ground rules.

In our personal lives, there are obviously situations where setting up ground rules is not workable. It is unlikely that you would turn to a perfect stranger and say, "I want to talk with you, but before we begin, let's set up some guidelines." Yet, in many instances in our lives, especially where we interact with someone over time — in our families, friendships, jobs, marriages, churches, synagogues, or professional associations — it may be appropriate to suggest to the other person the value of dialogue, and then talk about effective ways to practice dialogue.

Skill Two: Listen with Empathy.
Definition: *Listen with undivided attention to the other person, regardless of whether you agree with his or her beliefs, ideas, or mind set. Try to put yourself in the other person's place.*

Two computers can have an important exchange of information, but they cannot have dialogue. Dialogue requires listening between two or more persons, not only to the content of what they are saying, but also to the depth of who they are. This kind of listening is an art and needs to be practiced regularly to develop its full potential.

When most of us converse, we try to get other people to listen to us. Often we are unsuccessful, because the person who is being asked to listen is also urgently waiting for a chance to be heard. Frequently what looks like a conversation is a series of mutual interruptions: One person speaks, then the other interrupts because something the first said triggered a reaction, then the first interrupts back — on and on. We are like reactive, stop-and-start mechanisms with unacknowledged needs to express ourselves and be received. Because of this internal pressure to talk, we often cannot listen very well.

Even when we appear to be listening, we are often still

quite divided in our attention. We are reacting inside to what the other person said, thinking about our own agendas. This is greatly intensified in an adversarial situation: If one person says something with which another disagrees, the second person begins to prepare a rebuttal before the first has uttered a few sentences. Real listening requires receptivity. As Thoreau said, "It takes two to speak the truth — one to speak and another to hear."

Real listening requires a certain spaciousness within one's psyche. When the mind is filled with contentious beliefs and opinions, there is no capacity to receive the other person. By stepping back from one's own beliefs, we can become more receptive and curious about the other person's experience. Also, when the mind is calm, it is easier to listen from the depths of oneself to the depths of the other. The more we listen to and integrate our own inner divisions, the more we can listen to others with undivided attention.

The goal is to learn to listen at all three levels of human communication: intention, process, and content. Listening to the words of the other, we hear the content of what is being said. Listening to the dynamic of the other — e.g. body language, gestures, tone of voice — we hear the *process* of how it is being expressed. Listening to the other person behind his or her beliefs, we hear the *intention* — where the other person is "coming from" in terms of values and life experiences.

At the heart of dialogue is empathy — the capacity to put oneself behind the eyes of another person and to walk a mile in his or her shoes. No matter how much we may disagree with another person, the effort to look at things the way he/she does is critically important. This practice is at the root of our real hope for more effective communication and a more secure coexistence with each other.

No one can fully understand the experience and perspective of another. We live in parallel realities, separated by our own unique perception and perspective. A man cannot know what it's really like to be a woman and be pregnant. A white person cannot fathom the experience of a black person in East Harlem. A well-fed-and-housed person cannot really comprehend what it is like to be a malnourished and homeless person stranded on the streets.

Much of the time, we see each other only on the outside, with little recognition that behind every human exterior, there is a real person, a human soul. No one else can know what we know in the recesses of our own psyche. Yet, given these limits, the intention to seek to understand someone else is remarkably powerful.

Empathy is the art of feeling with the other person. When we empathize, we get outside our narrow and self-absorbed agendas for a few moments; we transcend ourselves by listening with undivided attention to the other. Empathy enables us to re-create the other person's point of view. Theo Brown once commented, "When I was a kid, I remember seeing somebody in pain and being able to switch my consciousness for a moment — to put myself behind their eyes or in their shoes. Being there for a moment or two made it impossible not to care about them. How can we teach that to all children?"

Listen to another person's story and ask yourself, "What would it be like to be this other person?" Picture yourself in his or her life experience. How would you see the world? What would you value? What are your hopes and fears? What do you really want?

You might experiment with listening attentively to people with whom you think you disagree. You can begin this practice anywhere — the co-worker you don't like, the conservative or liberal with whom you never talk politics, the weapons builder or the arms-control activist, the environmentalist or the developer. Whatever side of a controversy you identify with, try listening to the other side without the sirens of judgment. See if you can sustain contact with the person behind the position or stance. Seek to extend your understanding to include the other's point of view and life experience.

Skill Three: Restate with Understanding.
Definition: *Mirror back your understanding of what the other*

party is saying, free from your opinions and judgments. Then,
find out what you omitted or need to correct in order to obtain
a complete understanding.

In every communication, there is a sender and receiver.
We can send a message, but if no one receives it, the communication is left dangling and incomplete. Usually when
we express ourselves to another person, our first and most
basic goal is to be heard and understood. We want the
other to hear and comprehend what we are saying. Hearing
our words is not sufficient; we want the other to grasp
our meaning. Our communication is not complete until
that happens.

In this sense, dialogue is a continual feedback loop: Send
the message to the other person, group, or nation; find out
whether the message was received and understood; then
make adjustments or corrections until there is mutual understanding — and understanding does not mean agreement.

The commitment to accurately restate the other person's
way of seeing is a commitment to increase the depth and
precision of our listening. This is equally true in a personal
context or a policy dialogue. For example, in a policy dialogue,
if national experts or community leaders from left and right
summarize and restate one another's perspective, this can
help to establish the foundation for a more thoughtful and
substantive exchange.

Often in adversarial situations, we expect that the other
person will not try to grasp what we are saying. "Even if he
hears my words, I doubt if he will understand my point." It
is powerful to reflect back to the other person that you have
accurately understood what he or she is saying. Or, if you
did not, to ask honest questions with the intent to clarify
and better understand his or her perspective.

In Gainesville, Florida, we conducted a dialogue on
peace and security which was cosponsored by the Young
Republicans and the Young Democrats. The dialogue featured
the leading conservative and liberal spokespersons from the
area, two men who had been on bitter terms for years.
Before the dialogue began there were signs, placards, and a

general atmosphere of "Our side is right; yours is wrong" in the large room. Then there was a key moment, when the second speaker restated the other's point of view with such clarity and understanding that the first speaker was genuinely startled. He paused, obviously moved, and said to his opponent, "I never expected that you would want to take the time to really understand my perspective." After the successful restatement, the tone shifted, and the two long-time adversaries spent the evening really listening to each other.

There is much value in mirroring back the other person's perspective until you reach mutual understanding:

- You demonstrate your willingness to listen carefully. This often serves to gain respect from the other, who appreciates your effort to comprehend his or her point of view.
- You make certain that both parties are really talking about the same thing. Unless you listen and reflect back to the other, you cannot be sure that both of you are really talking about the same subject.
- You give the other person the opportunity to hear and reflect upon his or her own beliefs mirrored back. This feedback provides an opportunity for the person to gain new insights.
- You encourage the other person to clarify any ambiguities or misunderstandings in your restatement, and thereby obtain the satisfaction of knowing that he or she has been precisely understood.
- You are modeling a constructive process and giving to the other what you want to get from him or her.

In restating, paraphrase the important points the other person is saying: Verify that you understand them accurately by asking whether the paraphrase is correct. Reflect back to the other person by saying something like, "Let me make sure that I understand you," or "Let me share with you what I understood you were saying."

The restatement process should not be mechanical. No technique can be substituted for real attention. If we are paying attention to the other person and trying to understand his or her way of seeing things, we will be able to give accurate feedback. Remember that restatement is not an automatic repetition of the other's words, but rather an effort to let the other person know that we are understanding his or her meaning. This is a critically important distinction. To repeat the other's words without comprehension is useless, perhaps even counterproductive.

When we attach our judgments and opinions to the restatement process, it does not work. We are not interested in having our point of view criticized under the ruse of accurate feedback. There is an important place for criticism, but this is not it. If we want to increase contact and have a real dialogue, we need to step back from our judgments, whether positive or negative — to listen to and summarize what is true for the other person free from our opinions. Our job is not to add or subtract to the other's perspective, but to be a clear mirror.

Skill Four: Speak Your Truth.

Definition: *Express your point of view, as both an advocate for what you think is true and an empiricist who inquires after more data and increased understanding.*

When you are expressing your point of view, remember that your speaking is not a one-way communication, but always a two-way exchange. Listening is not the opposite of speaking, so that when you turn speaking "on," listening goes "off." Listening is the receptivity of your awareness, focused and attentive to what is happening, whether you are sitting quietly by yourself, speaking to another person, or lecturing to 5,000 people.

To become truly effective communicators, we must learn the art of empathetic speaking. This is the skill of expressing yourself fully while you are simultaneously attentive to how the other person is receiving what you are saying. The key is where you put your attention. If your attention is only on yourself, than you are unaware of the continuous feedback coming in from the other person or group. But if your attention is only on the other, than you are separated from the truth of your own experience. Neither of these two polarities serves to deepen real dialogue.

Frequently in our everyday interactions we relate to ourselves and others as objects. Our attention is either on ourselves as an object — "How do I look? Am I making a good appearance?" — or our attention is focused on the other person as an object — "Is he responding positively? Does he agree with my point of view?"

In both cases, whether we objectify self or other, we are trapped in a prison of self-consciousness. We are cut off and isolated from the underlying flow. We do not express ourselves or listen fully. Our attention is divided, thinking about and judging what we are doing even as we do it.

In speaking your truth, be honest and straightforward in a way that is appropriate to the situation and the person you are addressing. Given that the scope of your idea is wide, ask yourself, "What is the particular focus which is most appropriate and valuable to forward this dialogue?" Essential to the art of dialogue is knowing the appropriate level of information to communicate to the other person. "Appropriate" means what the other person is able to hear, and what will produce the result of deepening the interaction.

For example, if you want to take a picture with your camera, you need to take a light-meter reading on how wide to open the lens. Just so, in any interaction, it is most effective to take a reading on how wide to open the lens through which you are going to communicate your perspective. You want to find the aperture that is an appropriate fit to the other person's level of interest.

Be as clear and precise in what you say as you can. This is not easy; it requires discipline. So often our conversations degenerate into combat because we are imprecise with our language. We state our positions which are rhetorically extreme and which do not accurately represent what we really think. This leads to polarization and black-and-white thinking. Saying what we really mean is very important to sustaining thoughtful dialogue.

There are many different ways in which to express the same point of view, each with a different, unspoken message. For example, you can express your view in a tone of voice which implicitly says: "I am right and you are wrong." Or you can do the opposite, implicitly conceding, "You are right and I am wrong." If you want to sustain a dialogue with someone, make certain that your purpose is not to appease or surrender, nor to be superior or dominate. You are seeking to express yourself as clearly and powerfully as you want, yet in a tone that communicates regard for the other person and thereby maximizes the possibility of being received and understood.

Seek to be in contact with the truth of your perspective, while addressing the truth of the other person. A few keys: Humor is often the shortest distance between two people. Acknowledgment and sincere appreciation work wonders. In terms of building rapport, it often helps to start with where you can honestly agree with the other person. Start with whatever you can acknowledge as true for you in what the other said, even if it is only his or her commitment to be in dialogue with you.

Get to know yourself and your point of view. Spend time thinking and reflecting on why you think what you think. What are your underlying assumptions and beliefs? The more you honestly know your own perspective, the more you can afford to be aware of the other person's perspective. Practice the balance between advocacy and inquiry. Be an advocate for what you think is true, and an empiricist who always inquires after more data and new options. If you believe you have the most compelling or thoughtful point of view, by all means don't hold back. Yet, also be open to changing your view based upon new insight.

Most of all, speak from truth. As Mark Twain once put it, "When you tell the truth, you don't have to remember anything else."

CHAPTER TEN

Tools For Transforming Conflict

*To constitute a dispute there must be two parties.
To understand it well, both parties and all the
circumstances must be fully heard; and to accommodate the differences, temper and mutual
forbearance are requisite.*
— George Washington —

Conflict and contradiction are an essential part of life.
Without the interaction of conflict between opposites, there
would be no growth, no evolutionary development. Life
evolves in part through conflict and resolution.

Everyone of us can readily think of examples of conflict
in our own lives. Conflicts occur with friends, family, land-
lords, business associates, and others we encounter daily. At
the same time, we are aware of the serious and potentially
catastrophic conflicts that exist at national and global levels.
The common danger poses a threat to the survival and
health of every inhabitant on Earth. This reality makes it
clear that there is a compelling need for more effective ways
to manage conflict.

The creative management of conflicts ought not be
thought of as a mechanical process. No doubt there are many
helpful techniques, but a mechanical, paint-by-the-numbers
approach often misses the spirit or real intent behind what
is happening.

For example, put two people who are in the midst of
a conflict in a room. Both parties are trained in conflict-
resolution methods, but neither party has the intent to resolve

the conflict in a mutually acceptable way. Each wants to resolve it but only on his or her terms: "I win/you lose." Alternatively, put two "ordinary" people who are also embroiled in a conflict in a room. These two have no training or understanding of conflict resolution methods, but they both have a clear intention to resolve their differences in ways that result in mutual gain. Which pair will reach an accord first, or at all? It is clear that the second pair without any sophistication will figure out what's fair, because they are operating out of good will and common sense.

Meryl Lefkoff, a nationally known conflict-resolution specialist, says: "Eighty percent of any negotiation is getting through the resistance: everything that's in the way of both parties wanting to reach an agreement that will work. Once the acknowledgment of this commitment is clear, then you can work out the details of the agreement with relative ease."

When approaching conflicts, make the distinction between those conflicts that you have the intention to resolve, and those you do not. For example, there may be conflicts in your life which you are not ready to resolve. Often the psychological gradient is too severe. There is too much hatred or pain left, and you are not prepared to address the underlying issues. There is no need to blame yourself. For example, in a situation like an estranged marriage, where two people have inflicted a great deal of emotional harm onto each other, it may be completely premature to attempt to deal with the underlying issues until the wounds have healed.

Then, of course, there are the conflicts that we have no intention of ever resolving. Quite the contrary, we want to keep them around because we derive secondary benefits. Many couples maintain familiar sources of friction in order to give them a good excuse to have a fight and then make up. Similarly, with our children, the conflict is often not so much about the thing itself as it is about the need for consistent limits. What the child says, such as "I want to stay up later" or "I want that new toy," and what the child needs, and probably wants below the surface, are good, clear boundaries. Again, the conflict serves a larger purpose than simply resolving the apparent issues.

Discerning whether a particular conflict is ripe to be resolved, or whether a conflict even requires resolution, is very important. Once you have determined, "Yes, this is a conflict I want to resolve," then proceed.

Here are four tools which, if practiced and put to use, will help you to turn conflicts into mutual gain. Remember that most important is a sincere intention to really find a solution that works for everyone involved. Behind all the techniques is the question, "Do you intend to seek an outcome that works for all parties?"

Tool One: STOP . . . Take a Step Back.

Definition: *Step back from the conflict. Establish your intention and seek to determine the intention of the other.*

When hostility between two people or two nations escalates beyond a certain point, there is little chance of turning back. They have lost control of their impulses. They are caught in a mad spasm of action and reaction, each an escalation of the conflict. There is hardly a human being alive who has not experienced this feeling of being swept away by aggressive impulses. Someone cuts in front of your car without warning on the freeway, or someone insults or threatens someone you love, and you are thrown back to a survival mode. It's me against you, us against them — and only the winner will survive. You are reduced to kill or be killed, fight or be dominated.

When you find yourself in a conflict that is beginning to escalate, the first and most important step is to STOP. Take a step back from the dispute, and from your reactive mind.

This is difficult, as we all know. As Robert Fuller, former president of Oberlin College, once said, "I'm reminded of the short poem that runs, 'Let's stop hurting each other. You go first.' " For many of us, being the one who goes first is like exercising a muscle that we have rarely used before. Still, it is possible, especially if we practice. The discipline is to catch ourselves before we spin out of control into old reactive patterns. Sometimes it may be necessary to separate ourselves physically from the situation, to take a recess, to let some time pass until tempers and irrational responses have cooled. Taking a few deep breaths helps to calm the mind and re-establish our sense of center.

Once we are able to stop, all of the other steps will follow. Indeed, the other steps all depend upon our capacity to stop an escalating cycle and take a step back. An example: A husband and wife are having a dispute about house chores. The wife says: "The living room is not clean enough." The husband, whose job it is to keep the living room clean, immediately hears that he is being attacked and criticized personally. He counter-attacks, based upon his unchecked assumption that his wife is "getting on his case," and says: "The kitchen floors are dirty. They look like they haven't been cleaned for weeks." Even though he knows this is an exaggeration, he justifies it in terms of what his wife said to him. She attacks back about the trash, and so it goes, back and forth, until they are both hurling insults at each other the way nations at war hurl missiles.

This kind of escalation, not only between individuals, but between groups and nations, causes untold violence and suffering in our world all the time. Recent headlines in one day's newspaper screamed about the way we are trapped in escalating cycles:

"IRA Mourners Beat Soldiers to Death"
(Belfast, Northern Ireland)
"Iraqi Planes Hit Iranian Oil Depot"
(Nicosia, Cyprus)
"Israel Limits Access of Foreign Journalists"
(Hebron)
"4 Americans Hurt in Bomb Explosion"
(Athens, Greece)
"Extremists Blamed for 10 Sikh Deaths"
(Amritsar, India)
"China Blames Vietnam for Forest Fires"
(Hong Kong)

The remaining headline on the page pointed to an example of a profound de-escalation now in process between the two superpowers:

"Soviet Star to Record American Album"
(Moscow)

There is hope that we can stop ourselves from plunging into destructive escalations. It requires discipline, motivated by the recognition that the consequences of not stopping will mean that both parties will lose. Neither combatant is likely to get what he or she wants, because war is not an effective way to solve problems or reach mutually workable solutions. Indeed, the ultimate terror of global war in the nuclear age cannot be overstated.

Once you have established to yourself that your intent is to seek an "I win/you win" outcome, then seek to determine the intention of the other parties to a conflict. Where you have an on-going relationship with the other parties, ask yourself what their actions tell you about their motivations. In the final analysis, you can only ascertain the intention of other people based upon their deeds. As the Bible puts it, "By their fruits ye shall know them."

Start by telling the other person of your intent to find a workable solution for both yourself and the other. You want to send a balanced signal to the other party: "I am seeking the best outcome to meet both my concerns and yours. I do not intend to dominate you, nor will I allow myself to be dominated."

Lead with cooperation. Take small steps that involve no major risk and see what the other party does. If they respond with cooperation, continue step by step. If they respond with a mixed signal — part domination and part conciliation — set limits on the part that seeks to dominate. If they respond with the intent to control and defeat you, stop cooperating. Make it clear that you will not be controlled. Set clear and defensible limits so that the other person can see that all the advantages of a mutually beneficial process will be lost. Note the difference between retaliation and setting limits. In our earlier example, the husband retaliates by escalating. This leads to a tension-increasing spiral.

There are at least four possible intentions which we encounter, in ourselves and others, when dealing with conflict. To be effective, each requires a different kind of response:

Appeasement: The intent to make peace at any price. This is the passive position that seeks to deal with conflict by avoiding it, indeed by doing almost anything to prevent it. We have all met people who allowed themselves to be door mats just to keep things pleasant.

When Prime Minister Neville Chamberlain of Britain flew to Czechoslovakia in 1938 to make a deal with Hitler, he was acclaimed as a peacemaker. But when Hitler marched into Poland shortly thereafter, Chamberlain's bargain with Hitler became the classic example of appeasement. It is very important to not confuse being "nice" and conciliatory with acting as a real peacemaker.

Many of us need to acknowledge the place in ourselves that is afraid of conflict. Perhaps we sustained a trauma in our childhood, so that we associate conflicts with the wrath of a harsh parent. Or, perhaps we were taught that it is not OK to be directly assertive or angry. In any event, acceding to a domineering adversary will not lead to a mutually acceptable solution. You cannot help yourself or the other by "giving away" your perspective, goals, or interests. Remember: appeasement does not work. When you give in without regard to your real concerns, there can be no mutual, durable outcome. Similarly, when you encounter appeasement in others, empower them to claim their point of view and to express their goals and concerns.

Domination: The intent to exploit or control the other. When dealing with someone who has the intent to dominate, you can refuse to respond to the content of the other person's position, and focus instead on the fact that the process is not working. In such a situation it must be made clear that there is no way to proceed unless both parties agree to respect the legitimate interests of each side. If the other party's consistent intent is to destroy or dominate, then there are very few things about which you can have a dialogue. When faced with the intent to dominate, and your intent is to attempt to communicate, then you can make the following points to your adversary:

• "Any attempt to dominate will serve no productive purpose because I will resist and the result will be that neither of us will get what we want."

• "It will be a waste of time to have an interaction in which there is no open inquiry and no real exchange of information. There will be no value for us to go away only confirmed in the rightness of our positions."

• "I am interested in what you have to say, but I am not interested in having an interaction in which you try to dominate me. I will not respond to any of your concerns until you stop seeking to dominate or harm me. And if you are not willing to do this, I am not willing to have this interaction."

Such a strong response to one who seeks to dominate is essential if there is to be any chance of changing your adversary's underlying purpose. This is particularly true where interlocking conflicts and interests make continued interaction inevitable. An initial intention to dominate may evolve to another strategy if confronted with strong-willed resistance.

An example of this in international affairs was the beginning of real communication between the United States and the Palestine Liberation Organization in 1989. For thirteen years, three different American administrations refused to have any dialogue with the P.L.O. because it would not acknowledge Israel's right to exist or disavow the use of terrorism. The United States made it clear that the intention of the P.L.O. to destroy or dominate Israel made real dialogue impossible. In December, 1988 P.L.O. Chairman Yasser Arafat decided that he wanted to have substantive talks with the United States enough to change his stated positions. He publicly acknowledged the right of Israel to exist and renounced the use of terrorism. As a result, for the first time in more than a decade, Secretary of State George Shultz announced the willingness of the United States to participate in direct talks with the P.L.O. Whether these talks will lead to any productive changes in the Middle East remains to be seen, but it does demonstrate how a consistent policy can produce a shift in stated positions and establish the prerequisites for dialogue.

By making it clear that the intent to dominate is not an effective way to resolve conflict, you have established a minimum requirement for real dialogue. If the person or nation is willing to abide by this principle, then you can proceed. If not, you may have to break off the process until the other party is willing to do so.

Mixed Signal: The intent is part-conciliation, part-domination. Often it seems powerful to send a mixed signal, to keep your adversaries off guard, to not let them know what you are actually intending to do. Yet this kind of mixed signal easily leads to misinterpretation. The other party hears the part of your signal that seeks dominance and begins to escalate, setting off a dangerous spiral. Mixed signals between nations often lead to war, because each interprets the other's actions in terms of the worst-scenario fear.

When dealing with a mixed signal, set limits on the part that seeks to dominate and encourage the part that seeks to accommodate. Don't acquiesce and don't escalate. Seek to be as steady and unwavering as possible, encouraging the other party to cooperate by pointing out the advantages of a mutually beneficial agreement.

Cooperation: The intent to achieve real peace based upon mutual gain. The intent to seek a mutual gain has nothing to do with trusting blindly or being naive about the potential for harm. It does not mean that you agree with the other party's point of view, succumb to their opinion, or condone what they are doing. Rather, the willingness to be cooperative simply recognizes that by finding inclusive solutions which reconcile the interests of both parties, it is possible to gain a larger mutual benefit than you might otherwise.

Tool Two: LOOK . . . For Increased Understanding.
Definition: *Look at both perspectives. Start with where you agree, then where you disagree and your underlying assumptions.*

Seek to get a comprehensive picture of how each side sees the conflict. Try to look at the dispute from both perspectives. Ask the other person about his or her view of the conflict. Find out about his or her perspective and express your own.

Keep your mind open. Practice inquiry. You might begin with a round of listening and restating alternative points of view. This will allow you to clarify the juxtaposition of conflicting positions: Person A speaks. Person B restates. Person B speaks. Person A restates. (Review the section on "Skills for the Art of Dialogue" for a complete discussion of listening and restating.) It is particularly important to apply the practice of dialogue to a conflict situation. Looking both ways, you will begin to get a sense of the larger picture.

After you have done a set of opening statements of point of view, then start with where you can agree. So often in conflicts, we focus only on the area of disagreement. For example, a husband and wife may agree 90 percent on how to raise their children, but when they get into a fight, they will only focus on the other 10 percent that is in conflict.

By looking at where you agree, you can often shift the tone of the exchange and build a common basis of understanding. This allows you to deal more effectively with the more difficult areas of conflict.

Next, look at where you disagree. After establishing areas of mutual agreement, it is often quite possible to look at the areas of disagreement in a more inclusive, less combative manner. Examine the areas of real disagreement as opposed to perceived disagreement based upon stereotyping. So often in conflicts we are shadow boxing — fighting as much with what we think the other person represents as with the reality.

Getting clear on where you disagree is a major step

toward understanding the roots of the conflict. It helps to get all of the cards on the table, so that both parties can better see and appreciate what is at the basis of your differing positions.

Finally, examine the underlying assumptions of both parties. Our underlying assumptions compose the frame of reference through which we see and interpret the data of our experience. They are, as biologist Ken Norris puts it, "our windows to the world." Input from the outside world is filtered through our basic assumptions. One person's "fact" is another person's propaganda, depending upon the assumptions we have made.

For example, when one person assumes that the Soviet Union is an expansionistic empire driven by communist ideology, with an elite ruling class which justifies its existence by expanding the outside boundaries of the country; and the other person assumes that the Soviet Union is a peace-seeking nation that is driven by fear, ravaged by World War II, and determined to be defensively prepared; then their perceptions of the meaning of various actions by the Soviet Union will vary accordingly.

What are the roots of the disagreement in your conflict? Explore the underlying assumptions of both parties. What is your data and what is the source of your data? Is this information that you know firsthand? How is it that you believe this and I believe that? Do we have a different data base? Or are we interpreting the data differently based upon our different windows of perception?

Tool Three: LISTEN . . . For the Real Interests of Both Parties.

Definition: *Seek to determine the real concerns and needs behind the positions.*

In their book, *Social Conflict,* psychologists Dean Pruitt and Jeffrey Rubin described how the Camp David talks in 1978 produced a breakthrough between Israel and Egypt. When both countries sat down to negotiate at Camp David, it appeared their positions were absolutely irreconcilable.

Egypt demanded the immediate return of the entire Sinai Peninsula, which Israel had occupied since the 1967 Middle East War. Israel refused to consider returning even a small part of the occupied territory.

So long as the conflict was defined in terms of their two positions, no agreement could be reached. A compromise proposal in which each nation would control half of the Sinai was completely unacceptable to both sides. The breakthrough came when each nation expressed its real interest and underlying goal. What Israel really wanted was the military security that the Sinai provided, while Egypt was primarily interested in having sovereignty over it. The gridlock was broken. The two countries were able to reach an inclusive solution: Israel would return the Sinai to Egypt in exchange for a demilitarized zone in the Sinai maintained by United Nations' troops. Both countries achieved their respective goals in a fashion that was mutually satisfying and significantly reduced hostilities.

There is a fundamental cultural shift going on in the way we negotiate and bargain with each other to solve our conflicts. It is a shift from the old way of positional bargaining to a new way of interest bargaining. In positional bargaining, negotiations are viewed as a contest or struggle where one side will emerge victorious and the other will be defeated. In interest bargaining, both sides are willing to work together to achieve solutions that meet the goals and concerns of each one.

This change is happening at the roots of our culture — through neighborhood mediation boards and community conflict-resolution centers; policymakers working for common security and labor negotiators using mediation; corporations applying innovative methods for conflict management and universities offering programs in conflict-resolution theory; and ecologists, educators, psychologists, and other professionals teaching interdependent modes of thinking and problem-solving.

The essential step in interest bargaining is to look behind the positions to address the underlying goals and concerns.

What does the other party really require behind what they say they want — e.g. their current stance? What is their real motivation? What is driving the content of their position?

Start by listening to what is true for the other person or party in the conflict. What are his or her real concerns? Seek to distinguish between the real interests and the current positions about how to achieve those interests. Do not assume that you know what the other party's real concerns are; rather, ask questions to find out. The more you listen with undivided attention, the more you will be able to discern what underlies the other person's position or stance. You will begin to hear what is unspoken, the unexpressed needs and concerns.

Frequently, conflicts between individuals or nations cannot be healed or adequately resolved simply by dealing with the material interests that are at stake. It is also important to listen to the psychological underpinnings of what is happening, because often the objective interests are only part of what the fight is about. Never discount the importance of the psychological need which may also be operating in the other party. Listen for the difference between the psychological and the material dimensions of the conflict. This is a key distinction for learning to listen to someone with a very different point of view, someone whose version of the "objective facts" is likely to be very different from your own.

Tool Four: DISCOVER . . . Mutually Workable Solutions.

Definition: *Formulate inclusive options that meet the real needs and interests of both parties.*

You are looking for the overarching or umbrella solutions that address as many of the goals and concerns of both parties as possible. You are seeking to frame an agreement which is fair and durable, because both parties recognize that it is fundamentally in their best interest. Here are four different ways to arrive at workable solutions based upon mutual gain:

Meeting in the Middle. Here both parties recognize that

the stakes are high, and they are willing to be flexible in order to find the middle ground. Both parties become aware that the negative consequences of going to war with each other are far greater than the fear of loss from the give-and-take of compromising.

Conflicts may arise where finding a solution requires a compromise from one's ideal plan in order to avoid a battle. Take the example of divorced parents who share custody of their young daughter. They are bitterly divided about what to do about her schedule. Yet, in the course of their dealings, they both come to realize that they share one overarching goal: both want to provide a consistent and supportive atmosphere for her so that she will grow up healthy and happy.

Within the context of this shared goal, they have different positions. The mother thinks it is best for her daughter to stay at home and get as much nurturing as possible. The father thinks it is best for his daughter to go to pre-school and develop her skills with other children. If they fight it out, the child and ultimately both parents will lose. So they compromise. Their daughter goes to pre-school three days a week part-time. This way she begins to develop friendships with other children, while having some full days at home. Neither of the parents gets exactly what they initially wanted, but both receive far more in terms of their child's well-being than if they fought it out.

This kind of compromise is a distributive solution: 50/50 — I will meet you halfway. This is the method which most people think of when they hear phrases like "mutual gain" or "win/win," but in fact compromise is often the court of last resort. There are at least two other methods which in many situations may produce a larger joint benefit for all concerned parties.

Expanding the Fixed Pie. Often in conflicts, we assume that there is only a fixed amount of gain or profit, and that in order for me to win something I want, you must necessarily lose. There are of course many actual win/lose situations in our lives — in job promotions, admissions to college, sports and contests of all kinds, and in war. But we need not generalize from these experiences to include the whole spectrum.

By assuming that most conflicts are win/lose, we miss the point that almost always there is an overarching need to co-exist with the other person, interest group, or nation. The relationship itself has value to us, and the consequences of treating the conflict solely as a contest (I win/you lose) are not in our own best interests. Often when we are faced with conflicts which require us to be both competitive and cooperative, we focus only on the competitive aspect.

Max H. Bazerman in his article, "Why Negotiations Go Wrong," pointed out that this competitive orientation "produces a distributive rather than an integrative approach to bargaining." He used the classic example of the two sisters and the single orange, first presented by Mary Follett many years ago. One sister wants to make orange juice, the other wants to make a cake. After fighting over their single orange, they agree to a distributive compromise. Each sister takes half the orange. Thus one ends up with a very small glass of juice, and the other with a very small cake.

Dr. Bazerman's point is that the sisters overlooked what he called "an integrative solution" to their conflict. The first sister takes all the juice and the other takes all the peel. In this way, both get exactly what they want and twice as much as they did in the compromise solution. Often the pie is not as fixed as it appears because the real interests of the two parties can be reconciled and thereby yield a larger mutual gain than through simple compromise.

A small branch of the Perpetual Bank sits on the corner of Columbia and 18th Street, N.W. in the Adams-Morgan section of Washington, D. C. The bank building is noticeable because of its rather striking architecture. Built in a horseshoe shape, the bank is located at the very back of a large, pie-shaped lot, leaving the front part open as a large plaza. On weekends, an open-air market fills this plaza with booths, goods of all kinds, and people buying and selling. This arrangement is the innovative solution which two opposing forces reached in what was once a bitter zoning battle.

At the turn of the nineteenth century, this centrally located parcel of land was occupied by a theater, which collapsed in a snow storm. The old theater was torn down and the vacant lot became the place where craftspeople and farmers from outside the city came to sell their goods on weekends. This tradition of the open-air market continued for a few decades, until the bank bought the property in the 1950s and made plans to erect a bank building on the lot. Intense negotiations between the bank and the neighborhood residents produced the horseshoe design which met the conflicting needs of both parties.

In this case, both parties got exactly what they wanted and more: the bank got its building and increased goodwill in the community, and the residents, while keeping their open-air market, also expanded their local tax base.

Reframing the Situation. Sometimes it appears that people or nations of opposing views have come to an irreversible impasse. Yet, when we separate their real interests from their current positions, we can discover a larger frame of reference which offers new possibilities.

Consider the example which Roger Fisher and William Ury gave in their book, *Getting to Yes.* Two men are quarreling in a library. One wants the window open and the other wants it closed. They bicker back and forth about how much to leave it open: a small crack, halfway, three-quarters. No solution satisfies either of them. Enter the librarian. She asks the first man why he wants the window open. "To get some fresh air," he says. "It's stuffy in here." She asks the second man why he wants the window closed. "To avoid the draft," he says, "because I have a cold."

The librarian opens a window in the next room, bringing in fresh air without a draft. Thus both men obtain exactly what they want by reframing the situation, seeing it through the eyes of the librarian, a third and more inclusive frame of reference. Once you learn both sets of real goals and real concerns, then it is possible to discover new options through seeing the conflict from a larger and more comprehensive frame of reference.

Remember the story of the old man who wills his seventeen camels to his three sons and creates a seemingly irresolvable conflict. Then the village sage gives them his one camel, and the eighteenth camel transforms the situation. This is an example of how when we increase our frame of reference to take in new elements, a transforming possibility can emerge. When we reframe a conflict by holding the perspective of one point of view together with another point of view, then new insight and new data emerges. This new insight and data gives us access to more inclusive options.

These four tools for the constructive use of conflict are applicable to many levels of life. They are not panaceas or magical solutions. As we have seen, their usefulness derives from one's clear intention to resolve disputes in a mutually acceptable fashion. Used on a regular basis, the four tools will help you break old patterns and transform the way you deal with conflict.

Practice For Winning:
A Summary

Principles For a New Kind of Victory
Principle One: Interdependence
Definition: Everyone and everything is interconnected as part of the living Earth. We are bound together in a web of mutuality.

Principle Two: Consequences
Definition: We reap the consequences of our actions. For every action, there is a reaction.

Principle Three: Responsibility
Definition: The individual is the primary architect of human advancement. We all have a unique part to play.

Principle Four: Reciprocity
Definition: Treat yourself and others the way you want to be treated. Give what you want to get.

Steps For Shaping Our Future
Step One: Clear Vision
Definition: Seeing where we want to go. The ability to acknowledge what is, while sustaining a vision of what can be.

Step Two: Personal Integrity
Definition: Building the foundation for our vision. The sincere intent to match our words and our deeds, to be undivided in the resolve to achieve our goal.

Step Three: Open Inquiry
Definition: Exploring understanding from all directions. The

willingness to keep an open mind, to seek truth without prejudice, to inform ourselves from many points of view.

Step Four: Conscious Action
Definition: Taking the next step toward our vision. The commitment to take small actions, to make adjustments, and then take another step, again and again.

Skills For The Art of Dialogue
Skill One: Establish Ground Rules.
Definition: At the outset, express your commitment to listen and to learn with mutual respect. See if the other will agree to proceed using these guidelines.

Skill Two: Listen with Empathy.
Definition: Listen with undivided attention to the other person, regardless of whether you agree with his or her beliefs, ideas, or mind set. Try to put yourself in the other person's place.

Skill Three: Restate with Understanding.
Definition: Mirror back your understanding of what the other party is saying, free from your opinions and judgments. Then, find out what you omitted or need to correct in order to obtain a complete understanding.

Skill Four: Speak Your Truth.
Definition: Express your point of view, as both an advocate for what you think is true and an empiricist who inquires after more data and increased understanding.

Tools For Transforming Conflict
Tool One: STOP ... Take a Step Back.
Definition: Step back from the conflict. Establish your intention and seek to determine the intention of the other.

Tool Two: LOOK ... For Increased Understanding.
Definition: Look at both perspectives. Start with where you agree, then where you disagree and your underlying assumptions.

Tool Three: LISTEN ... For the Real Interests of Both Parties.
Definition: Seek to determine the real concerns and needs behind the positions.

Tool Four: DISCOVER ... Mutually Workable Solutions.
Definition: Formulate inclusive options that meet the real needs and interests of both parties.

Getting To
The Great Turning

*If the human race wishes to have a prolonged and
indefinite period of material prosperity, they have only
got to behave in a peaceful and helpful way toward
one another, and science will do for them all they wish
and more than they can dream.*
— Winston Churchill —

*Everywhere women ... are concerned with the direction
that we are taking. They want to know what they
can do. To them ... I say, "Educate yourselves.
Draw on the values and capabilities that have made
women strong. Then set America and the world on
the path towards peace."*
— Jihan Sadat —

*This is the true joy in life, the being used for a purpose
recognized by yourself as a mighty one. ... Life is no
"brief candle" to me. It is a sort of splendid torch
which I have got hold of for the moment, and I want
to make it burn as brightly as possible before handing
it on to future generations.*
— George Bernard Shaw —

*There are no passengers on Spaceship Earth.
Everybody's crew.*
— Marshall McLuhan —

*No one can grant freedom to anyone else. Gandhi's
act [the march to the sea for salt], however symbolic
and inspiring, only liberated those who had the courage
to take action of their own. ... Like the salt on India's
shores, our power is there for the taking ...*
— Marilyn Ferguson —

*There are only two powers in the world, the sword
and the spirit. In the long run, the sword will always
be conquered by the spirit.*
— Napoleon Bonaparte —

*When human lives are endangered, when human dignity
is in jeopardy, national borders and sensitivities become
irrelevant. Wherever men or women are persecuted
because of their race, religion or political views, that
place must — at that moment — become the center of
the universe.*
— Elie Wiesel —

*These techniques of finding common ground . . . will
be very useful. . . . I think it would be interesting for
American policymakers and Soviet policymakers to
try this process out . . . to see what kind of common
ground they could find. . . . It's a useful process in
helping to achieve a consensus about what an arms
control agreement would look like, or whatever the
particular issue . . .*
— Anne Cahn —

It was the second day of a mediated dialogue we facilitated involving one hundred citizen representatives and national security experts from around the United States. Dr. Angelo Codevilla from the Hoover Institute and Dr. Anne Cahn from the Committee for National Security were having an intense exchange about whether the Soviet Union had attained superiority in the arms race. Dr. Codevilla argued that during the 1970s the United States had fallen behind the Soviet Union in certain critical areas of our national defense. He cited extensive data to support his point of view. Dr. Cahn took the view that the United States had not only maintained parity in the 1970s, but also kept the lead in certain important areas. She too cited extensive data to support her opinion.

As each disagreed more vehemently with the other, they began to lock into an escalating spiral. This kind of verbal "gun fight" is the opposite of open inquiry. It hardens the positions, increases defensive reactions, and narrows the scope of thoughtful exchange. In a heated situation like this there is a threshold level where the hardening of positions makes it quite difficult to return to a more reasonable interchange. Without skillful facilitation, the room can quickly turn into a battlezone and spin out of control, much the way nation states escalate into war. Colonel Tim Klug, the commanding officer of Marine Corps Air Station, Camp Pendleton, spoke up:

> This to me is the perfect example (of) . . . our process here . . . (and) the efforts we've made with one another to see different points of view. . . . I was personally involved as a staff member [in the Pentagon] . . . in counting these things and figuring out what the counts would be and so on. I know for a personal fact that Anne's numbers are precisely exact. I also know Angelo's statements are precisely exact . . .
>
> I just ask you to remember . . . the facts are not the end point. They are the starting point. They are important to get correct, but what is far more important is to understand the meaning of those facts in the largest possible frame of reference . . .

His comment was greeted by a spontaneous round of applause from the room. When the dialogue resumed, the tone had shifted to one of respect and open inquiry. As a result, there was a real exchange of information between the participants and an increased understanding. This kind of mediated dialogue can provide the basis for a politics of interdependence. As Bruce Berlin, founder of the Trinity Forum, expressed it: "Each time any one of us is able to facilitate or inspire real communication between adversaries, we all move forward one step."

"Getting to the Great Turning" offers a broad strategy for the 1990s of how we can break the gridlock and help shift our decision-making to respond to the realities of interdependence. It provides a new model of mediated dialogue which enables parties or nations of differing views to build consensus. It offers strategies to build a dialogue movement, methods to create more peace in one's life, and ways to help restore the natural environment. It is a call to all of us to create the beginning of a Great Turning by the onset of the twenty-first century.

CHAPTER ELEVEN

Architects Of
A New Era

*When the building materials are all prepared and
ready, the architects will appear.*
— Walt Whitman —

In 1787, the founders of American democracy drafted
the U.S. Constitution "to secure the blessings of liberty for
ourselves and our posterity." They were the architects of a
new era of self-governance and human freedom, based upon
the proposition that all people are created equal, with the
right to life, liberty, and the pursuit of happiness.

During the last two centuries, many individuals and
groups have fought to secure these rights for themselves —
to make the initial vision real for increasing numbers of
people. Slowly, the narrow grip of privileged interests has
been loosened to now include women and men of different
economic, racial, and religious backgrounds. The reality of
our social and legal structure has begun to correspond to
the ideals of the Constitution.

Now, two hundred years later, we stand at the threshold
of a new period. Confronting the threats to our future, who
will be the architects of human survival and dignity? Who
will help to build the ethical foundation for a twenty-first
century that is not steeped in oppression and destruction?

Like the founders before us, our generation is called to
renew the roots of democracy and to reaffirm the highest
values of human will and spirit, dedicated to building a
more secure and peaceful future. We are challenged by our

historical circumstances to be the architects of a new era of human dignity and world peace.

Crisis As Opportunity

It is in meeting the great tests that mankind can most successfully rise to great heights. Out of danger and restless insecurity comes the force that pushes mankind to newer and loftier conquests. . . . The real solutions come from conquering difficulty, not avoiding it.

Isaac Asimov

There is an ancient story about a peasant village in China. The village was poor and was therefore known as an unfortunate village. One man in the village had a horse so he could plough more fields than anyone else. This man was known as the fortunate man in the village. Then one day, the man's horse ran away, and he was known as the unfortunate man in the village. Two days later, the man's horse returned and brought with it a wild horse from the mountains. Then the man was known as the fortunate man once again. Three days later, the man's son tried to ride the wild horse and was thrown off and broke his leg. Then the man was known as the unfortunate man in the village. One week later, the press gangs came through town to take all the able-bodied men to war, and they didn't take the man's son, because he had a broken leg. Then the man was called the fortunate man once again . . .

As this old wisdom-tale illustrates, it is difficult to judge the meaning of events in our lives until we come to understand the outcome, or consequences. We have all experienced seeming tragedies, or mishaps, which turn out to be blessings in disguise. Is the development of nuclear weapons, or the current environmental crisis, fortunate or unfortunate? The answer awaits the unfolding of future historical events. Whether our common danger is ultimately judged as fortunate or unfortunate is a function of how the human race responds to the evolutionary pressure and challenge that these threats exert. "Pain comes from seeing how arrogant you've been," writes the poet Rumi, "and pain brings you out of that conceit." The pain of the threat to life can serve to bring us out of our current arrogance and conceit.

Our word *crisis* comes from the Greek *krisis* and means: "1. a serious or decisive state of things . . . when an affair must soon terminate or suffer a material change; 2. in medicine, the turning point in the course of a disease, which indicates recovery or death." The Chinese character for the word *crisis* is composed of two symbols: one meaning *danger*, the other *opportunity*. Just as the danger we face is unprecedented, so the opportunities to create and come together in new ways are unprecedented. Just as this moment in history can become the greatest tragedy, so it can also be a doorway to the greatest victory.

By believing that things are hopeless, we overlook the immense possibility implicit in our time. The future need not lead to collective death and destruction. When we respond to our common danger by shutting down, we do not see the other half of the story. Often we act as though the game is lost, but it is not true. We are still here, quite alive and orbiting the Sun on our blue sphere. To paraphrase Mark Twain's famous remark, "The well-publicized reports of our demise are premature."

Have you observed the phenomenon that most people respond to crisis with great energy and commitment? The crisis is a kind of wake-up call. It punctuates the habitual patterns of daily life and calls us to a larger purpose. When the flood waters are rising, most of us do not hesitate to start lifting sandbags. And have you noticed that often in crisis the sense of community is heightened, that the recognition of a shared danger brings us together?

A few years ago there was a major flood in Northern California. It rained torrents for days and all the rivers and canals overflowed. Cars and people were stranded, traffic lights went out, the electricity went dead, bridges collapsed, and whole mountainsides slid down and buried houses. Things ground to a halt.

And yet, everywhere one could see people offering assistance — shoveling and putting up sandbags, talking to each other about the flood, pulling other people out of the muck. One young man who had a four-wheel drive truck with a winch spent two days driving around looking for cars and passengers who were trapped and then pulling them out. He said it was one of the best times in his life.

Crisis often brings out the best qualities in human beings. Crisis is the opportunity we have been waiting for to be fully alive. Just as necessity is the mother of invention, crisis is often at the root of evolution and innovative change. Crisis evokes and strengthens the lifeforce within us — the will to survive and to transcend our dangerous circumstances.

Because the common danger threatens everyone, it offers an unprecedented opportunity to come together. Each one of us is asked to do his or her unique part. Passivity will not suffice. If your small child were teetering on the edge of a swimming pool, you would do whatever you needed to do to make certain your child was safe. What we see to do, we are called to do.

A Renaissance of Human Dignity

Every era of renaissance has come out of new freedoms for peoples. The coming renaissance will be greater than any in human history, for this time all the peoples of the earth will share in it.

Pearl Buck

In the early 1980s, Robert J. Ringer wrote a book entitled, *How You Can Find Happiness During the Collapse of Western Civilization.* Mr. Ringer, who is also the author of the best-selling, *Looking Out for Number One,* began this second volume with a chapter called "Apocalypse Now." He argued that the rise of crime, violence, suicide among teenagers, and drug abuse all point to the decay of our civilization.

The shrewd individual, he said, will be able to carve out an island of security and success even as the continent of Western values and society is sinking.

This kind of thinking exemplifies what many have called the "Me Decade," a period in which the primary values have been based upon an attitude of "Me First — I can make it big in this life while you are suffering beside me." It has been a period that has celebrated individual success and self-improvement, but with little concern for the fabric of community or the welfare of the less fortunate. Success and the pursuit of self-interest are worthy goals. But if "Me First" is pursued to the exclusion of taking any responsibility for the well-being of one's community, one's nation, and one's environment, then we are in trouble.

A recent article from the Associated Press, entitled "Homeless Join Briefcase Crowd," described how New York City's homeless have found relief from the streets in the lobbies of some of Manhattan's most luxurious midtown office skyscrapers.

> The atriums were designed to be oases for office workers and passing pedestrians, but during the last few years the growing ranks of the homeless have sought comfort and shelter there, especially during the winter.
>
> While commuters rush quickly past "street people" who dwell in the city's subway stops, bus stations, and train terminals, the presence of homeless in the polished glass and steel symbols of corporate America seems harder to ignore.
>
> The juxtaposition of wealth and poverty is striking in the lobby of Park Avenue Plaza, a 45-story building between 52nd and 53rd streets off Park Avenue.... Under a waterfall and a forest of ficus trees, professionals in pin-striped suits eat $7.95 tortellini salad at an open-air cafe, while nearby dozens of ragged homeless men and women sleep, play cards, or stare aimlessly into space.

Peter Russell, in *The Global Brain*, used the metaphor of a cancer cell. The cells of a healthy body function in an interdependent fashion. Each cell makes its unique contribution to the whole system and sustains the health of the body. A cancerous cell is one that has gone astray; it is only serving its own interest of expansion, without a harmonious relationship to the entire body. Ultimately, cancer, like many parasites, kills its host and thus kills itself.

During the last century or so, much of human behavior might well be compared to cancerous cells. Individuals, as well as nations, have acted largely as if we were isolated units driven by competition and the desire to dominate. We have blindly and urgently used up natural resources and lived as though there were no tomorrow. Short-term immediate gain has driven most of us without a great deal of concern for the long-term consequences.

More and more people are recognizing that the values of "Me First" are not sufficient to solve the problems of our time. Instead of a book on happiness and the collapse of Western civilization, we need to operate in the spirit of a book entitled: *How You Can Find Happiness and Contribute to the Renaissance of Western Civilization.*

In a provocative article in the *Washington Post*, "The Coming of the 'We' Decade," Paul Taylor argued that there is "a yearning for national community and moral uplift." Taylor pointed to events like Hands Across America as representative of the early signs of a deep shift in our national psyche. Hundreds of thousands of Americans gathered on a Sunday afternoon in 1987 to join hands across the U.S.A. in an unprecedented display of national concern to end hunger. Similarly, the participation of leading rock stars and entertainers in a series of events, including We Are the World, Live Aid, Farm Aid, and the Amnesty International Rock Tour, point to a very different set of values than "Me First." These concerns reached millions of people and raised tens of millions of dollars for the hungry and homeless, for debt-ridden farmers and prisoners of conscience around the world.

After a decade or more in which ideals like "the betterment of all" or "compassion for the less fortunate" have been considered out of fashion or contrary to shrewd self-interest, a profound change in our national mood is under way. As Taylor puts it:

> Instead of Me-Decade materialism and muscular patriotism, the new mood seems to be about things like a national sense of community, moral revival, civic virtue, and the imperative of doing good.

The emergence of a "We" era is based upon the acknowledgment by ever-widening circles of people that the chances for real happiness are far better by reviving our commitment to the best of human values, restoring the environment which sustains our lives, and dedicating ourselves to a renaissance of human dignity and creativity.

Our challenge is no less than to rebuild and fashion a community of common resolve and mutual respect. We are challenged to reconstruct the foundations of decency and renew the bonds of trust and tolerance between individuals and groups, within neighborhoods and cities. We are asked to generate better understanding and unity of purpose across races, creeds, and factions of different points of view.

When the Founders gathered at the Constitutional Convention 200 years ago, they were divided between anti-Federalists, who believed that "character and virtue," the willingness of the individual to put the good of the community ahead of his or her private interests, should form the basis of the new American government; and Federalists, who believed in the "new science of politics," which held that self-interest was the necessary foundation of all political life.

Today, what is needed is an artful balance between self-interest and the public good. The imperative of our global survival requires that our own self-interest cannot be separated in the long run from the interests of the world. The key is both: both personal happiness and environmental health; both personal security and the security of reducing the threat of global war; both winning at our own lives and winning together for our world. The chances for real happiness are far better by renewing our commitment to the best of human values, and by dedicating ourselves to a renaissance of human dignity.

The Baby Boomers' Moment

You can't always get what you want, but if you try somehow, you just might find, you get what you need.

Mick Jagger

This book addresses "our generation" in the broadest sense of everyone who is living on Earth now at the end of the twentieth century. By virtue of our living at this time in history, we bear a special responsibility. Should there be such a rupture in human history — whether through ozone depletion or nuclear winter — it could disrupt or destroy human civilization as we know it. In this sense, we are the bridge between all that has been created by past generations and the continuity of future generations.

We, the authors, would like to address for a moment another generation, the "Baby Boom" generation born in the aftermath of World War II. Without in any way diminishing the responsibility that people of all ages have, we want to take notice of the particular responsibility and immense opportunity which the Baby Boom generation can play in making the Great Turning come to pass.

Soon the country will be in the hands of this "Boomer" generation, the 76 million Americans who were born in the aftermath of World War II between 1946 and 1964. Baby Boomers are the largest grouping in the population, the pig in the python, a moving bulge that affects everything as it goes through the different stages of life. When the Boomers began to graduate from universities in 1968, there were feature articles in major national publications. When the leading edge of the generation began to turn 40 in 1986, *Time* (May 19, 1986) and other national press ran cover articles. According to *Time*, the Boomer generation "represents some 60 percent of the electorate." Perhaps more than any other group, if for no other reason than sheer size and potential influence, the Boomers should begin to take responsibility for shaping our world.

Those of us who grew up in the 1950s and '60s were the children — at least those of us who were white and middle class — of postwar prosperity, television and freeways, rock 'n roll and jet airplanes. Everyone born after 1945 has been haunted by the specter of the atom bomb. Many of us can remember doing "duck and cover" exercises under our desks in elementary school. We sensed that the future was never really ours, not the way it had been for our parents. The atomic blasts at Hiroshima and Nagasaki made anything possible. Whatever we built in our lives could be taken away from us in a blinding flash. We grew up with that knowledge, though we rarely, if ever, spoke of it.

Occasionally there would be a rash of "end of the world" movies or "save the world" protests, but mainly we learned the taboo — not to speak up, to deny the danger. We learned to live behind a veil of unspoken fear and insecurity. We learned to live in a hurry, trying to get all that we could out of the world just in case it might explode. Janis Joplin, rock star and symbol of the 1960s, died in her twenties singing, "Get it while you can."

Our parents' generation fought and defeated the Nazis in World War II; they won a great victory for the continuation of human freedom. Their generation rebuilt a war-ravaged Europe under the Marshall Plan, brought a new democratic constitution to Japan, and resisted the totalitarian advances of Stalin in the post-war years.

The Baby Boom generation, growing up in the wake of World War II, was raised with this powerful story of victory. John Wayne and Audie Murphy refought the great fight against evil on our movie screens. From the *Sands of Iwo Jima* to the *Guns of Navarone*, we relived the world war that we never experienced. We sat around the campfires of our collective imagination and retold the great stories: Patton versus Rommel in North Africa; Churchill and Roosevelt mobilizing the Allied forces; Eisenhower at Normandy; and our soldiers recapturing Europe inch by inch. We were immersed in this myth of victory.

Later, in the early 1960s, President Kennedy evoked these images of victory and reframed their meaning in his call for a "New Frontier." Kennedy sought to inspire a generation in the battle to end war:

> Let us examine our attitude toward peace itself. Too many of us think it is impossible. Too many think it unreal. But that is a dangerous, defeatist belief. It leads to the conclusion that war is inevitable, that mankind is doomed, that we are gripped by forces we cannot control.
>
> We need not accept that view. . . . No problem of human destiny is beyond human beings. Man's reason and spirit have often solved the seemingly unsolvable, and we believe they can do it again . . .
>
> Is not peace basically a matter of human rights — the right to live out our lives without fear of devastation — the right to breathe air as nature provided it — the right of future generations to a healthy existence?

But John F. Kennedy was killed. Those of us who were alive then can remember where we were and what we were doing when we first heard the news: President Kennedy was dead, November 22, 1963. This tragic loss profoundly affected our sense of hope and expectation for the future.

From 1963 to 1973, the murders of President Kennedy, Dr. Martin Luther King, Jr., and Senator Robert Kennedy; the Watergate scandal, and perhaps, most of all, the Vietnam War, left many of us bitter and disenchanted. Why had the world not responded to our youthful dreams of love and peace? What had happened to our sense of the victory we could win?

In 1988 many people in the United States commemorated the twenty-fifth anniversary of John F. Kennedy's death. A letter to the editor of *Time* written in the aftermath of the twentieth commemoration said:

> The greatness of John F. Kennedy does not lie in his accomplishments but in his ability to inspire ordinary

men and women to believe that they could make the world better. Kennedy's death was a tragedy because it denied Americans the chance to find out if we really were capable of improving life on this earth.

The assassination of President Kennedy did not take away from ordinary men and women the inspiration and opportunity to make the world a better place. True, if we believe that it did, then his death will be seen as a closing chapter. But it is incumbent upon us, the ordinary men and women, to make this world a better place, beginning with our own lives. No one else can do it. John F. Kennedy, had he lived, could not have done it for us. Nor can any other leader. It is our privilege and responsibility to be the ones to write the next chapter of our history.

The Two Great Journeys

We shall not cease from exploration
And the end of all our exploring
Will be to arrive where we started
And know the place for the first time.
                                    T. S. Eliot

There are two great quests which have largely framed the story of human advancement. One is the *journey of exploration* — the impulse of human consciousness toward expansion and discovery. It is the drive behind science and the yearning to reach out to new lands, new worlds, the next frontier. As astronaut Michael Collins said: "It's human nature to stretch, to go, to see, to understand. Exploration is not a choice, really, it's an imperative." In our time, the next stage of this journey was initiated by John F. Kennedy's declaration in 1961:

I believe that this nation should commit itself to achieving the goal, before this decade is out, of landing a man on the Moon and returning him safely to the Earth. . . . We set sail on this new sea because there is new knowledge to be gained and new rights to be won ... and used for the progress of all people.

The second great saga is the *journey of wisdom* — the impulse of human consciousness toward self-knowledge and compassion. It is the drive behind religion, the source of ethics, and the yearning to develop a more harmonious relationship between self and world. It is the ethical vision expressed by our poets and prophets across the centuries. In our time the next stage of this journey was perhaps most eloquently expressed by Dr. Martin Luther King, Jr.

> I have a dream, deeply rooted in the American dream, that my four little children will one day live in a nation where they will be judged not by the color of their skin but by the content of their character ...
>
> I refuse to accept the cynical notion that nation after nation must spiral down a militaristic stairway into the hell of thermonuclear destruction.... I have the audacity to believe that peoples everywhere can have three meals a day for their bodies, education and culture for their minds, equality and freedom for their spirits.

The journey of wisdom is the quest to know the human mind and spirit and to live with justice and compassion toward others and all life.

The journey of wisdom must provide the ethical basis for our journey to new worlds. For if we explore the solar system as plunderers and polluters, with no respect and reverence for the mystery of the universe, we shall have gained nothing. Commenting on the environmental crisis, a recent *Newsweek* stated:

> We have evolved down to the present with a set of cultural and biological imperatives totally inappropriate to our level of technology. When we see something good, we gobble it up; we procreate to the limits of our ecological niche and when we've made a mess in one place we try to pack up and move on. But there's nowhere else to go.

Until we learn the lessons from the threatened destruction of our own planet, we are not ready to voyage beyond.

During the last half-century, the nations of the world have armed themselves with ever more destructive weaponry, reaching a crescendo of heightened expenditures in recent years. By 1985, global military expenditures topped $800 billion per year. This is a level which many contend exceeds the economic and environmental base necessary to sustain it. Lester Brown, president of the Worldwatch Institute, writing in *State of the World 1986*, concluded that declining economic and environmental conditions in the United States and the Soviet Union are a result of the over-emphasis on military spending and a neglect of economic and ecological support systems, both within their own borders and worldwide.

"The Mars Declaration," which advocates a United States space program leading to the human exploration of Mars by 2010, has been signed by many eminent people, including Walter Cronkite, Jimmy Carter, and Senator Jake Garn of Utah; and endorsed by major publications from the *New York Times* to the *New Republic*. The Soviets apparently have committed themselves to going to Mars, regardless of what the United States decides. There is growing support in both countries for a joint U.S.-Soviet mission to Mars.

The price of such a mission is estimated at $100 billion. And what will it cost to restore our environment — to clean up our filthy seas, to purify our air, water, and soil, and to reverse the greenhouse effect? Most scientists agree that the environmental challenge is not simply a matter of stopping harmful actions, but also taking positive long-term steps to revitalize the Earth's ecology. And what will it cost to end hunger, to assist the poor nations of the world to develop in ways that are more just and ecologically sound?

Now we have arrived at a point in human development where the two journeys must converge. The two visions, of exploring our solar system, and developing our personal/ global potential are two halves of one larger whole. We cannot do one without the other. We cannot go to space, certainly not for the long-term, unless we renew our home base. If we continue to militarize our planet, then it is likely that the two journeys will be seen as competing against each other for scarce resources. Advocates of each will see the other as a threat to their primary vision. But if we can demilitarize, step by step, through mutual, verifiable, tension reduction, then the resources will be freed to do both. The trillions of dollars that we as a nation and a world are currently spending in the search for military security can be gradually redirected toward the beginning of a vast, new enterprise.

At the turn of the nineteenth century, the great philosopher, William James, called for "the moral equivalent of war." May we suggest that the elements of this moral equivalent, and of our vision for the next century, are already present — the twin frontiers of outer space and personal/global development. We are compelled to restore the quality of life and environment on Earth, and we are beckoned by circumstances and our own curiosity to explore our solar system. These two journeys are two halves of one larger vision.

Two hundred and fifty thousand miles from the Earth in a flat, dry plain called the Sea of Tranquility, there is a footprint of the first human to walk on the Moon. Millions of us watched our TVs in July 1969 as Neil Armstrong climbed down a ladder, cautiously tested alien soil, and spoke his historic words: "That's one small step for a man, one giant leap for mankind."

The landing on the Moon set the stage for human exploration of space. When President Kennedy evoked our imaginations and declared our nation's commitment to put a man on the Moon by the end of the decade, he was exercising the human capacity to shape the future. He was using the power of intention. From the perspective of history looking back, it seems logical, even inevitable, that the Apollo space ship would land on the Moon in July 1969. It would appear to be the result of a series of events, an unbroken chain of cause and effect. But this kind of reasoning misses the key point — the human variable, the underlying spark of intentionality.

There is a famous story about Babe Ruth, the great baseball player. Standing in the batter's box at a critical moment in the World Series, he raised his hand and pointed over the centerfield fence. On the next pitch, he hit a homerun over the fence where he had pointed. Whether the details of this story are true, the spirit of this legendary event offers a vivid image of the power of intention.

The future is a function of what we are able to imagine and create in the present. In 1984, Gene Rodenberry, the writer and producer of *Star Trek*, talked about how people thought he was crazy as he began producing the first episodes in the mid-1960s. The show was cancelled after three seasons because the general public thought it was too outlandish. Ironically, *Star Trek* was taken off the air during the same month that Neil Armstrong walked on the Moon. Later the show caught on with college students, and an entire generation began to incorporate the futuristic images. "In the 1960s when we were writing *Star Trek*," said Rodenberry, "we made up the most fanciful communications and space technologies we could think of. Now, twenty years later, these fantastic images are becoming reality."

A volcano erupted 3.6 million years ago in what is now Tanzania, spewing ash onto the surrounding plains. In 1979 Mary Leakey, the paleoanthropologist, found footprints embedded in the ash which she believed were those of our earliest known ancestors. It has been a long journey from the footprints in Tanzania to the footprints on the Moon.

The human species now stands ready to embark upon the exploration of the solar system and beyond. Through the use of intention we have the capacity to give direction to our lives and to influence the course of history. It is this capacity which, when dedicated toward our common survival and a mature respect for all life, can bring the human mind from adolescence to conscious adulthood.

Our challenge is to project victory — to live a positive vision of a healing revitalization which creates the foundation for a more secure twenty-first century. Over time we can cultivate a garden Earth, a place of dignity and joy, from which we can embark on our voyage to other worlds. There is no future in believing that something cannot be done. The future is in making it happen.

CHAPTER TWELVE

The Politics Of Interdependence

Once a photograph of the Earth, taken from the outside, is available ... a new idea as powerful as any in history will let loose.
— Sir Fred Hoyle, 1948 —

To create the future we want, we need to change our personal lives, and this change must be translated into the way we do politics. As we have also seen, our current decision-making process — the politics of narrow, short-term interests — cannot get us to where we need to go. Policies to address issues such as international security, national and global debt, environmental pollution, and lasting peace cannot be achieved by the kind of divisive and factionalized approach that now predominates. So long as we are divided against ourselves, we will not be able to formulate clear, consistent, and long-term policies toward overcoming the common danger. Hence, we must change the way our policies are formulated.

Those of us living in the twenty-first century will have to adjust to the reality of interdependence — global, national, personal — whether we like it or not, and whether it happens through conscious policies or painful resistance. The paramount issues of human survival require us to move beyond narrow factionalism to a politics of interdependence.

The consequences of not changing our current direction are far worse than any perceived risk of cooperating with people of opposing points of view. Our common goal and shared intention to build a more secure and peaceful future can bring us together across our differences to change the process of the way we interact and make policies. By communicating and problem-solving through mediated dialogue and conflict management, we can arrive at new and more inclusive solutions. To formulate such conscious policies, we must transform the gridlock of win/lose politics to a bipartisan, unified effort.

Leading By Example

So let us not be petty when our cause is so great. Let us not quarrel amongst ourselves when our nation's future is at stake. Let us stand together with renewed confidence in our cause — united in our heritage of the past and hopes for the future, and determined that this land we love shall lead all mankind into new frontiers of peace and abundance.
John F. Kennedy

As we approach the end of the twentieth century, it is timely for the people of the United States to re-evaluate our country's international goals with a view toward developing policies that are global in scope and worthy of our highest values. The superpower which takes the lead in helping other countries successfully address the dangers which threaten our collective future is the nation most likely to win the respect of the community of nations in the twenty-first century. To safeguard our own future, we must help secure other nations against the poverty, hunger, environmental degradation, and spiritual desperation that could precipitate a global catastrophe.

Since World War II the United States, in pursuit of its goal of maintaining freedom and opposing communism, has from time to time used means that contradict its underlying ends. Our government has supported foreign governments who opposed communism even though these governments acted in ways that violated fundamental principles of human rights.

If we who live in the United States want to promote democracy — and the conditions that foster human dignity and make democracy possible — then the methods and practice of our foreign policy need to reflect our underlying intention. Similarly, if we want to formulate clear, comprehensive policies between factions within this country, our methods of communication and negotiation with each other must reflect this goal.

We, the American people, have a special responsibility to play a leadership role in laying the foundations for a more secure and peaceful future. Let us be clear that when we say America can lead, we do not mean that our country must try to enforce its views on other nations. United States leadership must take place in concert with the other countries of the world and with respect for their self-determination. The United States must lead by example — not coercion through strength or intimidation. The United States must solve its own contradictions and conflicts and then it can help to facilitate the international community of nations toward more effective means of solving the conflicts that underlie the common danger.

There are at least three reasons why the United States bears this great responsibility: First, it is the most powerful nation on Earth; second, it has one of the most diverse populations of any nation, and third, it has a democratic system.

While there are two military superpowers in the world, only the United States is also a superpower in other important ways: economically, culturally, and politically. Although United States' power, wealth, and influence have declined in relative terms, our nation is still looked to for leadership in shaping the course of international events.

America is a country of immigrants who have come from all parts of the world to create a new nation. This makes the United States' society something of a microcosm of the planet, and an appropriate setting for learning how to better resolve the cultural, racial, and religious issues which divide the peoples of the world.

Finally, the democratic system of government in the United States has the potential to model a new level of problem-solving that is essential to success in a complex and interconnected world. In theory and sometimes in practice, we have developed a system of government which allows for the participation of the concerned individual. While greed and narrow interests have often abused the principles of democracy, we still recognize a tradition of shared values — a nation, as Lincoln put it, "conceived in liberty and dedicated to the proposition that all men are created equal."

In the past, when Americans have been threatened by a grave danger, we responded with decisive clarity and commitment. After the attack on Pearl Harbor by the Japanese, Americans demonstrated an undivided national resolve. We began to transform ourselves from a sleeping giant — a passive, isolated nation — into the recognized leader of the Western world.

In the aftermath of World War II, as the nations of Western Europe lay in smouldering ruins, the United States created the Marshall Plan to rebuild and protect our allies against Soviet expansion. When areas of the world were hit by natural disasters, American citizens often responded quickly and compassionately. Similarly, Americans have been instrumental in mobilizing worldwide campaigns to eradicate smallpox, polio, and malaria.

Since the time of the American Revolution, our nation has had a deep sense of historic mission. Now, in response to our common danger, the American people have a profound opportunity to initiate policies on behalf of our own national interests and the interests of global survival. As the most powerful democracy on Earth, the United States has a choice: we can misuse the power of the nation-state, or we can dedicate that power to the survival and enhancement of all life on Earth. Our country is in a unique position; we have both the national strength and the freedom of expression necessary to initiate a new direction.

Breaking the Gridlock

*Societies thrive not on the victory of factions over each
other, but on their reconciliation.*

Henry Kissinger

The common danger presents an ultimate test for democracy. The problems which must be addressed are so complex, and the solutions needed are so comprehensive, that our decision-making process requires nothing less than our full ingenuity and intelligence.

In a democracy the development of consensus — i.e., the widest spectrum of agreement — is critically important to being able to implement consistent policies over time. As we discussed above, the United States has often been ineffective in exerting its necessary leadership toward real peace and global security because of deep divisions within the country.

The current gridlock in our political process prevents us from resolving disputes through consensual approaches. As we have seen, there are several reasons for this inability to achieve broad public agreement for policies to defeat the common danger: the domination of narrow-interest groups; a divisive and adversarial political process; too much of a short-term focus; and the insufficient quantity and quality of citizen participation.

In their book, *Breaking the Impasse*, Lawrence Susskind and Jeffrey Cruikshank argued that our narrow, adversarial process is virtually paralyzed. For example, efforts to build waste treatment facilities for hazardous waste have been regularly defeated; even though almost everyone agrees they are needed, no one wants them in their community. Similarly, efforts to construct highways, prisons, mental health facilities, or housing for low-income families are stymied by a jungle of competing interests. Susskind and Cruikshank pointed out that these public disputes cannot adequately be resolved through a narrow, adversarial process in which one side wins and the other loses.

At a time when we need clear and steady leadership to address the common danger, we are in a traffic jam. Elections are not effective in settling policy disputes in a win/win way. Candidates sell themselves, not the issues, and many critically important issues cross political boundaries and therefore require broader cooperation from regional and national authorities. Public disputes often end up in the courts. Litigation is costly and tediously slow. Moreover, the courts see their role as interpreting the law, not reconciling conflicting interests to meet the needs of all parties. Referendums tend to present complex questions in overly simplified, win/lose terms. In short, we have very few means within our current political process to formulate bipartisan, comprehensive policies.

What is needed is a new process of decision-making that enables us to reach national consensus. This is necessary to reconcile different interests and mobilize a common effort in response to our common danger. The separation of powers provided by the American Constitution makes broad agreement necessary in order to achieve major change on any issue. James Madison, the primary author of the Constitution, wrote in the *Federalist Papers*: "We have deliberately created an inefficient system in order to keep men free." One cost of this freedom is the fact that without broad public consensus the government cannot take consistent and comprehensive action.

By "consensus," we do not mean unanimity, but rather a broad "super-majority" — probably at least two-thirds of the public and our leaders. For if our political factions cannot reach such broad agreement, there is no consistent basis upon which to shape long-term policies to defeat the common danger. The ability to reach consensus on the national level is the first and most essential step in breaking the gridlock. Consensus provides a broad-based and multi-partisan foundation for policy. It permits us to undertake consistent action across the fluctuations of different administrations. It enables our nation to undertake long-term initiatives which are more comprehensive in purpose and scope. It reconciles the competing interests of many groups under the overarching need for a coherent direction and a unified purpose.

Without consensus, we will not be able to overcome our current, political paralysis. No one political party or interest group can orchestrate policies that reconcile the interests necessary to address the threats to our future. For example, the cooperation of both environmentalists and industrialists is required to make rapid and substantial progress toward reversing the greenhouse problem. Or, cooperation between peace-through-strength and peace-through-disarmament groups is required to reach consensus about how to maintain national security while reducing the risk of global war.

We are at a point where nothing less than a fundamental change in how we conduct politics will be adequate to meet the challenge we face. We can break the gridlock by changing our national political process in a number of ways. First, there must be a heightened emphasis on the need to cooperate in order to solve problems. Individuals and interest groups must realize that the solutions they seek will be achieved more through cooperative dialogue than through adversarial competition. Citizens and politicians need to recognize that, in spite of our many differences, we face common threats which can only be solved by working together with others in our nation and around the world.

Second, we need a broad base of citizens who have more accurate, factual information about the threats to our future and a sound understanding of various points of view about how to approach these problems. We need more information and more insight. We need to increase our understanding from many different points of view. The way to do this is to have more people who are better informed become effectively involved in our societal decision-making process. Just as in ecology — the greater the diversity of species, the stronger the base of life — so too in democracy, the greater the participation of diverse perspectives in thoughtful and informed ways, the stronger the democratic process.

Third, the quality of our national political process will

improve as increasing numbers of citizens learn basic skills for dialogue and conflict resolution. This will allow more citizens and politicians to communicate and search for solutions more effectively across our differences.

Fourth, the transition from our current stalemate to a politics of interdependence will require a significant increase in the numbers of citizens who participate. The bad news is that currently only a very small percentage of Americans participate in shaping our public policies. The good news is that the active participation of everyone or even a majority of Americans is not necessary to create a Great Turning in our nation's direction.

Mediated Dialogue: A New Model

Have you not learned the most in your life from those with whom you disagreed — those who saw it differently than you?

Walt Whitman

If we are to practice the "politics of interdependence," we must develop new forms of political discourse which enable us to move beyond narrow adversarial interactions and focus on ways we can work together to achieve common goals. A wide variety of approaches must be tried so that we can develop the best possible methodologies to achieve this end. Some version of the standard debate format has traditionally been the basis for most interaction between citizens and/or politicians who hold different views on how to approach a problem. Yet, the debate format is too inefficient and too divisive to solve the complex problems that make up our common danger.

Project Victory, in conjunction with other groups such as Search for Common Ground and the Trinity Forum, has worked to develop and refine a set of ten steps for a "mediated dialogue." Mediated dialogues have some of the structure of a traditional debate, but the underlying purpose and focus is different. A mediated dialogue might be described as a "cooperative debate;" it shifts the intention from an adversarial win/lose mode to a collaborative search for common ground and new options. A brief look at the ten steps of a mediated dialogue provides one example of how issue discussion can be structured to facilitate open inquiry, increased exchange of information, and cooperative problem-solving. The methods and skills outlined in "Practice for Winning" have been applied here to create a new mode for political decision-making appropriate to our interdependent reality.

The purpose of this ten-step process is to create a climate of mutual respect, so that people of different points of view can work together to effectively problem-solve. By changing the intention or underlying motivation in the room from one of adversarial debate to one of shared commitment to listen and seek to discover common ground, unimagined new possibilities emerge. This is the key: as we change the intention, the process or way things are discussed is changed, and then the content of the discussion is altered as well. If the shared intention is to seek common ground, then the process of communication will be thoughtful, in an atmosphere of mutual respect and open inquiry. Out of this changed atmosphere, new ideas and new options emerge.

STEP ONE: *Identification of a topic that includes the concerns of all parties.* Topics of discussion which are slanted in a particular direction or towards a specific point of view make it difficult to reach out to a wide range of participants. The topic for dialogue must be one that is inclusive of the basic problems and goals as they are perceived by people with divergent views.

STEP TWO: *Agreement on the goal of the dialogue and the guidelines by which it will be conducted.* Participants acknowledge that the purpose of the dialogue is to focus on ways to cooperate and agree to follow certain guidelines which will facilitate that cooperation. Basic guidelines for a mediated dialogue include: listening carefully to others, using language that is precise as possible, observing time limitations, and being open to learning from other points of view.

STEP THREE: *Statement and definition of the initial positions of the participants.* Each of the participants takes a few minutes to define his/her basic views on the topic and to suggest initial positions for consideration by others in the dialogue. These opening statements focus as much as possible on specific steps that should be taken in response to the topic.

STEP FOUR: *Restatement of the initial position given by someone of a different point of view.* Each participant in the dialogue restates the major points made by a representative of another point of view. Restatements are very brief (one to two minutes) and give the highlights of what a previous person has said. The process of restatement continues until the person who made the original statement is satisfied that it is accurate. Brief questioning among participants will also be allowed to help understand positions that have been presented.

STEP FIVE: *Questioning by the facilitator and the audience that begins to prode for areas of agreement and disagreement.* The facilitator and/or any audience that is present asks questions of the dialogue participants in order to begin to identify specific ways that they agree and disagree. The facilitator makes sure that the questioning is informative and not argumentative and also makes note for everyone when clear positions are identified on various issues.

STEP SIX: *Identification by participants of areas of agreement and disagreement.* The facilitator states the items of agreement that have already been reached and then leads the participants in an exploration of other ways in which they agree and disagree. The facilitator helps them explore the range of differences that exist and then moves them on to other topics. Careful records are kept by a recorder and at the end of this session a list of initial agreements and disagreements is posted.

STEP SEVEN: *Examination of the areas of disagreement through*

a focus on the interests (or goals) behind the different positions.
The facilitator turns the dialogue to a consideration of some
of the issues where the participants have found disagreement.
They are asked to step back from their specific positions and
examine their underlying assumptions, their basic beliefs,
differences in their data bases, the sources of their information, and their fundamental goals. The facilitator notes where
there is agreement on what they are trying to achieve and
has participants expand on those areas.

STEP EIGHT: *Brainstorming led by the facilitator in which
participants seek to discover new options for meeting the shared
interests they have behind their policy disagreements.* One by
one the participants look at the agreements they found in
step seven and list as many different ideas as they can think
of about how some aspect of those common interests can be
met. Participants are encouraged to think together and create
new options. They do not critique ideas presented, but merely
brainstorm to look for as many new ideas as possible.

STEP NINE: *Identification of any new ideas (or options) that
are agreeable to all participants.* The facilitator directs the
dialogue to a consideration of new ideas that have emerged
that may be acceptable to all parties. Participants are urged
to look briefly at many different ideas in an effort to identify
as many as possible that are agreeable to all concerned.

STEP TEN: *Discussion by participants of specific ways which
they might work together after the conclusion of the dialogue.*
All points of agreement are summarized and dialogue participants consider specific steps they can take to work together
to implement the things on which they have agreed.

Personal Responsibility, National Integrity

*What the nation does is done also by each individual, and
so long as the individual continues to do it, the nation
will do likewise. Only a change in the attitude of the individual
can initiate a change in the psychology of the nation, the*

great problems of humanity were never yet solved by general
laws, but only through the regeneration of the attitudes
of individuals.

Carl Jung

The personal and the political are inextricably linked. Although our democracy is imperfect in many ways, there is a direct relationship between our values as a people and our policies as a nation. Our values as individuals taken together create the cultural context and the climate of public opinion in which our national policies are formed. If we want to change our policies, we must change our cultural values. And if we want to change our cultural values, we must begin by changing our lives as individuals. This change then feeds back into the political process.

Our current American democracy might be pictured as a reciprocal, feedback process between the decision-makers — political, corporate, and interests groups — and the citizens, with their personal and cultural values. Most commentators would agree that our elected officials generally reflect the substratum of values of their constituents; conversely, the effort by those who have power to manipulate and shape these values through advertising and economic/political policies is also obvious. Both are true.

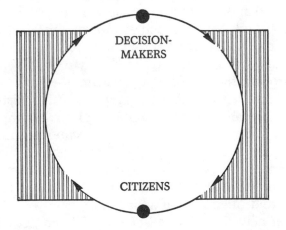

DECISION-
MAKERS

CITIZENS

If we are to mobilize the nation, individuals must take the initiative. There are many recent examples of individuals who have taken responsible leadership to influence national policy in ways that improve the quality of life. In 1980 Candy Lightner's thirteen-year-old daughter, Cari, was killed in an automobile accident caused by a drunk driver. She became so angry about the menace of drunk driving that she went to Washington, D.C. to protest at the White House in order to call attention to the issue. Her protest generated media attention and people began to contact her, asking what they could do. In response, she founded Mothers Against Drunk Drivers (M.A.D.D.)

M.A.D.D. has grown into a national campaign with chapters in 48 states. It has worked for tougher drunk-driving laws at both the state and national level. Largely because of M.A.D.D., over 400 laws have been changed across the country in the past eight years. Increasing numbers of people are no longer willing to be lenient toward drinking and driving. Mrs. Lightner's personal commitment helped to generate a movement of concerned people whose actions have changed values and laws all across the country. Her decision to focus her rage and her grief into constructive action has helped to prevent senseless tragedies for other families.

In the early 1980s, a group of conservative leaders became concerned that the American public was not being adequately informed about Soviet atrocities in Afghanistan. Under the leadership of Major General Milnor Roberts they formed the Committee for a Free Afghanistan which did extensive work around the country to educate the public, media, and political leaders about the war in Afghanistan. This educational campaign was influential in helping to win increased U.S. support for the Afghanistan resistance. Most observers agree that this support was one of the factors which led to the Soviet withdrawal. This is another example of how individual citizens can take initiative to change national and international situations.

In her new book, *When Technology Wounds*, Chellis Glendinning describes the story of Lois Gibbs, who emerged as the primary leader of the Love Canal effort to call attention to, and reduce hazardous waste. Love Canal was a canal that was seven miles long, built by William Love in the 1800s. It was sold in the 1920s and became a chemical disposal site, whose principle user was Hooker Chemical Company. In 1953, Hooker filled the canal and sold it to the Board of Education for one dollar. The Board of Education built a school on top of the disposal site, not believing there was any danger, and a community grew up around the school.

In 1978, people in the neighborhood began to realize that something was tragically wrong. There were miscarriages, birth defects, leukemia, other cancers, and respiratory problems. At the time, Lois Gibbs was a young housewife and mother of two children. She took the initiative to obtain redress for the community. She spoke, wrote letters, negotiated with state and federal officials, and eventually talked with President Carter. After two years of her tireless efforts, the government agreed to evacuate the families and replace their homes. Lois took her two children, both seriously ill, and moved to Arlington, Virginia, where she started the Citizens' Clearinghouse for Hazardous Waste, which today is the major national network to help people across the country take action to stop chemical contamination.

Our political process is based upon and reflects our societal values. These societal values are the reflection of our cumulative, individual behaviors. By changing our personal lives, we change the cultural foundation of our political process. If we intend to inspire and mobilize our nation to create policies that are truly responsive to the common danger, we must simultaneously begin to change our personal lives and our political process.

Changing Our Personal Lives — The goal here is to build a broadly-based cultural understanding of interdependence, and a shared recognition of the need for a new kind of victory. As tens of thousands of us begin to live a new way of managing conflicts to generate "I win/you win" outcomes, this will build the cultural and ethical foundation for the same shift to occur in the way we do politics. Similarly, as tens of thousands of us shift from the habit of waste to the practice of conservation, this change will be reflected in our political policies to achieve real environmental restoration.

Changing Our Political Process — The goal here is to build a shared ethical commitment across traditional lines of political ideology; to change our political process from the old win/lose adversarial mode to the politics of interdependence; and to use mediated dialogue and other forms of consensual decision-making to arrive at new and inclusive solutions to our common danger.

In many ways, the movement toward a politics of interdependence has already begun. Our culture increasingly recognizes that our common danger and its solutions are both rooted in interdependence, and this is being reflected in the American political process. Unfortunately, the conscious recognition of this interdependence is not growing as rapidly as the accelerating reality of the problems we face. Our task is to help speed up the recognition of the need for a new political process to break the gridlock of our current situation.

Massive financial and human resources must be put into educating the public about the common danger and the need for a politics of interdependence to overcome it. Both private and government resources must be brought to bear in this huge educational endeavor. We need to be realistic about the magnitude of this task. One does not change public attitudes in a country as large as the United States without an historic effort which is sustained over many years. But let us make it our goal that by the year 2000 we will have generated an irreversible momentum to implement policies based upon interdependence.

An Ethical Alliance

> *Man's capacity for justice makes democracy possible, but man's inclination to injustice makes democracy necessary.*
> Reinhold Niebuhr

Martin Niemoeller was a German Protestant minister who was seized by the Nazis and put in a concentration camp for his involvement in the resistance against Hitler. When he was released after the war, he was asked, "How did the Nazis manage to take power in Germany?" He responded:

> In Germany, the Nazis first came for the Communists and I didn't speak up because I wasn't a Communist. Then they came for the Jews and I didn't speak up because I wasn't a Jew. Then they came for the trade unionists and I didn't speak up because I wasn't a trade unionist. Then, they came for the Catholics and I didn't speak up — because I was a Protestant. Then they came for me and by that time, there was no one left to speak for me.

If in the late 1920s there had been a movement which built an ethical alliance among people of good will committed to stabilizing and strengthening the principles of democratic government in Germany — a coalition bringing together people of integrity across many points of view — Hitler and his terrorist thugs would never have been able to seize power.

Now, in the age of nuclear weapons and global environmental threats, when the fate of our Earth is at risk, we are challenged to build an ethical alliance committed to changing the way we interact with each other. We are challenged to move beyond the politics of gridlock and to address the paramount survival issues in ways that are thoughtful and inclusive of the relative insights of many points of view. We know that if we are going to survive and prosper, our politics and the advancement of human dignity must be interwoven into a tapestry of ethical development, and effective decision-making.

We need to create a spirit of good will and national reconciliation across political parties and points of view. Leaders from various traditions, disciplines, and ideologies who see the need for this change must take the lead in promoting it throughout the country. A relatively small group of committed leaders who bridge the traditional divisions can have a great impact in educating their groups on how our various factions are interdependent and how they must work together if our nation is going to craft coherent, consistent policies.

Although the information revolution and the global media provide us with ever-increasing amounts of knowledge about each other, many of us still live within narrow and somewhat isolated clubs of agreement. Many of us continue to define our experiences of community in terms of those with whom we agree or share the same world view, rather than in terms of those with whom we share humanity.

In almost every political or religious group, there are people with a sincere intention to live with integrity and to help create a better world. Similarly, in every belief system, there are individuals with little or no integrity, whose words and deeds do not match. Corruption and the willingness to abuse power cut across all ideological and ethnic distinctions.

By building an ethical alliance with those who have integrity — regardless of whether they currently agree or disagree with the content of our position — we create a different level of community. Here the victory is to be found not in setting our point of view into concrete, but in joining together with other individuals who share the common goal of advancing human dignity through changing the process of the way we relate to each other and formulate policy.

When the Great Turning comes to pass, it will not be as a result of the efforts of one particular group, political party, or religious tradition. It will happen because individuals of integrity across partisan and ideological lines recognize that the threats to our future compel us to acknowledge our shared ethical commitment to preserve and enhance life on Earth, and that all peoples and nations are allies in this struggle to achieve victory over the common danger.

CHAPTER THIRTEEN

What You Can Do

Never doubt that a small group of thoughtful, commit-
ted citizens can change the world. Indeed, it is the on-
ly thing that ever has.
— Margaret Mead —

The way to effect the future is by changing our thoughts
and actions in the present. A recent article in the *San Fran-*
cisco Chronicle vividly illustrates this insight:

> **Countdown Begins: 228 Years To Go**
> At Runnymede yesterday Queen Elizabeth planted an
> oak tree, in preparation for the 1,000th anniversary of the
> signing of the Magna Carta, in the year 2215.
> The tree planted by the queen — one of 60 planted
> by namesakes of medieval barons — should be 70 feet tall
> by then. The whole grove is intended to provide a
> background for ceremonies on the field below, where the
> document was signed.

By planting the small oak trees now, the British hope
to assure that the 1000th anniversary of the signing of the
Magna Carta in 2215 will be commemorated in the setting
of a mature oak grove. An American equivalent might be
planting small trees in Philadelphia in 1989 so that in 200
years, they will be fully grown for the 400th annivesary of
the signing of the U.S. Constitution. This is a profound
metaphor for our challenge — to take actions in the present
which will generate the conditions for a more secure and
compassionate world for future generations.

What are specific things that each of us can do on a regular basis to help create a Great Turning? A number of specific actions are discussed below which can be taken by every person who is concerned about the threats to our future. Most of them can be done on a regular basis without a great expenditure of either time or resources. All of them are examples of small, individual changes that will have enormous, positive consequences when practiced by large numbers of people. These suggestions are not intended to be complete. Hopefully, they will provoke you to think of other specific actions you can take in your life as well.

Just as "winning-peace" is not an end but a process, none of these actions is something we do once and for all. They are small actions which if done on a regular basis will enable us to turn our lives and our world.

Making a Personal Pledge

We are equal to whatever we resolve with full determination.
Thomas Jefferson

First and foremost, the Great Turning begins with each one of us when we step forward and say: "Yes, I will do my part." We are the fulcrum of the Turning. Just as our common danger is the result of the accumulated actions of individuals and nations, so too the Great Turning will happen as a consequence of the accumulated actions of individuals.

If we want our vision to come to pass, we must commit ourselves. A vision without commitment has no grounding in reality. The key phrase in Jefferson's quote above is "full determination." Divided and pulled in different directions, little is possible. If we are going to help construct a better world, less dangerous and more just, it will require our full determination.

Stop and reflect upon what really matters to you. What gives you meaning and purpose? Think for a moment about all the people that you love and other aspects of your life that are dear to you. What if everything you value was destroyed or damaged? What if our children or our grandchildren live in a world that has been stripped of the beauty we know as a result of our actions (or inactions)? With all you value in the forefront of your mind, make a commitment to do what you can to help overcome the common danger which threatens it.

You may find it helpful to write down a brief pledge or statement that expresses your commitment in your own words. What is it that you would like to help achieve in the world? If you write a pledge, you may wish to share it with at least one other person, perhaps someone in your family or a close friend. Telling someone else about a commitment you have made helps to seal it in a way that makes it more real.

Another important part of one's pledge is a commitment to take care of our personal health. Good health is the base for all our actions, the foundation for everything that we do and aspire to do in life. As Thomas Carlyle said, "Health is the only victory." Health requires balance. Extremes lead to distress. Balance requires us to be in harmony with our body, mind, and spirit. Body, mind, and spirit should not be seen as three separate units, as though we are machines and these are our parts. Body, mind, and spirit are three aspects of our totality. When one aspect is underdeveloped, it limits our capacity to live to our fullest potential.

The practice here is to design, if you have not already, a program to optimize your own health and vitality — addressing diet, exercise, and the management of stress. When your body is well-used and healthy, your mind clear and integrated, and your spirit dedicated to a larger purpose, there is joy, the satisfaction of living your life fully.

Making a pledge means something quite different for each person. No one can tell you what it means to you. It's about doing what you love to do best, dedicated to the larger purpose of building a more secure and compassionate world for everyone.

Creating Peace in Your Life

Peace, if it ever exists, will not be based on the fear of war, but on the love of peace. It will not be the abstaining from an act, but the coming of a state of mind.
                                        Herman Wouk

If our intention is to create a more secure and peaceful future, we need to begin by *making peace with ourselves* and extending this practice outward to *making peace with others.* It is a reciprocal feedback process: peace within, peace without. This does not mean that we are ever finished "making peace," whether with ourselves or others. As we have seen, peace is not an end-point, but a process, a way of living. And let us also remember that creating peace in our lives is not a prerequisite to taking other actions to help. To be most effective, our inner work needs to proceed simultaneously with our outer work, integrating self and world.

The key to *peace of mind* is integration. Whenever we are total, we experience an undivided sense of self. For some of us, this totality happens while we are skiing down a mountain, dancing, jogging, taking a long walk in nature, being involved in our work, playing with a child, or just sitting quietly. Each of us is different and so the way we experience peace of mind is also quite individual.

Find out what nourishes you and brings you a sense of totality, and commit yourself to spending time doing it. You might spend a few minutes every day listening to some favorite music. Or you might spend time each day "simply being:" sit for a few minutes, quiet and alert, let your mind and body relax, be aware of your breath coming in and going out. Seek to extend the experience of peace of mind to as much of your life as possible.

When we experience inner conflict — being divided between two or more competing pulls — we need to explore the opposing drives or wishes. Often, we can better understand these conflicts through an inner dialogue. Stop and take time to listen to your own differing points of view. You might write down each perspective. Sometimes this process can be best facilitated through talking things over with a friend. The more you can externalize and clarify the inner conflict, the more you will move toward integration. What are the real needs and insights of your differing points of view? And what is the outcome you really want, and intend to have happen?

The human mind operates through duality and division. Yet, whenever we turn inward to the essential person, the Observing Self, there is no division. We discover who we are behind the polarities. This process is similar to what happens when we listen to a beautiful piece of music. The mechanics of the piece can be dissected — the notes, the score, the various instruments — but the spirit of the music cannot be captured by dividing it up and translating it into another form. The music of who we are — our own unique symphony — already exists. The question is, will we take the time to listen to ourselves deeply enough to begin to know our own harmony?

Peace of mind begins by accepting and loving ourselves just the way we are. We cannot improve our character or behavior without first accepting that we are already worthwhile. Our sense of self-worth and self-esteem is the foundation for our efforts toward a better world: treating ourselves with the same respect and kindness that we would like to be treated with by others, and treating others with this same respect and kindness.

Making peace with others is fundamentally a consequence of one's intention. We cannot control or persuade another person to want to seek reconciliation. That is his or her choice. But we can sustain the intention to be at peace, to seek reconciliation, and eventually to be clear and complete with everyone before we die. With this intention, we do not invade the other person's freedom to hold a grudge or to be unwilling to resolve a particular conflict. What we do have power over is our own intention. And in the long run, we will find that if we are clear with ourselves about our intention toward everyone in our lives, this will free us.

Real relationships are not always congenial. Yet creating peace with people in our lives has nothing to do with not hating destructive actions, or fearing domination, or always being "nice people." Making peace has nothing to do with being vulnerable with those who would abuse you. Similarly, forgiveness is not about tolerating harmful behavior, but rather releasing the bitterness and anger inside ourselves. And, as Martin Luther King, Jr., said, "Forgiveness is not an occasional act, it is a permanent attitude."

Seek to make peace with everyone in your life. Make amends where appropriate, and clear up unresolved conflicts, whether emotional, economic, or spiritual. Seek to forgive those who have violated you, and forgive yourself for all the violations you have done against others. Reach out to people with whom you need to clear things and seek reconciliation. They may, or may not, be available or interested in this point in time. Yet, what is most important is your intention to create peace in your life. As Mother Teresa said, "All the works of love are works of peace . . . if everyone could see the image of God in his neighbor, do you think we should still need tanks and generals."

Informing Yourself and Others

I know no safe depository of the ultimate powers of the society but the people themselves; and if we think them not enlightened enough to exercise their control with a wholesome discretion, the remedy is not to take it from them, but to inform their discretion.

Thomas Jefferson

The human-caused threats to our future are complex. There are few, if any, simple answers. For democracy to be effective in addressing these threats, citizens must be sufficiently informed to make thoughtful choices and work to develop comprehensive strategies. When we remain uninformed, no matter how sincerely concerned, we cannot participate with understanding. Real education about any issue requires an open mind. Without looking at a particular concern from various perspectives, we are limited by our own preconceptions and prejudices. To fully inform ourselves, we need to seek data and insight from those with whom we think we disagree.

Educate yourself about the human-caused threats to our future, such as: the nature and causes of the depleted ozone layer and the greenhouse effect; U.S. environmental policy; future trends in environment, development, and population; the destructive capabilities of weapons; U.S. and Soviet foreign policy in regional "hot spots" around the globe; human rights and its threats to freedom from authoritarianism; hunger and poverty; and national/global debt; etc.

As is apparent from this partial list, the challenge of self-education is on-going and never fully completed. You do not have to become an expert on all or any of these questions. What is needed is a basic working knowledge of the key data and underlying issues.

Whatever your current understanding about our world-threatening dilemmas, begin to inform yourself from as many points of view as possible. Read newspapers and journals. Watch educational television and videos. Listen to experts from a wide range of perspectives and ask yourself about their assumptions. How did they get to their current position? Talk to people who have different perspectives than your own. As much as possible, try to avoid being positional about what you think is the "answer." Rather, seek to maintain an attitude of exploration and discovery. Become a truly informed and effective citizen of your nation and your world.

As you become more knowledgeable about the threats we face and various proposals for overcoming them, *the natural next step is to help educate others.* There are many varied and creative ways this can be done. For example, organize a community forum, where representatives of different points of view talk about a particular topic relating to the common danger. Send educational materials to local radio shows and suggest topics for their programs. Write letters to the editor of your local newspaper. Create a television show for local cable stations or other public access channels. Organize small study groups, where interested people meet weekly or monthly to discuss issues.

Restoring the Environment

The creation of a thousand forests is in one acorn.
Ralph Waldo Emerson

There are many ways that we can take action to begin to restore our natural environment. First, scientists increasingly agree that planting a tree (or many trees) will have a positive long-term effect. At first glance, it may sound simplistic, but in fact it is immensely practical. The World Resources Institute recently declared that the Earth needs about three billion more acres of trees to keep its atmosphere in balance. This means we must replant enough forest to cover an area the size of the United States plus 700 million more acres. Scientists have concluded that trees planted anywhere in the world will absorb carbon dioxide, no matter how distant the source.

We know that excess carbon dioxide generated from burning fossil fuels is gradually raising the Earth's temperature. We also know that carbon dioxide is recycled by plants, especially big ones like trees. Yet we are rapidly destroying our forests worldwide. Brazil's rainforests, for example, are disappearing at the rate of about one football field per second.

This accelerating destruction of our global forests, especially the rainforests, threatens to seal the extinction of tens of thousands of endangered species, and poses a threat to human survival as well. By cutting our forests at a staggering pace, we threaten world climatic conditions. A recent report by the Environmental Protection Agency said that global warming caused by industrial pollutants in the atmosphere is likely to destroy most coastal wetlands, shrink forests, reduce water quality, and cause extensive environmental damage in the United States over the next century.

If the trees die, humans and animals will die too. The forests have been called our global lungs. Planting millions of acres of trees between now and the first decades of the twenty-first century will help to renew habitats for wildlife, increase oxygen levels, and replenish the soil. Trees are the natural counter-balance for the greenhouse effect.

The tree of life is a symbol used by many cultures around the world to represent the lifeforce: it appears in Native American stories, Buddhist teachings, and biblical parables. The Iroquois taught that when the Tree of Peace returns to the land, a great time of peace will be at hand. During the American Revolution, some of the colonies used the tree on their flag to symbolize freedom, calling it "the Liberty Tree."

The physical act of planting a tree and seeing that it is cared for is a small yet practical step toward restoring the Earth's environment. It is a fitting symbol for our personal and shared commitment to the quality of life now and for future generations.

Second, you can begin to recycle, practice conservation, and encourage your community to do the same. Currently, Americans throw away 150 million tons of trash each year. Other industrial nations generate about half as much trash per person as Americans do, and recycle a major part of it. Estimates arc that at least 50 percent of this country's wastes can be productively recycled. Yet nationwide, only ten percent of America's waste is now recycled. Americans discard enough office and writing paper each year to build a twelve-foot-high wall between Los Angeles and New York. The glass bottles and jars we throw away would fill the World Trade Center in New York City every two weeks. Depending on which figures one uses, the average American generates between three and five pounds of garbage per day.

Prior to World War II, recycling was a part of almost every American's life. In rural communities where self-sufficiency was necessary, the re-use of waste materials and composting of organic matter was commonplace. Before 1920, 70 percent of cities in the United States operated recycling centers. During World War II rationing required American industry to re-use and recycle up to 25 percent of the total solid waste. With post-war affluence, cheaper consumer products, and the advent of the "disposable society," recycling declined. It was old-fashioned, associated with the hard times of the Great Depression.

Now, with heightened environmental awareness and with increasingly widespread concern over the national and global waste crisis, recycling is coming back with a passion. Recycling does not mean only collecting and separating re-useable trash. It also means the conversion of this "waste" into new useable products and raw materials.

Recycling preserves natural resources and avoids harmful disposal methods (such as burning with fossil fuels). It reduces energy use and pollution from new manufacturing. Recycling is often the lowest-cost method of solid-waste management. Whether it is immediately cost-effective or not, the long-term cost to society is too great to keep burying our trash and creating more and more landfills. You can work for state and national legislation which creates economic incentives and regulations for recycling.

You can be more aware of ways to conserve energy. Again, the United States leads the pack in energy consumption. America uses twice the energy to achieve the same standard of living as do Europe or Japan. You can take personal steps to conserve energy, and you can work for state and national legislation which promotes both energy conservation and significant investment in renewable energy sources. The practice of conservation involves almost every aspect of our lives. Ray Dasmann, the nationally respected environmental scientist, wrote:

> Conservation is a way of looking at the world and a way of action . . . to provide for the existence of the greatest possible diversity and variety of life on earth. A conservation viewpoint . . . must challenge the right of nations, human institutions, and individuals to engage in activities which impair the long-term well-being of other human

beings, other species, or the environments on which they all depend.

Third, you can work for legislation, international agreements, and the promotion of environmental awareness. You can help to promote educational programs to teach people the value of genetic diversity and the irreversible damage that occurs when whole species are brought to extinction. You can help to support campaigns to save endangered species and press for strong enforcement of the Endangered Species Act. You can work to pressure the World Bank and other development agencies to make certain their investments conserve the tropical rain forests. You can encourage economic development that is ecologically sound. You can support the establishment of comprehensive zoning plans, so that preservation goes hand in hand with development.

You can work for legislation to reduce the manufacturing of toxic chemicals, and thereby prevent them from ever reaching the environment. You can support national legislation and work for international agreements to reduce acid rain by limiting pollution from power plants and smelters. You can work to increase national and international funding for alternative energy sources, including solar and wind power. The development of less toxic and more organic, renewable sources of energy is critically important to preserving the quality of our lives — and life itself — in the next century. *Time*, (January 2, 1989) expressed our most compelling necessity:

> Every individual on the planet must be made aware of its vulnerability and of the urgent need to preserve it. No attempt to protect the environment will be successful in the long run unless ordinary people ... are willing to adjust their life-styles. Our wasteful, careless ways must become a thing of the past. We must recycle more, procreate less, turn off lights, use mass transit, do a thousand things differently in our everyday lives. We owe this not only to ourselves and our children but also to the unborn generations who will one day inherit the earth.

Resolving Conflicts: Win/Win

It is to our advantage to enhance the best that exists in each individual for everyone's mutual benefit.

Jonas Salk

It is not easy to stop old patterns of destructive conflict, but it can be done. It is our choice, moment by moment. The most important thing is to be clear about how you want to deal with conflicts. Renew your commitment again and again to take the initiative to find win/win outcomes.

As we discussed previously, the most essential step is to stop. When you start to become entangled in an escalating conflict — stop and take a step back. Make it a practice to step back from your old, reactive patterns and ask yourself, "What do I want here? What is my intention?" Then reaffirm to yourself that your goal is to obtain a satisfactory outcome for both your own needs and the needs of the other party.

To master this skill, choose a particular conflict in your own life which you would like to resolve effectively. It might be a conflict with a friend, a business associate, a neighbor, or a member of your family. It might be an organizational conflict. Think of ways that you can apply the skills of dialogue and conflict management to deal with it. It may help to review the material in this book under "Practice for Winning" or to consult other sources on creative problem-solving. You may also find it helpful to talk about what you plan to do with a friend. This often helps to clarify both your general intention and specific strategy.

After you have taken action, evaluate how well you were able to achieve your goal. Reflect on how you might be more effective next time. As you repeat this process, you will become more and more skilled at creatively resolving conflicts in your life.

The challenge of how to live in dynamic balance between our ability to manage conflicts and the power of our destructive technologies will not be accomplished in one generation. We must prepare and empower the next generation to continue the process of creating and sustaining this balance.

When our children reach adulthood, they will be compelled by world conditions to continue to address serious survival issues. They will be required to expand the scope of their vision to meet the realities of global interdependence. These challenges will require them to go beyond the logic of the past to a new level of creative thinking and problem-solving.

We need a twenty-first century curriculum which empowers our children to view themselves as intentional agents able to help shape their future; a curriculum which teaches them skills for communication across the divisions of ideology and race, and which gives them tools for resolving disputes with an all-win outcome. The foundation of this advanced curriculum is the capacity for empathy and a heightened respect for all life.

The question of how to raise our children with self-esteem is currently an area of active research and will be a major subject of discussion as we approach the next century. One thing is clear: we teach our children most effectively by example. If we want our children to respect themselves and others, this requires us — parents, grandparents, friends, and teachers — to treat them with respect. Similarly, experiencing awe and wonder for our living Earth is emerging as a major educational endeavor with school programs, books, videos, and public television programs.

We must do whatever we can to teach the children around us by living an ethic of respect for all persons and life itself. We must help generate support for educational excellence and for programs which teach self-esteem, personal responsibility, skills for citizenship, and tools for communication and conflict resolution.

Building a Dialogue Movement

With malice toward none, with charity for all ... let us

*strive on to finish the work we are in ... to do all 'which
may achieve and cherish a just and lasting peace among
ourselves, and with all nations.*

Abraham Lincoln

What do each of us as individuals have to contribute to
a Great Turning? We have our small, daily actions and we
have our circles of trust and influence, the people with whom
we already experience a sense of community. By linking these
circles together, we can form communities of trust. For if we
bring our sets of friends and associates together, dedicated
to a greater purpose of building a more secure future, then
we have established a larger network of real communication
and integrity.

In the 1880s when Marconi managed to send just one
letter in Morse Code across the Atlantic Ocean, this was
viewed as an awesome achievement. A century later we
have created a world-wide electronic circuitry through the
technologies of the telephone, the computer, and the satellite.
Now our challenge is to create a conscious human circuitry:
a network of mutual respect and shared intention, committed
to changing the process of our interactions.

We do not have to agree about the content of our positions
in order to share a commitment to change the process of the
way we communicate and resolve conflicts with each other.
If we are going to turn our world from an attitude of indif-
ference and fear to a network of dialogue and respect, then
we need to link first thousands, and then millions, of people.
This network can help to form the basis of the cultural shift
in values and thinking necessary to create the political shift
in the way we make policies.

You can start by helping to generate a *community dialogue*.
Those who are undertaking the practice of win/win can use
these methods to address issues of concern in their local
communities. For example, a community dialogue group
might decide to organize a series of mediated dialogues on
a local environmental dispute, or on how to reduce violent
crime or other issues of primary importance to residents.

You can take the findings — areas of agreement both in terms of analysis of the causes of the problem and the shared solutions — and present them to the media and those in power. If possible, invite major leaders and political figures to the dialogues.

Between now and the turn of the century, we need to build groups of people all around the country who are committed to the principles of dialogue and conflict resolution in both their personal interactions and in our political process. These community dialogue groups will form the backbone of a *national dialogue movement*. Bringing together people of integrity and concern, conservative and liberal, to participate in dialogue about the critical issues of our national future, will enable us to see from a wider perspective, and increase our understanding. By considering data and insight that have not usually been understood in light of each other, new options arise that are by definition more inclusive. Addressing the differing concerns of the participants will allow us to formulate policies that are comprehensive and will therefore help us to steer a steady course toward greater security, environmental restoration, and real peace.

Those of us who see what is at risk must work together to mobilize our country between now and the turn of the century. As Americans we must take the initiative for values and policies that not only reflect the needs and interests of our nation, but also reflect the needs and interests of our global survival.

As these world-threatening problems become more widely publicized and in some cases more acute during the 1990s, there will be an increasing demand on the part of informed citizens around the world for *global dialogue*. While the alliance of forces necessary to act effectively on a worldwide basis is not yet fully in place, the critical problems of the environment and threat of war will compel us to work together. What form this global dialogue between the citizens and leaders of different nations will take is not yet fully apparent. It may happen through the United Nations or through a unique forum, such as a "World Convocation." The real point is that if we are to survive, we must arrive at workable global agreements.

While it may not seem obvious how the average person can create better communication and understanding across different nationalities, there are many opportunities which already exist, or can be created. These include: groups which promote "citizen diplomacy;" cultural and educational exchanges; programs to increase awareness about international issues and concerns: interactive satellite television; and international computer networks. All of these educational programs have arisen as a result of individuals and groups taking the initiative to promote global dialogue.

In December 1964, Dr. Martin Luther King, Jr. was awarded the Nobel Peace Prize. On that occasion he said:

> I accept this award in the spirit of a curator of some precious heirloom . . . to hold in trust to its true owners — all those . . . in whose eyes the beauty of genuine brotherhood and peace is more precious than diamonds or silver or gold. I accept this award today with an abiding faith in America and an audacious faith in the future of mankind . . .

And who are these *true owners* who will accept and sustain the legacy of this precious prize? Who will speak and act on behalf of the dream which Dr. King and other great leaders have seen — a dream of what America can be both for itself and for the world?

Is it perhaps you and I? And is it not our responsibility to renew this great legacy for ourselves and for the children of the next century? The real peace prize, the one to which Dr. Martin Luther King, Jr. dedicated his life, must be sought after and achieved by each generation. The real peace prize must be won in our lives for our time.

An Invitation:
Create The Turning

It is possible that all the past is but the beginning
of the beginning, and that all that is and has been is
but the twilight of the dawn. It is possible to believe
that all the human mind has ever accomplished is but
the dream before the awakening.

Out of our lineage, minds will spring, that reach
back to us in our littleness to know us better than we
know ourselves. A day will come when beings who are
now latent in our thoughts, shall stand upon this earth
as one stands upon a footstool, and shall laugh and
reach out their hands amidst the stars.

H. G. Wells, 1902

If the four billion years of Earth's history were com-
pressed into one year, the time line it created would give
us a startling perspective. For the first three months, the
planet is hot, filled with volcanos and molten lava. There
is little atmosphere. By March the oceans have formed
making life possible. In April or May, life first appears —
first single-celled organisms and then over the summer
months, the oceans are teaming with life. The first amphi-
bians emerge from the ocean onto land into October and the
dinosaurs appear in November. Finally, on December 31st
at 10:00 in the evening, human beings step out on the stage
of Earth's history.

This time line helps us to grasp the magnitude of the
choice which is upon us. After four billion years of evolution,
we have come to the point where we have the destructive
capacity to negate all that has been created. We must act to

ensure that we do not interrupt the continuation of life on our planet.

The question is: will you become a partner in helping to achieve a Great Turning? What does it mean to answer "yes" to this question? It means you will have a different intention, which will create different actions. Your life will be different because you commit to the ongoing practice of ways to bring about a new meaning of victory for yourself and the world. As you think about saying "yes," you may have resistance because you feel that the changes necessary are inconvenient or difficult. Or you may say it doesn't really matter what you do because you are only one person.

Any new idea or behavior worth doing requires some effort. The best and most meaningful things in life often require us to take a stand. Yet, the rewards you will receive from practicing new ways of winning will be in many aspects of your life: deepening your communication with family and friends; improving your skills for handling conflict in your work; and helping to restore the quality and safety of life, now and for your children. The effort we contribute on behalf of creating a Great Turning is not a sacrifice, it is an investment from which we will reap benefits far greater than the outlay. By practicing these methods we will enrich and empower our own lives and our world.

How many people are needed to form a dialogue movement powerful enough to change American culture and politics, and thereby help to catalyze a global dialogue for the next century? Remember Albert Einstein's statement that two percent of the people can catalyze the necessary change. Two percent of Americans living a new understanding of victory in our daily lives can generate a wave of historic proportions. Two percent of the world's population living this change can be the Turning. Most social movements have happened because a small number of people have made significant changes in their own lives and thus created a larger wave in the world. Will you be one of the two percent, or whatever percentage it requires? Gandhi once observed:

"Anything you do will seem insignificant, but it is very important that you do it."

Many of us have dreams, but only some of us commit to realizing our dreams. If we want our vision to come to pass, we must commit ourselves. Our resolve is the bridge between the vision and the reality. Perhaps the power of true resolve has never been expressed as clearly as it was by W. H. Murray:

> ... Until one is committed there is hesitancy, the chance to draw back, always ineffectiveness. Concerning all acts of initiative (and creation), there is one elementary truth, the ignorance of which kills countless ideas and splendid plans: that the moment one definitely commits oneself, then providence moves too.
>
> All sorts of things occur to help one that would never otherwise have occurred. A whole stream of events issues from the decision, raising in one's favor all manner of unforeseen incidents and meetings and material assistance, which no man could have dreamt would have come his way.
>
> I have learned a deep respect for one of Goethe's couplets:
> Whatever you can do, or dream you can, begin it.
> Boldness has genius, power and magic in it.

The key assertion here is, that the moment one definitely commits oneself, then providence moves too. Though it cannot be proved except by one's own experience, whenever we are truly undivided and take action in the direction of our vision, there often is a convergence of events and assistance which we cannot foresee or reasonably expect.

We humans who have evolved from this Earth can choose to say that the journey is infused with meaning. Whether there is a higher power and purpose to our existence, no one can prove to anyone else. But we can choose to live as though there is a God, a Creative and Eternal Source; and as though respect and compassion for our fellow humans and other fellow creatures matters. We can choose to affirm that the universe, or the great mystery, or the lifeforce, does not want us to destroy life, but to choose life consciously, to take responsibility to help steward the evolutionary process to the next step of our development. Again, this cannot be proved. Yet, simple observation of the lifeforce all around us — in plants and animals — suggests there is an underlying impulse shared by all living beings to survive, grow, transcend old boundaries, and strengthen the richness and diversity of life.

When we assess the overwhelming dimensions of our common danger, we may think that the challenge is too great, or beyond our capacities. It is in these moments of genuine concern about the fate of our nation and planet that we need to remember what the wise teachers have told us across the centuries: When we commit ourselves to serve not only our own needs, but also the whole, we gain access to the help of a higher power. Providence moves with us like an unseen, but felt presence.

The human mind has sought to control nature but has never succeeded. We can turn winter into summer, move mountains, build underwater cities, travel through the solar system, but still we humans are only part of the miracle of evolution. We cannot control the universe — that which brought us into being. We who are finite cannot master the Infinite. And when we awaken to the reality of our relationship to the Infinite, we are brought to our knees with wonder. As Albert Einstein put it:

> The most beautiful experience we can have is of the mysterious — the sense of awe. It is the fundamental emotion which stands at the cradle of true religion, art, and science. Whoever does not know it and can no longer marvel is as good as dead and his eyes are dimmed.

What, after all, is our destiny if not to come to know, in our own way, the mysterious connection between ourselves and the universal force which sustains and evolves life itself?

Those of us living now have the power to destroy human civilization and perhaps extinguish life on Earth as we know it. This fact adds a depth of meaning to our time as no other time. Moses, as he followed the will of a higher power to free the Hebrew slaves from bondage in Egypt, could not have known the meaning of acting to free the entire Earth. Harriet Tubman, called "the Moses of her people" for leading hundreds of slaves to freedom via the Underground Railroad, could not have envisioned working to lead an entire world to safety. Thomas Jefferson, as he labored to create the democratic foundations of a great nation, could only glimpse what we now see more clearly — a Great Turning for our nation and all peoples.

From this perspective, we are fortunate to live at this moment in human history when we can help create the unfolding of a destiny as great as any before us. For if we are successful in building the foundations for a more secure and peaceful world, then future generations will celebrate our achievement long after we are gone.

Let us be bold. Let us do something unprecedented together — something that will assure the survival and well-being of our children and their children in the next century. Let us have the courage of our deepest aspirations and the pragmatic vision of our clearest thinking. Let us move beyond our narrow biases, and begin to listen to each other and work together across our differences.

The World Monument at White Sands, New Mexico — "to commemorate a new era of human dignity and world peace" — has yet to be built. Yet there are already tens of thousands of people helping to contribute their part to the foundation. It is a monument for our children — for their future, and far beyond.

By living the Turning — the turn of the century and the turn of the millennium, the turning of our lives and the turning away from catastrophe to a positive future — we will come to know a transcendent meaning in our everyday lives. By living in the vision that the Great Turning has already begun — that peace and dignity, kindness and justice will prevail — we will come to know and embody a new meaning of victory.

Bibliography

Ashe, Geoffrey. *Gandhi*. Stein and Day, New York, 1968.

Axelrod, Robert. *The Evolution of Cooperation*. Basic Books, Inc., New York, 1984.

"The Baby Boomers Turn 40," *Time*, May 19, 1986, pp. 22-41.

Barbour, Ian G., ed. *Western Man and Environmental Ethics*. Addison-Wesley, Reading, Massachusetts, 1973.

Bateson, Gregory. *Mind and Nature: A Necessary Unity*. E. P. Dutton, New York, 1979.

Batra, Dr. Ravi. *The Great Depression of 1990*. Dell Publishing, New York, 1985.

Blight, James. "Preventing Nuclear War." *Journal of Humanistic Psychology*, Vol. 28, No. 2, Spring, 1988, pp. 7-58.

Brown, Joseph Epes, ed. *The Sacred Pipe: Black Elk's Account of the Seven Rites of the Oglala Sioux*. Penguin Books, Baltimore, Maryland, 1953, 1971.

Brown, Robert McAfee. *Religion and Violence*. Stanford Alumni Association, 1973.

Broyles, William, Jr. "Why Men Love War." *Esquire*, November 1984, pp. 55-65.

Buber, Martin. *I and Thou*. 2nd ed. Charles Scribner's Sons, New York, 1958.

Byrd, Rear Admiral Richard E., U.S.N. (Ret.). "A Message from Admiral Byrd to the Young People of America." *Book of Knowledge*, The Grolier Society, Inc., 1950.

"Campaign '88: The Smear Campaign," *Newsweek*, October 31, 1988, pp. 16-19.

Campbell, Joseph. *The Hero With a Thousand Faces*. Bollingen Series, Princeton University Press, Princeton, New Jersey, 1949, 1973.

_____, with Bill Moyers. *The Power of Myth*. Doubleday, New York, 1988.

Carlson, Don, and Craig Comstock. *Citizen Summitry*. St. Martin's Press, New York, 1986.

Dalai Lama, The Fourteenth. *Kindness, Clarity, and Insight*. Snow Lion Publications, Ithaca, New York, 1984.

Dasmann, Raymond F. *Environmental Conservation*, Fourth Edition. John Wiley & Sons, Inc. New York, 1959, 1976.

————. *The Last Horizon*. The Macmillan Co., New York, 1963.

Deikman, Arthur. *The Observing Self*. Beacon Press, Boston, 1982.

Deutsch, Morton. "Conflict Resolution: Theory and Practice." *Political Psychology*, Vol. 4, No. 3, September, 1983, pp. 431-453.

Dunning, F. W. et al. *The Story of the Earth*. Cambridge University Press, New Rochelle, New York, 1986.

Dyson, Freeman J. *Weapons and Hope*. Harper and Row, New York, 1983.

Eastham, Scott. *Nucleus: Reconnecting Science & Religion in the Nuclear Age*. Bear & Co., Santa Fe, New Mexico, 1987.

Ehrlich, P., J. Harte, and M. Harwell. "Long-Term Biological Consequences of Nuclear War." *Science 222*, 1983, pp. 1293-1300.

Eiseley, Loren. *The Immense Journey*. Random House, New York, 1946, 1959.

Elgin, Duane. *Voluntary Simplicity*. William Morrow & Co., Inc., New York, 1981.

Ellul, Jacques. *The Technological Society*. Alfred A. Knopf, Inc., New York, 1964.

"Endangered Earth," *Time*, January 2, 1989, pp. 24-30.

Erikson, Erik H. *Gandhi's Truth: On the Origins of Militant Nonviolence*. W. W. Norton & Co., Inc., New York, 1969.

Ferguson, Marilyn. *The Aquarian Conspiracy: Personal and Social Transformation in Our Time*. J. P. Tarcher, Inc., Los Angeles, 1980.

Fischer, Louis. *The Life of Mahatma Gandhi*. Collier Books, New York, 1950, 1969.

Fisher, Roger and William Ury. *Getting to Yes*. Penguin; Houghton Mifflin Co., Boston, 1981, 1983.

Frank, Jerome D., Ph.D., M.D. *Sanity & Survival: Psychological Aspects of War and Peace*. Random House, New York, 1967.

Frankl, Viktor E. *Man's Search For Meaning: An Introduction to Logotherapy*. Washington Square Press, Inc., New York, 1963.

Freud, Sigmund. *Civilization and Its Discontents*. Trans. and ed., James Strachey. W. W. Norton & Co., Inc., New York, 1961.

Gandhi, Mohandas K. *Autobiography: The Story of My Experiments with Truth*. Dover Publications, Inc., New York, 1983.

Glendinning, Chellis. *Waking Up in the Nuclear Age: A Vision for Survival*. William Morrow & Co., Inc., New York, 1987.

————. *When Technology Wounds: From IUDs to Atomic Bombs*. Beechtree/William Morrow, New York, 1989.

Graham, General Daniel. *High Frontier: A Strategy for National Survival*. Tom Doherty Associates, Inc., New York, 1983.

Gromyko, Anatoly, and Martin Hellman, eds. *Breakthrough: Emerging New Thinking*. Walker and Co., New York, 1988.

Ground Zero. *Nuclear War: What's in it For You?* Simon & Schuster, New York, 1982.

————. *What About The Russians — and Nuclear War?* Simon & Schuster, Inc., New York, 1983.

Heschel, Abraham Joshua. *Man Is Not Alone: A Philosophy of Religion*. Harper & Row, New York, 1951, 1966.

Hoffer, Eric. *The True Believer*. Harper & Brothers, New York, 1951.

Holt, Robert. "Can Psychology Meet Einstein's Challenge?" *Political Psychology*, Vol. 5, No. 2, June, 1984, pp. 199-225.

Huxley, Aldous. *The Perennial Philosophy*. Harper and Row, New York, 1945.

Jandt, Fred E., with Paul Gillette. *Win-Win Negotiating: Turning Conflict Into Agreement*. John Wiley & Sons, New York, 1985.

Jones, Landon Y. *Great Expectations: America & The Baby Boom Generation*. Coward, McCann & Geoghegan, New York, 1980.

Keen, Sam. *Faces of The Enemy*. Harper and Row, San Francisco, 1986.

————. *To A Dancing God*. Harper & Row, New York, 1970.

Kelley, Kevin W., ed. *The Home Planet*. Addison-Wesley, Reading, Massachusetts, 1988.

Kent, Ian, and William Nicholls. *I AMness: The Discovery of The Self Beyond The Ego*. The Bobbs-Merrill Co., Inc., Indianapolis, Indiana, 1972.

Kidron, Michael, and Dan Smith. *The War Atlas: Armed Conflict — Armed Peace*. Simon & Schuster, New York, 1983.

King, Coretta Scott. *The Words of Martin Luther King, Jr.*. Newmarket Press, New York, 1983, 1987.

King, Dr. John L. *How to Profit from the Next Great Depression*. New American Library, New York, 1988.

Knudsen-Hoffman, Gene. *Ways Out*. John Daniel and Co., Santa Barbara, California, 1988.

Kozol, Jonathan. *Illiterate America*. New American Library, New York, 1986.

Krishna Kripalani, ed. *All Men Are Brothers: Life and Thoughts of Mahatma Gandhi*. Navajivan Publishing House, Ahmedabad, India, 1960.

Kull, Steven, "Nuclear Arms and the Desire for World Destruction." *Political Psychology*, vol. 4, no. 3, September, 1983, pp. 563-591.

Leopold, Aldo. *A Sand County Almanac.* Random House, New York, 1949, 1966.

Lifton, Robert Jay, and Richard Falk. *Indefensible Weapons: The Political and Psychological Case Against Nuclearism.* Basic Books, Inc., New York, 1982.

Maslow, Abraham H. *Religions, Values, and Peak-Experiences.* Ohio State University Press, Columbus, 1964.

May, Rollo. *Power and Innocence: A Search for the Sources of Violence.* W. W. Norton & Co., New York, 1972.

McDonnell, Thomas P., ed. *A Thomas Merton Reader Revised Edition.* Doubleday & Co., Inc., Garden City, New York, 1938, 1974.

Merton, Thomas. *Contemplation in a World of Action.* Doubleday & Co., Inc., New York, 1965, 1973.

Nixon, Richard M. *1999: Victory Without War.* Simon & Schuster, New York, 1988.

————. *The Real War.* Warner Books, Inc., New York, 1980.

Nye, Joseph S., Jr. *Nuclear Ethics.* Macmillan, Inc., New York, 1986.

Oates, Stephen B. *Let the Trumpet Sound: The Life of Martin Luther King, Jr.* Harper & Row, 1982.

"Onward to Mars," *Time,* July 18, 1988, pp. 46-53.

"Our Filthy Seas," *Time,* August 1, 1988, pp. 44-50.

Pais, Abraham. *'Subtle is the Lord . . .' The Science and the Life of Albert Einstein.* Oxford University Press, Oxford and New York, 1982.

Peck, Scott. *The Road Less Traveled.* Simon and Schuster, New York, 1978.

Peterson, Jeannie. *The Aftermath.* Pantheon Books, New York, 1983.

Pipes, Richard. *Survival Is Not Enough.* Simon and Schuster, Inc., New York, 1984.

Proceedings, *Prescription for Prevention.* Palo Alto, California, 1983.

Pruitt, Dean, and Jeffrey Rubin. *Social Conflict.* Random House, New York, 1985.

Ringer, Robert J. *How You Can Find Happiness During the Collapse of Western Civilization.*

————. *Looking Out for Number One.* Fawcett, New York, 1983.

Russell, Peter. *The Global Brain.* J. P. Tarcher, Inc., Los Angeles, 1983.

Schlesinger, Arthur M., Jr., and Morton White, eds. *Paths of American Thought.* Houghton Mifflin Co., Boston, 1963.

Schmookler, Andrew. *Out of Weakness.* Bantam Books, New York, 1988.

Schweitzer, Albert. *Out of My Life and Thought.* Holt, Rinehart and Winston, Inc., New York, 1933, 1949.

_____ . *Reverence For Life.* Thomas Kiernan, ed., Philosophical Library, New York, 1965.

Shipler, David K. *Russia: Broken Idols, Solemn Dreams.* Penguin Books, New York, 1983.

"Special Report: The Greenhouse Effect," *Newsweek*, July 11, 1988, pp. 16-24.

"Special Report: The Pacific Century: Is America in Decline?," *Newsweek*, February 22, 1988. pp. 42-63.

Stone, Ronald H. *Reinhold Niebuhr: Prophet to Politicians.* Abingdon Press, Nashville, Tennessee, 1972.

Sullivan, Harry Stack, M.D. *The Interpersonal Theory of Psychiatry.* W. W. Norton & Co., Inc., New York, 1953.

Susskind, Lawrence, and Jeffrey Cruikshank. *Breaking The Impasse: Consensual Approaches to Resolving Public Disputes.* Basic Books, Inc., New York, 1987.

Swimme, Brian. *The Universe Is A Green Dragon.* Bear & Co., Santa Fe, New Mexico, 1984.

Talbott, Strobe. *Deadly Gambits.* Alfred A. Knopf, New York. 1984.

Thich Nhat Hanh. *Being Peace.* Parallax Press, Berkeley, California, 1987.

Thomas, Lewis. *The Lives of a Cell: Notes of a Biology Watcher.* The Viking Press, New York, 1974.

Thompson, James. *Psychological Aspects of Nuclear War.* John Wiley and Sons Ltd., New York, 1985.

Tillich, Paul. *The Shaking of the Foundations.* Charles Scribner's Sons, New York, 1948.

Timberlake, Lloyd. *Only One Earth: Living for the Future.* BBC Books, London, 1987.

Walsh, Roger, and Frances Vaughan. *Beyond Ego.* J. P. Tarcher, Inc., Los Angeles, 1980.

Walsh, Roger, M.D. *Staying Alive: The Psychology of Human Survival.* New Science Library, Boulder, 1984.

Washington, James M., ed. *A Testament of Hope: The Essential Writings of Martin Luther King, Jr.* Harper & Row, San Francisco, 1986.

Weiner, Jonathan. *Planet Earth.* Bantam Books, New York, 1986.

Westphall, Victor. *David's Story: A Casualty of Vietnam.* Center For The Advancement Of Human Dignity, Vietnam Veterans Chapel, Springer, New Mexico, 1981.

————— . *The People's Revolution for Peace*. Morgan Printing &
  Publishing, Austin, Texas, 1984.
Wiesel, Elie. *Town Beyond the Wall*. Schocken Books, Inc., New York,
  1978, 1982.

About Project Victory

Project Victory is a national organization dedicated to helping to achieve a victory over the human-caused threats to our future, particularly the threat of global war and environmental catastrophe. Project Victory is founded on the belief that the dangers we face in common necessitate an evolutionary shift of mind — the recognition of our increasing global interdependence, and the willingness to take conscious responsibility for our future.

Project Victory assists individuals, organizations, and our nation to find more effective ways of resolving the conflicts which potentially threaten the future of all life. Project Victory believes we must create a new era of human dignity, environmental restoration, and real security between now and the year 2020. This "Great Turning" in the way nations manage conflicts without resorting to violence and with respect for the global environment will come about through "smaller turnings" in the lives of individuals and groups.

The United States can play a pivotal role in helping to achieve long-term solutions to the human-caused threats to our future. Yet our current political approach creates a gridlock of narrow, short-term interests. We are not addressing these paramount issues effectively. In order to achieve longer-term comprehensive policies to address the common danger, we must change the process of the way we formulate policies — we must generate a new politics of interdependence.

Project Victory has developed tools to enhance the art of dialogue and conflict management. These tools are derived from insights of psychology, the principles of conflict resolution, and the ethical precepts of the world's great religious and philosophic traditions.

Project Victory seeks to build in the 1990s an ethical alliance which bridges individuals and groups of different points of view who share the intention to preserve and enhance life on Earth. It affirms that what is needed is both a personal and political transformation — a shift in the way we communicate and resolve conflicts in our personal lives, and a shift in the way we interact politically and make policies.

Project Victory has a two-tiered strategy for helping to catalyze the beginning of a Great Turning by the turn of the century.

- *Personal Responsibility* — Programs which help individuals and groups to develop better skills for communication and conflict resolution to generate "I win, you win" outcomes.
- *Policy Dialogues* — Programs to facilitate mediated dialogues and nonadversarial communication between community and national leaders on issues concerning the global threats to our future.

Since it founding in 1985, Project Victory has conducted dialogues, conferences, and training programs in more than forty cities around the United States. It was worked with a wide spectrum of national organizations, from defense organizations to disarmament groups, from religious and psychological groups to veterans and military organizations, from environmentalists to business leaders. Through these efforts, Project Victory seeks to generate a growing movement of individuals and groups who want to practice "a new meaning of victory" in an interdependent world.

If you want to know more about Project Victory, or want to become involved in its programs, or order other written materials and audio cassettes, please contact:

Project Victory	Project Victory
560 Oxford, #1	2005 Massachusetts Ave, NW
Palo Alto, CA 94306	Washington, DC 20036
(415) 424-9622	(202) 265-2554

About The Authors

Craig F. Schindler, J.D., Ph.D.

Craig Schindler received his B.A. from Stanford University (1968), his law degree from Stanford Law School (1972), and his Ph.D. in Psychology and Ethics from the Graduate Theological Union and the University of California, Berkeley (1978). He is the recipient of a number of fellowships, including the Danforth-Kent Fellowship, the Rockefeller Fellowship, and a number of awards for his excellence as a teacher.

He has taught at Stanford and Harvard, and most recently was an Assistant Professor of Environmental Ethics at the University of California, Santa Cruz. He resigned from the university in 1984 to devote himself full-time to the work of Project Victory.

Dr. Schindler is the president and a co-founder of Project Victory. He also maintains a consulting practice in personal and organizational development. For the past few years he has designed and led workshops on communication, and facilitated mediated dialogues around the country. He is widely sought after as a speaker, and gives talks to a diversity of national organizations.

Gary G. Lapid, M.D.

Gary Lapid received his B.A. from the University of California at Berkeley (1967), his M.D. from the University of Pennsylvania (1971), and his post-graduate specialty training in psychiatry at Stanford University Medical Center. Currently he is an Associate Clinical Professor in Psychiatry at Stanford University, and has a private practice in Palo Alto, California.

He has served as the president of the Stanford/South

257

Bay Chapter of Physicians for Social Responsibility (P.S.R.), and was chairperson of P.S.R.'s National Psycho-Social Task Force from 1985 to 1987. He was the recipient of the Outstanding Clinical Teacher Award at Stanford Medical School's Department of Psychiatry.

Dr. Lapid is the chairman and co-founder of Project Victory. He has designed and facilitated mediated dialogues, communication workshops, leadership seminars, and policy conferences around the country. He lectures widely and is a consultant to schools on children and self-esteem.